Accountable Care Organizations: A Roadmap for Success

Guidance on First Steps

Bruce Flareau, MD

Joanne Bohn and Colin Konschak

Foreword by Bert Reese

Edited by Rebecca J. Frey, PhD

First Edition

This publication is intended to provide accurate and authoritative information in regard to the subject matter covered. The statements and opinions expressed in this book are those of the authors.

ISBN-13: 978-0-615-43602-9
ISBN-10: 0615436021

Convurgent Publishing, LLC
4445 Corporation Lane, Suite #227
Virginia Beach, VA 23462
Contact Information
Phone: (877) 254-9794, Fax: (757) 213-6801
website: www.convurgent.com;   email: info@convurgent.com

Special Orders.
Bulk Quantity Sales. Special discounts are available on quantity purchases of 25 or more copies by corporations, government agencies, academic institutions, and other organizations. Please contact Convurgent Publishing's "Sales Department" at sales@convurgent.com or at the address above.

Bibliographic Data:

Flareau, Bruce
  Accountable Care Organizations: A Roadmap for Success. Guidance on First Steps / by Bruce Flareau, Joanne Bohn, and Colin Konschak –1st ed.
  p. cm.
1. Healthcare administration. 2. Health reform. 3. Healthcare quality
ISBN: 978-0-615-43602-9

Contributions:
Corresponding author, Joanne Bohn (joanne.bohn@clinicalhorizons.com)
Copy editor, Rebecca J. Frey, PhD (rebeccafrey@snet.net)
Cover design prepared by Emily Kneipp

About the Authors

Bruce Flareau, MD, FAAFP, FACPE, CPE, is Chief Medical Informatics Officer and Vice President of Physician Alignment for BayCare Health System in Clearwater, FL. As a Family Physician, Academician, President of the Florida Academy of Family Physicians and Physician executive, Dr. Flareau has over 20 years of healthcare experience.

Joanne Bohn, MBA is founder of Clinical Horizons, Inc. Ms. Bohn focuses on research, planning, and communications initiatives related to healthcare industry transformation and innovation including health information technology and healthcare provider issues. She holds an MBA with a concentration in healthcare and economics studies.

Colin Konschak, MBA, FACHE, FHIMSS is the managing partner of DIVURGENT, a healthcare management consulting firm. Mr. Konschak is a registered pharmacist, has an MBA in health services administration, is board certified in healthcare management, and is a certified Six Sigma Black Belt. Colin leads DIVURGENT's Advisory Service consulting practice focused on operational and information technology strategies including those related to Accountable Care Organizations. Colin can be reached at colin.konschak@divurgent.com.

PREFACE

Accountable Care Organizations: A Roadmap for Success: Guidance on First Steps is a summary of important and timely issues affecting healthcare providers, clinical practices and practitioners, insurers, government agencies, and legal professionals with regard to the movement toward establishment of accountable care organizations. The past decade has yielded numerous insights derived from demonstrations and pilot projects related to healthcare quality and payment reform, and has brought our nation to the present point of transition in the system of healthcare delivery. Recognizing that many issues are still unfolding for accountable care organizations through both legislation and initiatives in the private sector, we have examined a number of these issues and reviewed pertinent healthcare literature, regulatory guidance, and past legislation to support the ideas and concepts presented here. We have also developed a number of models and illustrations and provide them in these pages as visual expositions of the most critical underlying issues.

We have placed a hypothetical roadmap to issues related to the establishment of accountable care organizations at the end of Chapters 3, 4, 5, 6, 7, and 8. Though there are countless potential configurations of stakeholders, we have attempted to assemble a high-level guide to major activities and issues related to the development and establishment of ACOs.

Our Goal

We offer this book as part of a tool kit to stimulate ideas; provide a consolidated set of reference materials; and foster momentum for working toward clinically and financially integrated high-performance accountable care organizations. Given the federal legislative measures passed since 2008, the health system in the United States is undertaking significant changes that will impact the healthcare services available to future generations. Accountable care organizations are only one vehicle emerging from a decade of pilot projects, demonstrations, and healthcare reforms that can help us attain the goal of providing higher-quality care for all our citizens.

ACKNOWLEDGEMENTS

We wish to acknowledge the contributions of Philip Felt of DIVURGENT, to the conceptual development of this book and thank BDC Advisors' Dale Anderson, MD for critique of several chapters and illustrations provided in Chapter 7. Medicity, Inc.'s, Greg Miller contributed to the development of Chapter 5 regarding health information exchange along with illustrations on the subject. Additionally, our team is sincerely appreciative for the Foreword statement and guidance provided by Mr. Bert Reese of Sentara Healthcare.

All the authors wish to thank our families and colleagues for their encouragement and patience during the time required for this project.

TABLE OF CONTENTS

FOREWORD.

Improving the quality and cost of care in America lies at the heart of accountable care organizations as they become an integral part of the fabric of our U.S. healthcare delivery system. In this first edition of *Accountable Care Organizations: A Roadmap for Success,* the authors have done a commendable job, providing thoughtful insights into and summaries of several issues addressed by industry leaders regarding this emerging vehicle for carrying out health reform initiatives. Recognizing the complexity of care delivery at the local level as each accountable care organization must do, the authors offer several conceptual models illustrating key points to assist physician leaders, researchers, legal professionals, health information technology leaders, academicians, clinicians, and other industry participants working on the implementation of these new care delivery models.

The roadmaps at the end of several chapters integrate a vast amount of material, providing a set of high-level multiyear pictures of key activities to be considered in regard to each of our own industry efforts. This book should be considered a useful supplement to anyone focused on strategic, legal, or health information technology issues; clinical transformation; or other planning and education-related activities for the startup of an accountable care organization. The industry is at an early stage in the life cycle of accountable care organizations, as they are newly formed entities that will mature for decades to come. While every issue for accountable care organizations is not covered in depth and a number of issues have yet to unfold through both legislative rule making and private sector policy developments, the book addresses a number of critical topics, including:

- Physician leadership,
- Importance of patient-centered medical homes as part of the foundation of accountable care organizations,
- Foundational technologies (later discussed as and incorporated under an ACO Technology Framework) that will affect meaningful use of electronic medical records enabling health information exchange within and across accountable care organizations, possibly tying into a future national health information network.

- Long-term focus on working toward a multipayer model of accountable care organizations,
- Antitrust and other legal issues.

Accountable care organizations will be an organizational and clinical transformation journey for all of us. Whether you are just starting to investigate the implementation of, or find yourself immersed in a current implementation project, this book should serve as a value-added guide on your own journey toward improving the quality of care for the community that you and your organization serve.

Bert Reese
Chief Information Officer
Sentara Healthcare

Chapter 1. History and Case for Action

Introduction

The healthcare system in the United States is at a turning point in its history. The convergence of many factors—including experience with health maintenance organizations, shortages in the healthcare workforce, expansion of the uninsured segment of the population, rising healthcare costs, and challenges to the quality and accessibility of care—has led to a number of reform initiatives. This process is not unprecedented, however: the recent history of American healthcare indicates that it has undergone transitions of this type every 10 to 20 years. Specific examples range from the creation of Medicare in 1965 and the passage of the Health Maintenance Organization Act of 1973 to the introduction of Diagnosis-related group (DRG) hospital reimbursement methodologies and the formation of Physician-Hospital Organizations (PHO's) in the 1980s as well as the Clinton administration's efforts to reform healthcare in the 1990s. Each transition has had various impacts on the larger society and resolved some—though certainly not all—issues in its respective decade. Of course, as Albert Einstein once said, "We can't solve problems by using the same kind of thinking we used when we created them." And so it is no surprise that emerging Accountable Care Organizations will need to manage healthcare differently than the way in which it has been traditionally handled in the United States.

In 1999, the Institute of Medicine's (IOM) Committee on the Quality of Health Care in America issued their landmark report *To Err is Human*, which increased awareness of the prevalence and impact of medical errors. The committee issued a second report in 2001 that noted the challenges confronting fundamental redesign of the U.S. healthcare system.[1] This report also outlined six aims to improve the quality of healthcare services

---

[1] Institute of Medicine, Committee on Quality of Health Care in America. Building organizational support for change. In: *Crossing the Quality Chasm: A New Health System for the 21st Century*. Washington, DC: National Academies Press; 2001: 117–118.

provided throughout the United States. Figure 1 illustrates these six aims, which provide a foundation for many organizations seeking to improve the quality of contemporary healthcare.

Figure 1. Six Aims for Improvement in Quality Healthcare

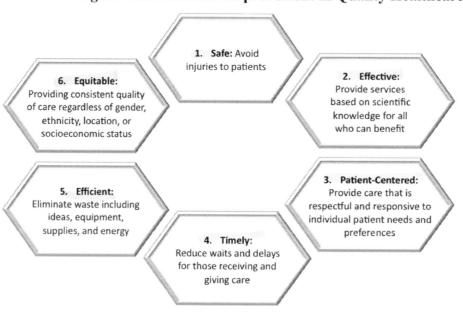

These six aims have individually and collectively fostered numerous strategic initiatives across the healthcare industry since 2000. The United States has experienced significant increases in the overall cost of medical care as well as the rate of growth in healthcare costs since the 1980s. The quality and accessibility of healthcare services have improved for some disease conditions, geographic areas, patient subpopulations, and patient satisfaction with the quality of services in recent years; however, medical errors still occur and inefficiencies still exist, leaving much room for further improvement.

The fee-for-service (FFS) payment system has not led to optimal performance. In fact, the IOM released a report in 2006 that called attention to problems with the FFS payment system. The Institute maintained that the FFS system "reward(s) excessive use of services; high-cost, complex procedures; and lower-quality care."[2] These incentives have resulted in a volume-driven system that, in many ways, contributes to reduced or stagnant quality of care in addition to concurrent rises in the cost of healthcare services.

In the recent past, healthcare expenditures in the United States have risen at an annual rate 2.4% faster than the rate of growth in gross domestic product (GDP).[3] In fact, the Centers for Medicare and Medicaid Services (CMS) stated in 2009 that total national health expenditures for 2008 reached $2.3 trillion—16.2% of GDP.[4] National health expenditures as a share of GDP are projected to increase to 19.6% by 2019.[5] Figure 2 illustrates the trend in national health expenditures from 1960 to 2008 as a percentage of GDP.[6] Many leading economists believe that expenditures above 20% of GDP will have a significant negative impact on the U.S. economy.

---

[2] Institute of Medicine, Committee on Redesigning Health Insurance Performance Measures, Payments, and Performance Improvement Programs. Summary. In: *Rewarding Provider Performance: Aligning Incentives in Medicare.* Washington, DC: National Academies Press; 2006: 4.

[3] Kaiser Family Foundation. Trends in health care costs and spending. March 2009. Available at: http://www.kff.org/insurance/upload/7692_02.pdf

[4] Center for Medicare and Medicaid Services. National health expenditures 2009 highlights. Available at: http://www.cms.gov/NationalHealthExpendData/downloads/highlights.pdf

[5] Center for Medicare and Medicaid Services. National health expenditure projections 2009-2019 (September 2010). Available at: http://www.cms.gov/NationalHealthExpendData/Downloads/NHEProjections2009to2019.pdf

[6] Kaiser Family Foundation. Industry trend charts. Available at: http://facts.kff.org/results.aspx?view=slides&topic=3&start=1

Figure 2. National Health Expenditures as a Share of GDP, 1960-2008

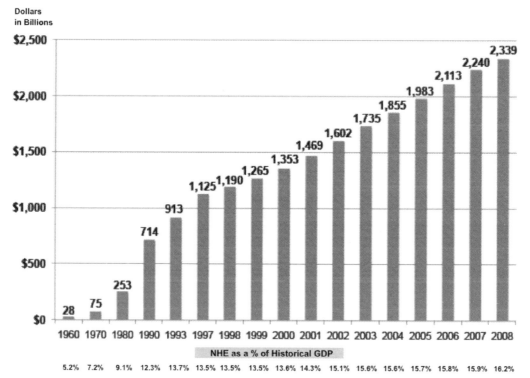

Source: Center for Medicare and Medicaid Services Statistics. Historical National Health Expenditures. Table 3. Accessed online at http://www.cms.gov/NationalHealthExpendData/downloads/tables.pdf

Because of rapid and continuous escalation in the cost of delivering healthcare and its impact on the nation's economy, the 2006 IOM report recommended that the Center for Medicare and Medicaid Services (CMS) move toward a pay-for-performance (P4P) system. The recommendation was intended to reward physicians and provider organizations for improving coordination of care, eliminating unnecessary tests and procedures, and improving overall quality of care as well as patient satisfaction with services received. The reason for the incentive lies in the history of health maintenance organizations (HMOs). Private insurer reimbursement programs and health plans grew rapidly after 1973, when Congress passed the Health Maintenance Organization Act. While HMOs did in fact reduce the rate of growth in national health care expenditures, they were poorly received by patients and providers alike. Similarly, the American public was—and still is—largely unwilling to accept the concept of the physician as gatekeeper, a model that turns the physician from a provider of quality medical care into a restrictive guardian of access to care. Physicians themselves experienced a lowering of their professional reputation as a result of their appearing to be obstacles to care delivery rather than the patient advocates they had always been in the past. If one looks closely at the graph representing national spending on healthcare, the only time the cost curve flattened out occurred when HMOs and physician–hospital organization programs were put in place. Consequently, many observers argued from a financial perspective that health maintenance organizations and physician-hospital organizations were in fact successful. A few solid models have survived, such as Kaiser Permanente and Geisinger; they are well positioned in this new era.

Consumer Issues

Two issues we wish to discuss in the context of rising costs are consumer-directed health plans and the escalating premiums paid by consumers for health insurance coverage with private payers in the U.S. healthcare system. Both issues concern the percentage of care directly paid by the consumer. To begin with consumer-directed health plans, these were introduced when HMOs became a major vehicle for employers to provide access to the healthcare delivery system.[7] Consumer-directed plans may be loosely defined as plans that give more responsibility to consumers to make decisions or set priorities regarding their healthcare needs. Some of the consumer-directed plans that have been developed and implemented include flexible spending accounts (FSAs) and health savings accounts (HSAs). These plans have opened a way to move consumers from an entitlement mindset in regard to healthcare ("if it's free it's for me") to an attitude of shared responsibility for decision making. In these plans, the individual consumer must pay for some portion of healthcare service consumption from his or her "own" account. Consumers are more frugal in their consumption of healthcare resources when they are closer financially to the burden of expense.

---

[7] Konschak C, Jarrell L. *Consumer-centric Healthcare: Opportunities and Challenges for Providers.* Chicago, IL: Health Administration Press; 2010.

This difference in mindset is a major distinction between health care systems in other countries compared to the system in the United States. In Switzerland, for example, the public favors fiscal responsibility in the utilization of health care resources. In contrast, the predominance of the indemnity approach to insurance in the United States encourages an entitlement mentality and the self-fulfilling tragedy of the commons, in which each member of a group demands their immediate share of finite resources at the long-term expense of all. The more rapidly people consume limited resources, the higher the total spending curve. Fortunately, greater transparency of reporting and such available technologies as the Internet coupled with the consumer movement and advocacy groups have led to improved knowledge of health issues in the general population over time. On the other hand, consumer-directed health plans may have an adverse impact on health in some cases. Consumers given increased personal responsibility for healthcare decisions in the face of limited resources may make unfavorable decisions.

To give a specific example, the consumer may choose to forgo preventive health screening; thus disease conditions may present later when treatment costs are higher and outcomes poorer. While flexible spending accounts and health savings accounts are making a comeback, and while many observers consider these plans as a reasonable alternative to other insurance products as standard premiums become increasingly unaffordable, such consumer-directed health plans would in fact have a long-term detrimental effect if they are decoupled from the basic benefits of wellness screening and access to care for chronic disease management. In addition, these types of plans in the past were available only to employers (who saw them as a means of offsetting the growing cost of employee healthcare) and not to self-employed individuals in most states.

The second issue concerns the escalation of indirect healthcare expenditures through rising insurance premiums both in aggregate as well as the portion required from consumers. This increase is part of the trend toward increased consumer cost sharing for high- and low-value healthcare services.[8] Figure 3 provides a picture of the historical trend

---

[8] Robinson JC. Applying value-based insurance design to high-cost health services. *Health Aff* (*Millwood*). 2010;29 (11): 2009-16.

toward escalating out-of-pocket expenses based on the consumer portion of healthcare expenditures with private insurers; it is a subset of the overall historical trend depicted in Figure 2.[9]

Figure 3. Annual Consumer Out-of-Pocket Expenses 1960-2008

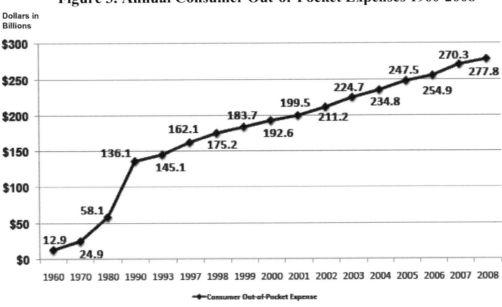

Source: Center for Medicare and Medicaid Services Statistics. Historical National Health Expenditures. Table 3. Accessed online at http://www.cms.gov/NationalHealthExpendData/downloads/tables.pdf

From the patient's perspective, premiums are a significant concern, as is the impact of rising out-of-pocket expenses. Value-based insurance design initiatives have been introduced that have proven to curb rising healthcare costs;[8] however, these initiatives have also affected utilization by consumers faced with choices regarding their healthcare needs based on out-of-pocket expense requirements. Whether public or private payers are involved in payment for healthcare services, consumers will still be responsible for insurance premiums and co-payments for services rendered.

---

[9] Center for Medicare and Medicaid Services. Statistics. Historical national health expenditures. Table 3. Available at: http://www.cms.gov/NationalHealthExpendData/downloads/tables.pdf.

After noting the historical patterns, we now turn to future projections of national health expenditures along with their projected percentages of gross domestic product. Current CMS estimates forecast increases in private plans, Medicare, Medicaid, and out-of-pocket consumer expenses over the ten years between 2010 and 2019.[10] This trend accounts for the expansion of insurance coverage planned under the 2010 Patient Protection and Affordable Care Act (PPACA) in that Medicaid coverage will expand significantly and the uninsured portion of the U.S. population is expected to decrease from 44.3 million in 2009 to 24.4 million by 2019. While more consumers will receive Medicaid coverage and their overall out-of-pocket expenditures will increase, the rate of acceleration in out-of-pocket expenses is projected to slow after 2014[11]

The general trend toward marked increases in national health expenditures[12] is illustrated in Figure 4. It is a known challenge for the United States and a major factor driving reform legislation. Further evidence of the financial challenges facing CMS, given these forecasted increases in healthcare expenditures for Medicare Parts A, B, and D, is provided in Appendix A with an excerpt from the August 2010 annual report of the Medicare Board of Trustees.

---

[10] Centers for Medicare and Medicaid Services. National health expenditure projections 2009–2019 (September 2010). Available at: http://www.cms.gov/NationalHealthExpendData/downloads/NHEProjections2009to2019.pdf. The reader is referred to Table 2 for a detailed breakdown of projections.

[11] Sisko AM, Truffer CJ, Keehan SP, Poisal JA, Clemens MK, Madison AJ. National health spending projections: the estimated impact of reform through 2019. *Health Aff* (*Millwood*). 2010;29(10): 1933-1941.

[12] Centers for Medicare and Medicaid Services. National health expenditure projections 2009–2019 (September 2010). Available at: http://www.cms.gov/NationalHealthExpendData/downloads/NHEProjections2009to2019.pdf . The reader is referred to Table 1.

Figure 4. Projected National Health Expenditures as a Share of GDP, 2010-2019

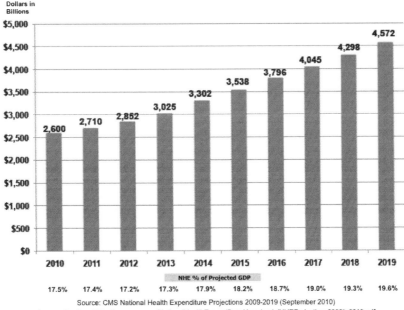

Source: CMS National Health Expenditure Projections 2009-2019 (September 2010)
Accessed online at http://www.cms.gov/NationalHealthExpendData/downloads/NHEProjections2009to2019.pdf

Figure 5 illustrates the projected increases in consumer out-of-pocket expenditures as a subset of the overall escalation in healthcare expenditures.

Figure 5. Projected Consumer Out-of-Pocket Expenditures 2010-2019

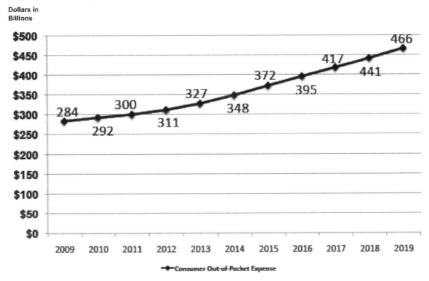

Source: Center for Medicare and Medicaid Services Statistics. Historical National Health Expenditures.
Table 3. Accessed online at http://www.cms.gov/NationalHealthExpendData/downloads/tables.pdf

Throughout this book we will touch on some of the new approaches to reimbursing physicians and hospital organizations for healthcare services and motivating them to adopt more advanced health information technology. These new approaches are addressed throughout the PPACA; they have been and will be tested in various payment reform models across the industry.

Structural Issues and the Formation of the ACO

The issue of business restructuring has also been a very important factor throughout the history of modern medicine and in working toward the IOM's six aims of higher-quality care. As early as 1933, organization was one of the foundational recommendations for provision of medical care made by the Committee on the Costs of Medical Care (CCMC), a group of fifty economists, physicians, public health specialists, and major interest groups funded between 1926 and 1932 by eight philanthropic organizations that included the Rockefeller and Millbank Foundations. According to the CCMC's 1933 report, "Medical service should be more largely furnished by groups of physicians and related practitioners, so organized as to maintain high standards of care and to retain the personal relations between patients and physician."[13] The managed care organizations of the mid-1970s can be viewed as an attempt to implement the CCMC's recommendation.

Two organizational structures that emerged from the managed care era were the physician-hospital organizations (PHOs) and integrated delivery networks (IDNs). These entities are two among others that will be discussed in more detail in Chapter 3. Physician-hospital organizations and integrated delivery networks began in the 1980s, when hospitals and physician groups within specific geographic areas came together in a structured manner to achieve stronger alignment, economies of scale in contracting, and provision of better patient care through their contractual relationships with health maintenance organizations.[14] A number of benefits and barriers resulted as these organizations evolved

---

[13] Falk I, Rorem R, Ring M. A summary of the findings. In: *The Costs of Medical Care: A Summary of Investigations on the Economic Aspects of the Prevention and Care of Illness*. Chicago, IL: University of Chicago Press; 1933: 582. Available at: http://www.deltaomega.org/costsof.pdf

[14] Morrisey MA, Alexander J, Burns LR, Johnson V. Managed care and physician/hospital integration. *Health Aff* (*Millwood*) 1996;15: 62-73.

over the next thirty years. Benefits included better negotiating power with health insurance payers while barriers included a lack of incentives to improve quality of care.[15] While these newer structures and arrangements helped the industry move in a positive direction, they were still challenged by dealing with contracts, limitations on patient choices, and antitrust laws imposed by the Federal Trade Commission to ensure that competition in specific geographic markets was not restricted or negatively affected. This issue will be discussed in depth in Chapter 4.

Last is the issue of transition from a model of individual health management to population-based health management. The American healthcare system focused on the individual patient during the era of health maintenance organizations and the consumer-driven healthcare movement—particularly with the consumer-directed health plans discussed above—which resulted in a shift away from the provision of proactive patient-centered care. By contrast, a model that focuses on improved quality of care, reduced cost of care, and responsibility for the health of a defined segment of the population returned to physicians will move the United States toward a higher level of population health management. This model will allow the country to provide better management of chronic conditions and diseases and predictive modeling over time for multiple clinical conditions as health information technology continues to advance. Putting such technology in place across the nation will in turn enable wider sharing of patient health data and information on clinical practices.

The trends and lessons learned from the managed care era and earlier history of the healthcare industry fostered a number of innovations in care delivery, quality improvement, and payment reform since 2000. One such innovation—the focus of this book—has been the emergence of the accountable care organization (ACO) model. The remainder of this chapter will introduce a number of topics that will be explored in more detail throughout the book.

---

[15] Casalino LA, Devers KJ, Lake TK, Reed M, Stoddard JJ. Benefits of and barriers to large medical group practice in the United States. *Arch Intern Med*. 2003;163: 1958-64.

The Medicare Physician Group Practice Demonstration Project[16] provided sufficient evidence for the public sector to support the formal advancement of the ACO model. The ACO was first introduced as a conceptual term by the Medicare Payment Advisory Commission (MedPAC) in November 2006[17] and by Dr. Elliott Fisher[18] in an article published in December 2006. Dr. Fisher described ACOs as partnerships between physicians and hospitals for coordinating and delivering healthcare services with greater efficiency and higher quality while lowering cost. ACOs accept ultimate accountability for clinical performance risk but are not responsible for insurance risk. Both public and private sector models of these organizations strive to improve coordination and delivery of patient care as well as optimize the reimbursement system. While this book will discuss a number of challenges to implementation, the authors maintain that the ACO model has the potential to improve quality, efficiency, and cost of care for services.

As the public and private sector ACO models evolve, what are some of the key principles for establishment? Drs. Fisher, McClellan, and colleagues summarized three key design principles for ACOs in a 2009 *Health Affairs* article. We have in turn represented these principles in Figure 6.[19]

---

[16] Centers for Medicare and Medicaid Services. Medicare Physician Group Practice Demonstration Project. Available at https://www.cms.gov/DemoProjectsEvalRpts/downloads/PGP_Fact_Sheet.pdf.

[17] Medicare Payment Advisory Commission public meeting November 8-9, 2006. 384. Transcript available at http://www.medpac.gov/transcripts/1108_1109_medpac.final.pdf

[18] Fisher ES, Staiger DO, Bynum JP, Gottlieb DJ. Accountable care organizations: the extended medical staff. *Health Aff* (Millwood). 2007;26 (1): w44–w57.

[19] Fisher ES, McClellan MB, Bertko J, et al. Fostering accountable health care: moving forward in Medicare. *Health Aff* (Millwood) 2009;28(2): w219-w231.

Figure 6. Key Design Principles for Accountable Care Organizations

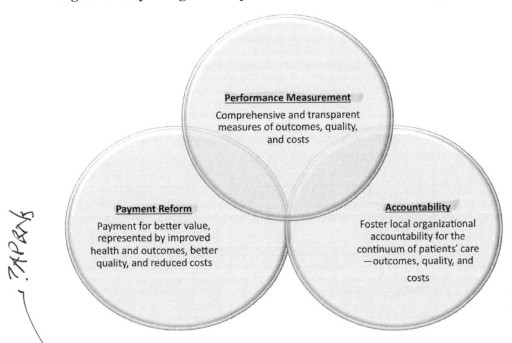

These three principles serve to anchor industry leaders as they collaborate in crafting the language and legislation to guide the implementation of ACOs across the United States. The principle of accountability refers to returning the power and leadership of these organizations to physicians. The second principle, measuring performance to provide greater transparency to patients and other stakeholders who assess the value of the care provided, will continue to be strengthened under the ACO model and will build on the performance measurement requirements in the patient-centered medical home (PCMH) to be discussed in Chapter 2. Third, payment reform will hinge on the transition to the P4P model, which relies on incentives for chronic disease management and preventive health care rather than such episodic outcomes as hospital stays to truly move the mark. As an industry, we must move from individual episodic P4P to population-based P4P by managing patient cohorts (groups of patients with like conditions) from primary prevention to chronic disease management, increasing opportunities to lower total healthcare expenditures. This transition will move the industry away from the FFS reimbursement model and partial capitation for reimbursement of services.

We can also refer to Figures 3 and 5 above in the context of the payment reform principle, as these figures illustrate the trend toward rising out-of-pocket premium expenses borne by consumers. One strategy described in the ACO literature regarding this issue is to offer consumers options on tiered premiums and tiered co-payments, depending on the ACO they select for their primary and specialty care services.[20]

ACOs and HMOs Compared

Recognizing the impact of health maintenance organizations on payment for services across the healthcare industry, we provide a brief comparison between HMOs and ACOs in Table 1 below:

Table 1. Historic HMOs vs. Public Sector ACOs

General Characteristic	HMO	ACO
Geographic coverage	Defined region	Primary coverage based on primary care provider but also responsible for services provided outside the local area
Stakeholders	Hospitals, physician organizations	Hospitals, physician organizations
Patient mix		Public ACO: minimum of 5000 Medicare patients (mixed patient demographics) Private: varies according to payer plan
Care coordination	Restricted through contracting options	Increased flexibility
Payment model	FFS shifting to P4P	P4P, partial capitation, bundled payments[21]
Performance measure	HEDIS	Public: PQRI, meaningful use Private: HEDIS, NCQA, Premier
Locus of control	Payer organization	Physician ⤳ APRN

---

[20] Sinaiko AD, Rosenthal MB. Patients' role in accountable care organizations. *N Engl J Med* 2010;363:2583-2585.

[21] de Brantes F, Rosenthal MB, Painter M. Building a bridge from fragmentation to accountability—the Prometheus Payment model. *N Engl J Med*. 2009;361(11): 1033-1036.

This tabular comparison shows that locus of control is one reason for the introduction of the ACO and a major characteristic that differentiates it from the HMO. When health maintenance organizations were launched in the 1980s, they became gatekeeping organizations for patients who needed access to appropriate healthcare services in a timely manner.[22] While there have been successful efforts between some insurance payers and provider organizations in refining their administrative processes in order to improve services, there has not been enough progress at a macro level across the industry to curb the high and unsustainable growth in costs or to provide a more flexible delivery system that meets the needs of patients in the United States. The continual rise in costs and lack of care options in HMOs after 1990 led to dissatisfied patients and advocacy organizations that were unable to control costs as originally intended while simultaneously ending in lower quality of care. In light of this fact, one of the key tenets for ACOs is to ensure that each is physician-led and physician-directed. We will later address clinically integrated networks (CINs) and the ways in which creation of these entities may serve as a transitional strategy in moving from a fee-for-service environment toward one increasingly capable of managing both clinical and financial risk as an ACO.

Legislative Background

In light of the industry initiatives, economic trends, and forecasts that emerged since 1980 along with guidance from such organizations as the IOM, the Institute for Healthcare Improvement, and others, two landmark pieces of legislation affecting the American healthcare system were passed in 2009 and 2010. First was the Health Information Technology for Economic and Clinical Health Act (HITECH), part of the American Recovery and Reinvestment Act (ARRA) enacted in 2009. HITECH provided $25B in funds[23] and incentives to physicians and other healthcare providers to stimulate the implementation and adoption of health information technology between 2010 and 2015.

---

[22] Mirabito AM, Berry LL. Lessons that patient-centered medical homes can learn from the mistakes of HMOs. *Ann Intern Med* 2010;152(3): 182-185.

[23] Kocher R, Ezekiel EJ, DeParle NA. The Affordable Care Act and the future of clinical medicine: the opportunities and challenges. *Ann Intern Med*. 153(8): 536-539.

Second was the 2010 enactment of the Patient Protection and Affordable Care Act (PPACA).

This legislation, while controversial and far-reaching, is one of the most significant attempts to overhaul the U.S. health system in the last 50 years. The intended effects of this legislation were summarized best in a 2010 article in the *Annals of Internal Medicine*:

> [The law] guarantees access to health care for all Americans, creates new incentives to change clinical practice to foster better coordination and quality, gives physicians more information to make them better clinicians and patients more information to make them more value-conscious consumers, and change the payment system to reward value.[24]

As noted by Dr. Kocher and colleagues, the PPACA will encourage the formation of ACOs, leading to opportunities for physicians to continue forming larger organizations, finding new efficiencies, benefiting from new health information technology, and acquiring the managerial skills and resources necessary to move these organizations forward. With demonstration projects advancing the ACO model, Section 3022 of the PPACA, known as the Medicare Shared Savings Program, gives the Department of Health and Human Services (HHS) the authority to establish new regulations for public sector ACOs on a broader scale. The section becomes operational on January 1, 2012.

Hospitals, physician group practices, health systems, and other qualifying organizations will be able to form ACOs under this new program. We have extracted some of the high-level requirements from Section 3022 for the CMS version of the ACO model that will be described in detail throughout the book (Table 2). The requirements for Medicaid versions of the ACO or ACOs established in concert with private insurance payers may differ from these CMS requirements.

---

[24] Kocher R, Ezekiel EJ, DeParle NA. The Affordable Care Act and the future of clinical medicine: the opportunities and challenges. *Ann Intern Med*. 153(8): 536-539.

Table 2. General Requirements for a CMS ACO per PPACA Section 3022

Topic	Description
Management	Formal legal structure: ♦ ACO professionals in group practice arrangements ♦ Networks of individual practices of ACO professionals ♦ Partnerships or joint venture arrangements between hospitals and ACO professionals ♦ Hospitals employing ACO professionals ♦ Other groups of service providers and suppliers deemed appropriate by HHS ♦ Each ACO to have shared governance and leadership making joint decisions in operations and providing administrative and clinical systems
Time commitment to venture	Each ACO to have an agreement with HHS to participate in the ACO program for no less than 3 years
Number of Medicare beneficiaries	Minimum of 5,000
Structure	ACO to receive and administer payment of shared savings to participant organizations
Patient-centeredness criteria	Patient and caregiver assessments or individualized care plans
Health information technology	Care coordinated through the use of telehealth, remote patient monitoring, and other enabling technologies
Defined processes	Promotion of evidence-based medicine and patient engagement
Performance reporting	Specific quality measures to be identified by HHS but will include care transitions across care settings Reporting to incorporate requirements of the physician quality reporting initiatives (PQRI)
Benchmark setting	HHS to establish a benchmark for each ACO's 3-year period with the most recent 3 years of per-beneficiary expenditures assigned to the ACO. Benchmarks to be set by HHS "using the most recent available 3 years of per-beneficiary expenditures for parts A and B services for Medicare fee-for-service beneficiaries assigned to the ACO.[i]"
Shared savings	ACOs surpassing established benchmarks to receive a percent of the difference with the program retaining the remainder HHS to establish limits on shared savings that can be paid out

The PPACA represents the most important piece of legislation affecting the American healthcare system since the creation of the Medicare and Medicaid programs in 1965. While the ACO is a significant new program within the PPACA, many other healthcare services and the industry at large will see changes as a result of its enactment. Some examples are provided in Table 3.

Table 3. Sample of PPACA Reforms

Insurance Market Reform		
Section	**Topic**	**Action**
1311	Affordable choices among health benefit plans	Establishes new state-level health insurance exchanges
1511–15	New requirements on insurance for employers to offer employees	Changes to employer responsibilities for employees' insurance coverage
1101	Immediate access to insurance for uninsured individuals with preexisting conditions	Mitigates challenge faced by segments of the population with preexisting health conditions
2718	Lowering the cost of health care coverage	Changes in medical loss ratio threshold affecting payer organizations
10202	Incentives for states to offer home- and community-based services as long-term care alternatives to nursing homes	Qualified state Medicaid programs have opportunities for medical assistance incentive payments

Table 3. Sample of PPACA Reforms, ctd.

Research and Healthcare Education Reform		
Section	**Topic**	**Action**
937	Dissemination of and building capacity for research	New grants to fund comparative effectiveness research and the dissemination of findings from Section 6301 initiatives
6301	Creation of a new patient-centered outcomes research institute	Establishment of a new nonprofit corporation, the Patient-Centered Outcomes Research Institute, along with a research agenda
5301	Training in family medicine, general internal medicine, general pediatrics, and physician assistantship	Establishment of a new 5-year grant program for primary care training programs ($125,000,000 total appropriated funds)

Other Reforms		
Section	**Topic**	**Action**
3002	Improvement of the physician quality reporting system	Requiring integration of physician quality reporting and electronic health record reporting
5601	Funding of federally qualified health centers (FQHC)	Increased appropriations for years 2010–2015 and beyond

Some of these reforms will interact with ACO initiatives. For example, the insurance-related reforms should indirectly affect the relationships of employers, patients, and private payer organizations in regard to payments to ACO participants for health services.

A major concern in regard to Section 1101 is that the numbers of patients granted coverage will likely result in millions of new Medicaid enrollees. In addition, Section 10202 stipulates that state Medicaid programs must come up to 100% of Medicare for the first few years of this program's enactment; however, there is neither sustainable funding as of early 2011 nor a guarantee to keep the subject program operative.

Given the new path that ACOs represent, comparative effectiveness research projects will likely be conducted in time as demonstrations, pilot programs, and new ACO joint ventures begin to yield results. Last, the mandated changes to physician quality reporting will affect reporting requirements for primary and specialty care physician groups belonging to ACOs.

Next, four specific programs included in the PPACA are of particular relevance to the ACO program. We have provided a short summary of each program below; they will be referenced throughout the book.

I. Section 3021, "Establishment of Center for Medicare and Medicaid Innovation within CMS." This new Center for Medicare and Medicaid Innovation (CMMI) will provide opportunities to fund innovative projects through 2019 related to improvement in care coordination, implementation of medical homes, increased use of health information technology, and models for payment reform—all of which will support the advancement of ACOs. The PPACA currently calls for $10B to be appropriated between 2011 and 2019 to fund projects in preliminary testing stages and provide follow-on funds for continued operation and demonstration when experimental models prove to be successful.

II. Section 2706 of the Act establishes the Pediatric Accountable Care Organization Demonstration Project, scheduled to launch on January 1, 2012. This program follows the same rules established under Section 3022 but serves as a separate program for pediatric medical care providers and state Medicaid agencies.

III. Section 3502, "Establishing community health teams to support the patient-centered medical home (PCMH)." This new program will be chartered to provide contracts and grants for the purpose of creating new interdisciplinary teams to support primary care and obstetrics and gynecology practices. The health teams will comprise "medical specialists, nurses, pharmacists, nutritionists, dieticians, social workers, behavioral and mental health providers (including substance use disorder prevention and treatment providers), doctors of chiropractic, licensed complementary and alternative medicine practitioners, and physicians' assistants."[25] These teams will be responsible for providing valuable clinical support services to aid implementation of PCMHs within their geographically defined areas. These in turn will assist the implementation of ACOs within which the PCMHs will operate. Appendix B provides additional details regarding the clinical support services these teams are chartered to provide in the communities they will serve.

IV. Section 3001, "Establishment of a Hospital Value-based Purchasing Program." This section of the Act provides for a new demonstration program offering value-based incentive payments based on discharges during a 3-year demonstration period. The program will become operative on October 1, 2012 (fiscal year 2013) [26] to hospitals that meet the performance standards based on selected measures. For fiscal year 2013 these measures will come from two areas: conditions and procedures, and the Hospital Consumer Assessment of Healthcare Providers and Systems survey, commonly referred to as HCAHPS. The five specific conditions or procedures used as measures will include acute myocardial infarction; heart failure; pneumonia; surgical care improvement project measures; and healthcare-associated infections. Second, measures of patients' experiences with nurses, physicians, and hospitals from HCAHPS will be factored in as part of the formula for determining hospital value-based purchasing incentives and will be determined through the federal rule-making process prior to the start of the program.

A third set of measures will be included in fiscal year 2014—efficiency measures based on Medicare spending per beneficiary and adjusted for demographic factors. Total incentive payments made to organizations shall consist of a base operating diagnosis-related group payment and a value-based incentive payment percentage for the hospital for the applicable fiscal year.[27] In addition, starting in 2014 the value-based measures shall include efficiency measures on Medicare spending per beneficiary based on key patient

---

[25] H.R. 3590, Patient Protection and Affordable Care Act, §3502(b)(4), Eligible entities for community health teams to support patient-centered medical homes (2009).

[26] H.R. 3590, Patient Protection and Affordable Care Act, §3001(a)(1)(B), Start date for hospital value-based purchasing program (2009).

[27] H.R. 3590, Patient Protection and Affordable Care Act, §3001(a)(6)(B), calculation of value-based incentive payments (2009).

population demographics. This program poses an interesting relationship to the ACO program. Figure 6 below illustrates this relationship.

Figure 7. Benefits Alignment: ACO and Value-based Purchasing (VBP)

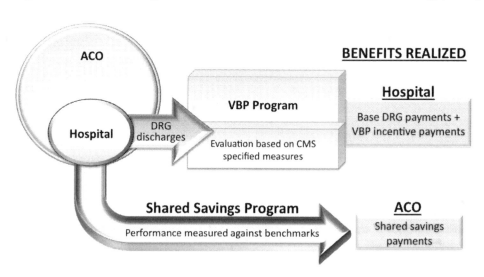

On closer examination of this model, the reader can see that when a hospital is part of the ACO as a collective (discussed further in Chapter 3), the entity should benefit financially from the ACO shared savings, base diagnosis-related group payments, and value-based purchasing incentive payments. While only the hospital can receive the value-based purchasing program and diagnosis-related group incentive payments, one can see how the structure created by formation of the ACO with its governance, leadership, and health information technology elements will yield opportunities for these rewards to support the total ACO structure in certain cases.

ACO Pilot Programs and Demonstrations

A number of pilot projects and demonstrations have been and are being conducted across the country. We shall discuss the landscape of these efforts in two separate categories: public sector ACO-related projects and private sector-related ACO projects and preparatory efforts.

Public Sector

The original public sector demonstration that is ongoing as of early 2011 is the Medicare Physician Group Practice Demonstration Project that was launched in 2000.[28] The program was initially established as a 5-year program involving ten different physician groups and health systems. Its purpose is summarized in the 2009 CMS program fact sheet:

> The demonstration creates incentives for physician groups to coordinate the overall care delivered to Medicare patients, rewards them for improving the quality and cost efficiency of health care services, and creates a framework to collaborate with providers to the advantage of Medicare beneficiaries.[29]

This group consists of the Dartmouth-Hitchcock Clinic, Geisinger Clinic, Marshfield Clinic, Park Nicollet Health Services, Forsyth Medical Group, Middlesex Health System, St. John's Health System, Billings Clinic, the Everett Clinic, and the University of Michigan Faculty Group Practice. Thirty-two ambulatory and preventive care measures were selected to evaluate improvement in outcomes. The 32 measures identified in relation to three disease conditions (diabetes mellitus, congestive heart failure, and coronary artery disease) and preventive measures as key categories are provided in Table 4.

---

[28] Centers for Medicare and Medicaid Services. *Roadmap for Implementing Value-driven Healthcare in the Traditional Medicare Fee-for-Service Program*, Physician PGP Demonstration. Available at http://www.cms.gov/QualityInitiativesGenInfo/downloads/VBPRoadmap_OEA_1-16_508.pdf, 13.

[29] Center for Medicare and Medicaid Services. Physician Group Practice Demonstration Program. Available at https://www.cms.gov/DemoProjectsEvalRpts/downloads/PGP_Fact_Sheet.pdf

Table 4. Physician Group Practice Demonstration Quality Measures[30]

Diabetes Mellitus	Congestive Heart Failure	Coronary Artery Disease	Preventive Care
HbA1c Management	Left Ventricular Function Assessment	Antiplatelet Therapy	Blood Pressure Screening
HbA1c Control	Left Ventricular Ejection Fraction Testing	Drug Therapy for Lowering LDL Cholesterol	Blood Pressure Control
Blood Pressure Management	Weight Measurement	Beta-Blocker Therapy – Prior MI	Blood Pressure Control Plan of Care
Lipid Measurement	Blood Pressure Screening	Blood Pressure	Breast Cancer Screening
LDL Cholesterol Level	Patient Education	Lipid Profile	Colorectal Cancer Screening
Urine Protein Testing	Beta-Blocker Therapy	LDL Cholesterol Level	
Eye Exam	Ace Inhibitor Therapy	Ace Inhibitor Therapy	
Foot Exam	Warfarin Therapy for Patients HF		
Influenza Vaccination	Influenza Vaccination		
Pneumonia Vaccination	Pneumonia Vaccination		

As a result of improved outcomes—all ten participants surpassed their goals for 28 measures—five of the physician groups shared in $25M of incentive payments out of $32M in total cost reductions for improving quality of care based on the specified ambulatory care and preventive care measures. The 2009 report noted a number of improvements; factors that contributed to their achievement included:

♦ Having clinical champions (doctor or nurse) responsible for quality reporting at each practice

♦ Redesign of clinical care processes

♦ Investment in health information technology, electronic health records, and patient registry improvements that allow practices to better identify gaps in care, alert physicians to these gaps during patient visits, and provide interim feedback on

---

[30] Centers for Medicare and Medicaid Services. Physician Group Practice Demonstration Program Fact Sheet (August 2009). Available at: https://www.cms.gov/DemoProjectsEvalRpts/downloads/PGP_Fact_Sheet.pdf, 3.

performance.

Appendix B provides an additional summary of these ten organizations, their individual approaches, and benefits derived from their demonstrations. Chapter 6 will also touch on some specific performance measure results from their efforts.

A second public sector example is related to Section 2706 and the pediatric accountable care organization demonstrations. These projects will have some inherent differences from the Medicare shared savings program even though they will be governed by the same rules. An instructive example is the Nationwide Children's Hospital organization in Columbus, Ohio.[31] Already organized as a pediatric accountable care organization under their Partners for Kids physician hospital organization, this hospital organization has over 760 physicians caring for over 285,000 pediatric patients across central and southeastern Ohio. Payments are arranged through capitated Medicaid fees for pediatric Medicaid patients from three Medicaid programs.[32]

While most of the literature surrounding ACOs focuses on initiatives related to adult patients, a key point regarding pediatric ACOs should be made—namely, the fact that each state has its own Medicaid office and can influence the focus and transformation of these ACOs separately from the Medicare- or private payer-based ACOs. As federal rules are defined, state rules will emerge from state Medicaid offices that will include differences to be reported in such other areas as pediatric-specific quality measures.

Private Sector

In the private sector, a number of organizations have led efforts to prepare physician practice groups and health systems for ACO implementation. The Premier Accountable

---

[31] Nationwide Children's Hospital Accountable Care Organization. Available at: https://www.nationwidechildrens.org/accountable-care-organization.

[32] ACO discussions begin; pediatricians will play a role. *Hospitalist News* [serial online], September 9, 2010. Available at: http://www.ehospitalistnews.com/news/practice-trendsleaders/single-article/aco-discussions-begin-pediatricians-will-play-a-role/38db10d39d.html

Care Organization Collaboratives[33] and the Accountable Care Organization Learning Network,[34] a joint initiative between the Brookings Institute and the Dartmouth Institute for Health Policy and Clinical Practice, are two of the leading programs in the industry. These collaboratives are meeting vital industry needs in helping organizations prepare for implementation of the ACO model. First, they facilitate forums for participants to mitigate risks through sharing lessons from organizations that have started the process of implementing an ACO. Second, the collaboratives provide opportunities for those organizations further down the path to help with guidance and serve as valuable case studies of early adopters.

The Premier Collaborative has 24 health systems engaged in their implementation collaborative[35] and 49 health systems in their ACO Readiness Collaborative,[36] both as of September 24, 2010. The Dartmouth-Brookings collaborative has engaged three different health systems for pilot ACO projects: Carilion Clinic in Roanoke, Virginia; Norton Healthcare in Louisville, Kentucky; and Tucson Medical Center in Tucson, Arizona.[37] Each organization in these demonstration projects is at a different stage in their ACO readiness or implementation. Norton Healthcare is partnering with Humana and Tucson Medical Center with United Healthcare, while the Carilion Clinic is partnering with multiple insurers that include United Healthcare, CIGNA, Anthem, and Southern Health.[38]

---

[33] Premier Accountable Care Organization Collaboratives. Available at: http://www.premierinc.com/quality-safety/tools-services/ACO/index.jsp

[34] Brookings-Dartmouth ACO Learning Network. Available at: https://xteam.brookings.edu/bdacoln/Pages/home.aspx

[35] Premier ACO Implementation Collaborative Participants (as of 9/24/10). Available at: http://www.premierinc.com/about/news/10-may/aco-impl-roster-with-map-092410.pdf.

[36] Premier ACO Implementation Collaborative Participants (as of 9/24/10). Available at: http://www.premierinc.com/about/news/10-may/aco-impl-roster-with-map-092410.pdf .

[37] Taylor M. The ABCs of ACOs. Accountable care organizations unite hospitals and other providers in caring for the community. *Trustee*. 2010;63(6):12-14.

[38] Tucson Medical Center picked to pilot program to improve patients' health, reduce costs. *Tucson Business* 3/12/10. Available at: http://www.azbiz.com/articles/2010/03/12/news/doc4b9a74a555d04943487875.txt; Norton, Humana involved in pilot program emphasizing wellness, preventive care. *Courier Journal* 11/21/10; Roberson J. Growing an ACO—easier said than done. *Physician Executive*, September-October 2010.

Part of the ACO concept is its ability to maintain flexibility. Just as the case studies of organizations participating in the CMS Physician Group Practice Demonstration Program showed that each organization focused on improving different aspects of their clinical processes and programs (Appendix C), the industry will learn about benefits realized and lessons derived from innovations implemented by these participating organizations in such different areas as infrastructure, leadership, and cultural change as well as payment model reform with their private payer partners. In addition, each ACO participant will concentrate on such technical issues as advanced application of electronic health records to strengthen care coordination and other goals in conjunction with PCMH and CMS meaningful use requirements.

An example of the formation of an ACO-like arrangement in the private sector is the Blue Cross/Blue Shield of Massachusetts (BCHSMA) Alternative Quality Contract Program.[39] Launched in 2009, this program focuses on implementing an "innovative global payment model that uses a budget based methodology, which combines a fixed per-patient payment (adjusted annually for health status and inflation) with substantial performance incentive payments (tied to the latest nationally accepted measures of quality, effectiveness, and patient experience)." As of early 2010, BCHSMA had contracted with nine provider groups in its network to engage in the program, which provides participants support with training, metrics dashboards, reporting, regular communications, and best practices sharing. While not established identically to the ACO concept and not specifically calling for a physician-led provider entity as is the case with the ACO model, the program is set up as a 5-year arrangement for participating providers and focuses on payment reform and performance measurement, looking at both ambulatory and hospital-based measures.

---

[39] Blue Cross Blue Shield of Massachusetts Alternative Quality Contract Program. Available at: http://www.qualityaffordability.com/solutions/alternative-quality-contract.html.

Summary and Conclusion

We observe in closing that the foundation of many key initiatives is in place with the strategic direction set by the Institute of Medicine, Department of Health and Human Services, and Center for Medicaid and Medicare Services, and other key industry stakeholders over the last decade. Having addressed public and private ACO models separately, we must also point to the importance of keeping a long-term perspective on working toward a multi-payer ACO model[40] that meets requirements for all payers and provides the benefits of improved population-based health management, reduced cost of care, improved reporting, and strong accountability. This issue will be addressed at various points throughout our book.

The United States faces tremendous challenges in the coming decades for providing needed healthcare services as well as managing their cost, and continuing to improve the quality of care offered. Many physicians practicing in the field are skeptical of the changes that lie ahead. A 2010 survey conducted with over 100,000 physicians after the release of the PPACA found strong sentiments expressed regarding anticipated increases in patient volume that must be handled with resources already stressed. Other respondents were even more concerned that the legislation will lead to the closing of more private practices.[41] Even amidst these challenges, ACOs, the industry shift to P4P, value-based purchasing, population health management, rising consumer expectations, and other agents of change are preparing to advance our nation's healthcare industry services.

---

[40] MedPAC Report to Congress: Improving Incentives in the Medicare Program (June 2009), Chapter 2: Accountable Care Organizations. Available at: www.medpac.gov/documents/Jun09_EntireReport.pdf, 55.

[41] Physicians Foundation. Health reform and the decline of physician private practice. Available at: http://www.physiciansfoundation.org/uploadedFiles/Health%20Reform%20and%20the%20Decline%20of%20Physician%20Private%20Practice.pdf , 45.

Chapter 2. Setting the Foundation
Patient-Centered Medical Home

Background of the Patient-Centered Medical Home

The patient-centered medical home (PCMH) is a major industry initiative for the primary care sector that was first introduced in 1967 by the American Academy of Pediatrics (AAP). After a slow start, it gained significant momentum after 2000. A basic element of the contemporary PCMH is the chronic care model that emerged in 2002.[42] This model provides components of care intended to meet key challenges for redesigning the healthcare system, as described in the Institute of Medicine's 2001 report titled *Crossing the Quality Chasm*.[43] These challenges are illustrated in Figure 8 below, and are responsive to both the need to reform primary care services and the conceptual need for the ACO model.

---

[42] Bodenheimer T, Wagner EH, Grumbach K. Improving primary care for patients with chronic illness: the chronic care model, Part 2. *JAMA*. 2002;288:1909-1914.

[43] Institute of Medicine, Committee on Quality of Health Care in America. Formulating new rules to redesign and improve care. In: *Crossing the Quality Chasm: A New Health System for the 21st Century*. Washington, DC: National Academies Press; 2001: 61–62.

Figure 8. IOM's Six Challenges for Redesign (2001)

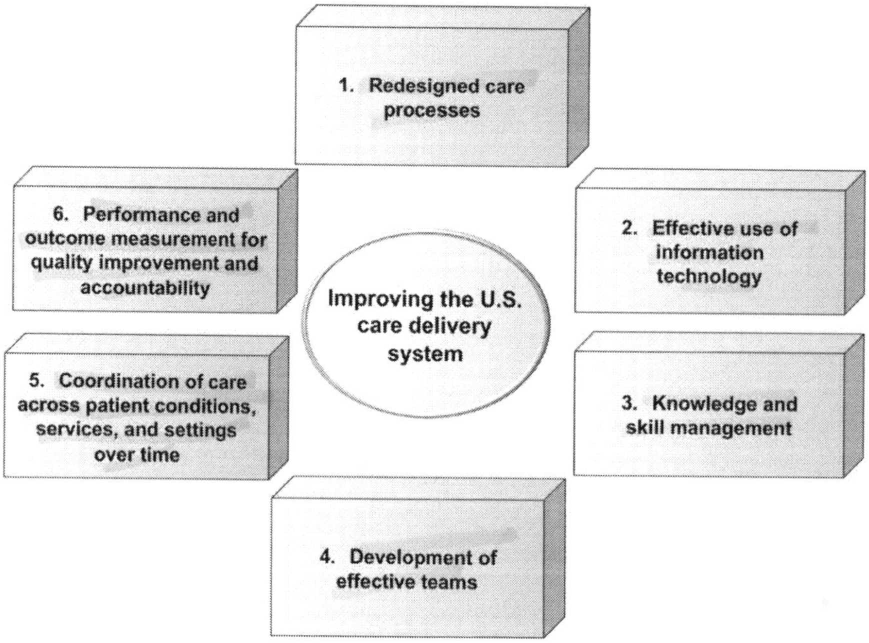

Looking at the IOM's redesign challenges for healthcare organizations identified in 2001, we can see that all six are addressed in the central design principles of the ACO as well as in the foundational elements and principles of the PCMH model.

The PCMH is based on a set of principles approved jointly by the American College of Physicians (ACP), the American Academy of Family Physicians (AAFP), the American Academy of Pediatrics (AAP), and the American Osteopathic Association (AOA) in 2007. These principles are:

↗ APRN

- Physician-directed medical services
- Quality and safety
- Personal ~~physician~~ → provider
- Whole-person orientation
- Payment reform
- Coordinated and integrated care
- Enhanced access to care

PCMH implementation focuses on improving coordination and integration of care; strengthening partnerships among physicians, patients, and their families; adopting and using electronic health records; and implementing methods of tracking performance measures based on industry-recognized requirements. Improving patients' access to care through open-access scheduling, flexible scheduling, appropriate use of the team concept, and proactive management between office visits are only a few of the activities conducted in the medical home. For many physicians, however, these changes represent disruptive innovations to traditional office practice. The uncertainty of moving to on-demand same-day appointment scheduling or corresponding with patients electronically are challenges that must be met. True roll-up-your-sleeves work is required to overcome the older embedded patterns. This task parallels the substantial changes that ACOs will require of hospitals and hospital systems. While certification as a medical home is not the only measure of success, it is one way to obtain recognition and assist in making the transformation.

The National Committee for Quality Assurance (NCQA) is recognized as the primary industry certification and recognition program for the PCMH model across the healthcare industry in the United States. Physician Practice Connections®–Patient-Centered Medical Home (PPC-PCMH™) is the present name of the certification. It has nine standards for physician practice reward and incentive payment eligibility. As achieving this certification provides part of the foundation for any ACO, we will mention three topics central to the NCQA program, including some that are specifically addressed in NCQA guidance for physician practices: program standards; steps to achieving recognition; and program scoring. First, the nine standards identified by the NCQA for attainment of PPC-PCMH™ recognition are summarized in Figure 9.

Figure 9. PPC-PCMH™ **Standards**[44]

Standards and Sections	Points	Standards and Sections	Points
Standard 1: Access and Communication		**Standard 5: Electronic Prescribing**	
a. Access and communication processes **	4	a. Electronic prescription writing	3
b. Access and communication results	5	b. Prescribing decision support-safety	3
	9	c. Prescribing decision support-efficiency	2
			8
Standard 2: Patient Tracking and Registry Functions		**Standard 6: Test Tracking**	
a. Basic system for managing patient data	2	a. Test tracking and follow-up**	7
b. Electronic system for clinical data	3	b. Electronic system for managing tests	6
c. Use of clinical data	3		13
d. Organizing clinical data**	6		
e. Identify important conditions**	4		
f. Use of system for population management	3		
	21		
Standard 3: Patient Tracking and Registry Functions		**Standard 7: Referral Tracking**	
a. Guidelines for important conditions**	3	a. Referral tracking**	4
b. Preventive service clinician reminders	4		4
c. Practice organization	3		
d. Care management for important conditions	5		
e. Continuity of care	5		
	20		
Standard 4: Patient Self-Management Support		**Standard 8: Performance Reporting/ Improvement**	
a. Documenting communication needs	2	a. Measures of performance**	
b. Self-management support**	4	b. Patient experience data	3
	6	c. Reporting to physicians**	3
		d. Setting goals and taking action	3
		e. Reporting standardized measures	3
		f. Electronic reporting to external entities	2
			1
			15
		Standard 9: Advanced Electronic Communications	
		a. Availability of interactive website	1
		b. Electronic patient identification	2
		c. Electronic care management support	1
			4

** Indicates "must pass" elements

The reader should note that ten must-pass elements are included within the nine standards.

By meeting these must-pass standards, each primary care practice can achieve improved chronic care management and patient compliance on prescribed interventions; stronger performance reporting; and the adoption and competent use of health information technology. Each physician or physician practice applying for PPC-PCMH™ certification must complete a rigorous process.

Second is the matter of "Steps for the Physician/Practice" as stated by the NCQA. Table 5 lists the NCQA's seven steps to recognition.

---

[44] NCQA Standards Workshop. Physician Practice Connections—Patient-Centered Medical Home, 2009. Slide 4. Available at: http://www.ncqa.org/.

Table 5. Steps to Recognition[45]

Step No.	Description
1	Review program information
2	Participate in a standards workshop
3	Obtain a survey tool
4	Participate in a WebEx ISS demonstration of the survey tool
5	Use survey tool to self-assess current performance
6	Submit completed application, agreements, fee, and results to NCQA
7	Receive final recognition decision and Level in 30-60 days"

The survey tool is central to the certification process and achieving required scores on the nine standards. This instrument helps practices assess their progress in preparing to submit an application and is required for recognition.

The third concern is program scoring. The NCQA established a three-level qualification model based on the nine certification standards. Table 6 defines scoring at each level.

Table 6. NCQA PPC-PCMH Scoring Levels and Structure[46]

Level of Qualifying	Points	Must Pass Elements at 50% Performance Level
Not Recognized	0-24	< 5
Level 1	25-49	5 of 10
Level 2	50-74	10 of 10
Level 3	75-100	10 of 10

[45] NCQA Standards Workshop. Physician Practice Connections—Patient-Centered Medical Home, 2009. Slide 94. Available at: http://www.ncqa.org/.

[46] NCQA Standards Workshop. Physician Practice Connections—Patient-Centered Medical Home, 2009. Slide 5. Available at: http://www.ncqa.org/.

The structure of this model is important because it is linked to the financial incentives that physicians/practices can receive based on performance for attaining and maintaining the standards at their respective level.

Common Ground: PCMH and ACO

The PCMH model has been identified as a starting point for successful implementation of the ACO. Figure 10 illustrates the close alignment between the seven joint principles of the PCMH and the three core principles of the ACO.

Figure 10. Alignment of PCMH and ACO Principles

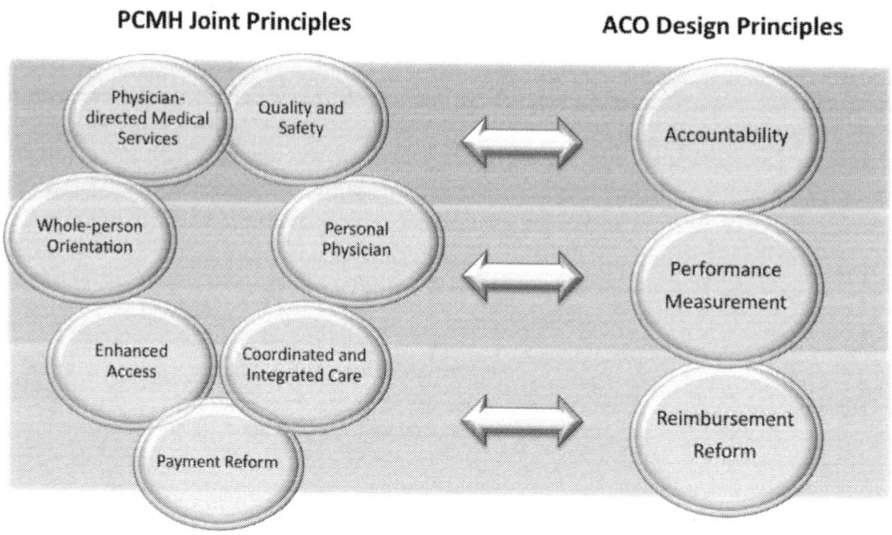

We will look at each of the three ACO design principles in relationship to the PCMH principles in order to provide perspective on this common ground. One additional area of commonality to note first, however, is the established process of PCMH certification and recognition and the conceptual certification criteria for future formal ACOs.

As indicated in Table 6, the PCMH model follows a three-level certification and recognition process based on standards and elements to be met by all physician groups applying to the NCQA for recognition. In the case of ACOs, industry experts and the

NCQA have explored the issues related to qualification and certification. In two articles published in 2010, Shortell and colleagues proposed a three-tier qualification model for CMS to consider adopting and adding to the federal rules on structuring public sector ACOs.[47] In the article that appeared in the *Journal of the American Medical Association*, the authors recommended a three-level qualification process for ACOs that could be combined with a set of envisioned characteristics set forth in their article in the May 2010 issue of *Health Affairs*.[39] These qualifications and characteristics are arrayed in Table 7 below.

---

[47] Shortell SM, Casalino LP, Fisher ES. How the center for medicare and medicaid innovation should test accountable care organizations. *Health Aff (Millwood)*. 2010;29(7):1293-1298. Fisher ES, Shortell SM. Accountable care organizations: accountable for what, to whom, and how. *JAMA*. 2010;304(15):1715-1716.

Table 7. ACO Qualification Levels and Characteristics

Level	Qualification Level[48]	Characteristics[49]
1	ACOs without electronic health records: could rely for the near term on key measures derived from claims data	◆ Legal entity with basic health information technology and performance reporting capabilities ◆ Shared savings for meeting quality and cost targets without downside risk ◆ Adoption of core starter set measures: quality, efficiency, and patient experience
2	ACOs with site-specific electronic health records and registries: expected to add more advanced measures (such as patient-reported health outcomes for selected conditions)	◆ Strong infrastructure in place with advanced health information technology and care coordination staff ◆ Larger shared savings with accountability for cost performance ◆ Adoption of core starter set measures: quality, efficiency, and patient experience
3	ACOs with comprehensive electronic health records across all sites: may be used to test and implement measurement systems to drive practice improvement and accountability in areas that challenge the industry (such as informed patient choice and health outcomes for a variety of conditions)	◆ Advanced infrastructure, full complement of services, and reserve requirements ◆ Risk-adjusted partial capitation coupled with performance bonuses ◆ Strongest performance and reporting targets

Recognizing that these qualifications and characteristics are only proposals based on recommendations from industry experts, we anticipate that final rules from CMS will contain guidance on a certification process and requirements that may be applied to both

---

[48] Fisher ES, Shortell SM. Accountable care organizations: accountable for what, to whom, and how. *JAMA*. 2010;304(15):1715-1716.

[49] McClellan M, McKethan AN, Lewis JL, Roski J, Fisher ES. A national strategy to put accountable care into practice. *Health Aff* (*Millwood*). 2010;29(5):982-990.

public and private sector ACOs. We shall now consider each of the ACO design principles in terms of its alignment with the joint principles of the PCMH.

Accountability

Accountability is central to the existence of the ACO. For the healthcare industry to move away from the FFS system and the HMO-dominated private insurer market, placing physicians as the leaders of ACOs is of paramount importance. In terms of the model depicted in Figure 9, one can draw an immediate parallel between physician-directed medical services, having a personal physician, and an emphasis on quality and safety on the one side and the ACO element of accountability on the other. All three areas can be directly related to the importance of having physicians in leadership roles in each ACO.

Similarly, having access to clinical information and placing physicians as leaders of the ACO holding themselves and the entirety of the ACO accountable to predetermined performance measures is an important distinction in comparison to the failed payer-driven physician-hospital organizations of the past.

Accountability extends beyond the single encounter or episode of care. From this perspective we are moving toward measures of ongoing health and health maintenance. Last, no discussion of accountability is complete without considering the patient. The health care team can accomplish much, but they cannot do it alone. Personal responsibility on the part of the patient is integral to moving forward. The ACO is designed to better equip patients to take ownership of their healthcare. Reminder notices, follow-up visits, simplified navigation of complex health care systems—all better enable patients in this regard. Thus engaging patients in their own care and partnering with them are essential features of both the medical home and the ACO in this model of accountability.

Performance Measurement

Defining the benchmarks of ACO evaluation will be important in establishing the performance measures of process, outcomes, and cost. The central principles of whole-person orientation, coordinated and integrated care, and enhanced access to care will all be traceable to specific measures in these areas of performance evaluation. Chapter 6 will address this topic in greater detail.

Reimbursement Reform

Reimbursement reform is central to success for both the PCMH and the ACO. As discussed above, moving away from the FFS/episode-of-care model of reimbursement in the direction of adoption and implementation of advanced methods—including bundled service payments, partial capitation, value-based purchasing arrangements, and the ACO's shared savings incentives—is critical to success. More specifically, paying the physician and the care team to provide care between episodes of treatment is essential to making the model work. Some of these methods have been tested previously and will be tried further in new models under Section 3021 of the PPACA in projects launched and funded under the Center for Medicare and Medicaid Innovation.

There is one significant point of difference between the PCMH and ACO models as indicated in a 2009 report by the American Academy of Family Physicians Task Force. This report noted that

> The Accountable Care Organization model mainly differs from the Joint Principles of the PCMH in that the PCMH focuses on physician practice structure and processes improvements (e.g. electronic health records, patient registries, same-day appointments, etc.) and not on accountability for cost and quality for a defined patient population.[50]

---

[50] AAFP Accountable Care Organization Task Force Report, October 2009. Available at: http://www.aafp.org/online/etc/medialib/aafp_org/documents/policy/private/healthplans/payment/acos/acotfreport.Par.0001.File.dat/AAFP-ACO-Report-NoRecs-20091010.pdf

What we derive from this observation is that while there is common ground, the PCMH provides many foundational elements that can be integrated within the ACO model. The major difference between the two models should not be seen as a shortcoming but rather as evidence of the ongoing evolution of the healthcare delivery system to better serve its patients and their surrounding communities.

Successful PCMH Models Leading ACO Industry Initiatives

At this point we wish to describe two models of care in the United States that have been acknowledged as successful PCMH models and are breaking ground in their communities for future ACO initiatives.[51]

Vermont Blueprint for Health

First is the Vermont Blueprint for Health Project.[52] This novel initiative began in 2006 as a state-based health care reform program with two phases, the first being an enhanced medical home model and the second, implementation of an ACO model. The state of Vermont provides a unique payer environment, as it has only three commercial payers and a history of collaboration on reform initiatives. Vermont's model "creates a shared savings incentive pool based on projected medical expenses, which is distributed on the basis of agreed-on quality measures and population health targets."[53] By the end of 2009, three enhanced medical home community pilot programs had been established. These pilots have five specific components, listed in Table 8.

---

[51] Fields D, Leshen E, Patel K. Analysis and commentary. Driving quality gains and cost savings through adoption of medical homes. *Health Aff (Millwood)*. 2010;29(5):819-826.

[52] Hester J Jr. Designing Vermont's pay-for-population health system. *Prev Chronic Dis.* 2010;7(6):1-6. Available at: http://www.cdc.gov/pcd/issues/2010/nov/pdf/10_0072.pdf.

[53] Hester J Jr. Designing Vermont's pay-for-population health system. *Prev Chronic Dis.* 2010;7(6):1-6. Available at: http://www.cdc.gov/pcd/issues/2010/nov/pdf/10_0072.pdf.

Table 8. Components of the Vermont Pilot Program[54]

Component	Description
Financial reform	Payers (Medicaid, Medicare, and the three commercial payers) agreed to make changes that included monthly per capita payments to each practice and funding of a community health team, similar in nature to the new program required by Section 3502 of the PPACA.
Community health teams	Varied multidisciplinary clinician teams focused on providing direct services to support the program's physician practices.
Health information technology	Each practice uses a Web-based patient data tracking system called DocSite Registry, mapped to both electronic health records and state-driven health information exchanges to provide population-based reports.
Community activation and preventive care	Three tasks assigned to the community health teams include: development and management of community risk profiles; setting priorities for preventive care interventions; and design and implementation of a "local prevention plan in coordination with the delivery system."
Evaluation	The program's effectiveness will be evaluated over a period of 20 months for the patient population based on "NCQA Patient-Centered Medical Home scores, clinical process measures, health status measures, cost and utilization measures from a multi-payer claims database, and population health indicators." Results will be compared to matched samples of patients outside the program's area.

The first phase of the program sets the foundation for the second phase and the implementation of the ACO. A central feature of the planning for the Vermont program was a focus on the Institute for Healthcare Improvement's Triple Aim Project.[55] The three tenets of this project are 1) control of total per capita medical costs; 2) improvement of

---

[54] Hester J Jr. Designing Vermont's pay-for-population health system. *Prev Chronic Dis.* 2010;7(6): 6. Available at: http://www.cdc.gov/pcd/issues/2010/nov/pdf/10_0072.pdf. The reader is referred to the section titled "Phase I: Enhanced Medical Home."

[55] Institute for Healthcare Improvement (IHI). The Triple Aim Project. Available at: http://www.ihi.org/IHI/Programs/StrategicInitiatives/TripleAim.htm.

population health; and 3) improvement of consumers' healthcare experience. While the ACO is still in the planning stage as of January 2011, the foundation is in place and the state's positive collaboration with payers should provide valuable insights for future ACO implementations.

Geisinger

The second PCMH model under consideration is that implemented by the Geisinger Health System (Geisinger). Geisinger is an integrated delivery system headquartered in Danville, Pennsylvania, with three acute care hospitals along with nearly 61 clinical practice sites that provide adult and pediatric primary and specialty care. Geisinger serves a population of over 2.6 million patients as of early 2011. Geisinger is recognized as an industry leader for innovation in delivery system initiatives; is one of 10 participants in the CMS Physician Group Practice Demonstration Project; is a member of Premier's ACO Collaborative Implementation Workgroup; and is a recipient of a BEACON Community Grant from the Office of National Coordinator for Health Information Technology. Two pioneering innovations that have contributed to Geisinger's successful PCMH implementation and ACO model preparation are its Personal Health Navigator and Geisinger Proven Care®.[56] The Personal Health Navigator system and its services include 24/7 access to primary and specialty care; a nursing care coordinator at all community practice sites; predictive tools to identify risk trends; virtual care management support; and evidence-based care to reduce hospitalization.

Additional features of the Geisinger PCMH model include access to electronic health records for physicians, patients, and care managers; practice-based payments that include base monthly payments to physicians, a stipend for each practice, and incentive payments shared by the physicians and care teams; and performance reports that are jointly reviewed by members of each community practice in concert with their payer group.

---

[56] Paulus RA, Davis K, Steele GD. Continuous innovation in health care: implications of the Geisinger experience. *Health Aff* (*Millwood*). 2008;27(5):1235-1245.

The second innovation by that has strengthened Geisinger's position as an industry leader of early ACO implementation is their acute-episode care program called Geisinger ProvenCare.® This program, which focused initially on coronary artery bypass graft procedures, has three primary elements that include putting best practices in place across the full episode of care; creation of risk-based pricing with an up-front discount to the payer for the historical readmission rate; and establishment of a path to patient engagement. Given the success of these programs and others at Geisinger, the system is a leader to watch for best practice implementation as the ACO model evolves.

In closing this section, we present in Table 9 a set of must-haves for any ACO as noted by Shortell in 2009:[57]

Table 9. ACOs Must Haves...

No.	Element
1	Have a governance structure that is the focal point for accountability
2	Able to measure costs, productivity, quality, and outcomes of care
3	Able to aggregate data from individual units
4	Have a sufficient number of patients to detect statistically significant differences in performance from established targets
5	Able to report data to external groups
6	Have the information technology and work process design capability to improve care on a continuous basis

This list embodies several of the key tenets already described and others that will be discussed throughout this book. In addition to the list in Table 7, we want to offer a seventh must-have:

Relentless drive to achieve new levels of integration for the benefit of improving quality of care across targeted patient populations.

---

[57] Shortell SM. Organizing healthcare for higher quality and lower cost. Slideshow presented at: Capstone Conference; May 14, 2009; Menlo Park, CA. Available at: http://www.slideshare.net/capstoneconference09/stephen-shortell-organizing-health-care-for-higher-quality-and-lower-cost-1456226.

We hope that this last element may serve as part of an inherent mission and framework for every ACO in focusing its future operations.

INFOCUS: **Challenges and Risks to Overcome**

Having an understanding of the common ground shared by the PCMH and ACO models, we know there are several challenges and risks to confront in order to guarantee future success for ACOs across the country. We have discussed key elements of the PCMH, the common ground between the PCMH and ACO, and presented examples of PCMH model organizations that are leaders of ACO adoption and implementation. So what are some of these challenges in relation to the primary care foundation with PCMH models? Table 10 below identifies a number of these along with a suggested set of mitigation strategies.

Table 10. Chapter 2: Challenges and Risks

Challenges	Risks
2a) Implementing an integrated performance reporting system.	2g) Revenue lost in transition to new reimbursement models.
2b) Achieving agreement across ACO participant PCMHs on integrated clinical guidelines and equitable savings allocation.	2h) Negative impact on individualized patient care services during the shift to population-based disease condition management.
2c) Aligning advanced PCMH objectives with ACO qualification level criteria.	2i) Lack of investment capital and acceptance of financial risk.
2d) Assigning patients to ACOs [58].	2j) Inability to hold an ACO accountable for a patient's care received outside their region [59].
2e) Having sufficient resources to	2k) Not managing organizational change

---

[58] Luft HS. Becoming accountable—opportunities and obstacles for ACOs. *N Engl J Med.* 2010;363(15):1389-1391.

[59] Luft HS. Becoming accountable—opportunities and obstacles for ACOs. *N Engl J Med.* 2010;363(15):1389-1391.

manage large-scale complexity, overcome tradition, and change activities required across a multiyear ACO implementation.	across ACO participants.
2f) Managing the impact on the revenue cycle impact for hospitals when chronic disease management has been optimized but payment methods have not caught up.	2i) Negative economic impact on consumers related to potentially higher out-of-pocket expenses and increased cost of navigating the care system.

Potential Mitigation Strategies

√ **Impact on patient care**: Use of predictive modeling tools[60] for identification of chronic illness population segments for targeted prevention efforts.

√ **Impact on patient care:** Implementing care management programs[44] to proactively support and manage the patient's needs following treatment or interventions.

√ **Lack of investment 1:** Engaging resources to establish financial plans that identify options for securing needed investments to cover capital, training, and expenses of the transition period.

√ **Lack of investment 2:** Encouraging physicians in need of capital infusion to consider partnering with health systems and large entities.

√ **Mitigating financial impact**: Physicians and providers negotiate rapid-cycle implementation of new payment methods to account for new and improved levels of healthcare services across the continuum of care.

√ **Organizational transformation**: Utilize change management disciplines and process improvement methodologies to minimize risk of failure.

---

[60] Boland P, Polakoff P, Schwab T. Accountable care organizations hold promise, but will they achieve cost and quality targets? *Manag Care*. 2010;19(10):12-6, 19.

Chapter 3. Governance and Alignment Strategies

Establishing the structure, formation, and leadership of each ACO is a critical element to success as ACOs come in many different shapes and sizes.

ACO Participants

A number of different healthcare organizations and physician practice arrangements can fit into the ACO model. Table 11 identifies seven potential entities that may independently or collectively form ACOs.

Table 11. Provider Organizations That May Participate in ACOs[61]

Independent practice associations (IPA)	Hospital medical staff organizations (MSOs)[62]	Integrated delivery networks (IDNs)
Multispecialty physician groups (MSPG)	Physician-hospital organizations (PHOs)	Primary care physician practices
Extended hospital medical staff[63]		Clinical integrated networks (CINs)

Other participants in an ACO will include the payer organizations (private and public), along with such ancillary care entities as home health caregivers, nursing homes, skilled nursing facilities, and rehabilitation facilities. From a stakeholder perspective, an ACO

---

[61] Devers K, Berenson R. Can accountable care organizations improve the value of health care by solving the cost and quality quandaries? Robert Wood Johnson policy analysis paper, October 2009. Available at: http://www.rwjf.org/files/research/acobrieffinal.pdf.

[62] Smithson K, Baker S. Medical staff organizations: a persistent anomaly. *Health Aff* (*Millwood*). 2007;26(1):w76-w79.

[63] Fisher ES, Staiger DO, Bynum JP, Gottlieb DJ. Creating accountable care organizations: the extended hospital medical staff. *Health Aff* (*Millwood*). 2007;26 (1):w44-w57.

should also focus its attention on its patients. While a Medicare ACO will be required to have a minimum number of beneficiaries covering a specific subpopulation, there will also be Medicaid and private payer ACOs. Though operating under the basic principles of ensuring accountability and payment reform innovation, each ACO may have different performance measurement requirements based on the patient population that it serves. Such other factors as patient communications, the ability of the information system to collect and track data, physician agreement on measurements, and clinical workflow processes that enhance patient satisfaction must also be taken into account. Each type of provider organization will relate to patients at different points across the continuum of care with the long-term goal of forming an entity that will meet all of a patient's needs effectively, efficiently, at the lowest cost, and of the highest quality.

Dr. Fisher described the extended hospital medical staff in a 2006 *Health Affairs* article as "essentially a hospital-associated multispecialty group practice that is empirically defined by physicians' direct or indirect referral patterns to a hospital."[64] This definition is based on the notion that physicians and groups of physicians who operate separately from an IDN or other hospital-type organization as independent practices can actually be viewed as part of an extended singular virtual organization. Dr. Fisher's study was based on quantitative analysis of Medicare claims data but also identified a number of challenges and barriers that included local market structures, physician-community cultural issues, legal hurdles, physician practice-hospital organization alignments, and performance measurements and evaluation. A number of these issues are noted in the *INFOCUS* section at the end of this chapter; they are also being addressed across the industry with ongoing reform efforts.

Leadership

Engaging the right persons to lead ACOs is critical to long-term success. This section will cover two key topics: styles of leadership to fit the goals and culture of each ACO, followed by a discussion of why physician leadership is central to the ACO's success.

---

[64] Fisher ES, Staiger DO, Bynum JP, Gottlieb DJ. Creating accountable care organizations: the extended hospital medical staff. *Health Aff* (*Millwood*). 2007;26 (1):w45.

Leaders of healthcare organizations have confronted challenges in the past in addition to those related to the present transformation of the healthcare industry resulting from the need for higher quality care and achievement of greater economic gains for the industry. Some of these challenges include:[65]

- A highly professional workforce concentrated in silos;
- Traditional physician training that tends to inhibit collaboration;
- Lengthy and demanding training to develop clinical skills and knowledge that may delay the development of leadership skills;
- An increasingly complex external environment (such as insurance payer compensation, state licensing requirements, and antitrust laws) requiring a high level of astuteness and business acumen to function in the primary/specialty care or hospital environment.

There are several specific points regarding leadership styles that support and expedite the development of ACOs, given the industry's continued movement toward collaboration and integration. As each community and its complement of healthcare providers is unique, the leadership required from physicians to help achieve the goals of improved population health and lowered cost of care across America has never been greater. In addition to dealing with these challenges as described at the close of Chapter 2, the ACO carries with it an increased need for skills and knowledge related to change management. Such large-scale organizational transformation initiatives—to be discussed in detail in Chapter 8—make it essential that leaders understand the emotional turmoil that their personnel will undergo and the complex interdependencies that will develop among participants as innovations are introduced to enhance the ACO's ability to deliver care at the right time in the right place.

A 1996 quotation from Dr. Donald Berwick may serve as a summary of this section: "Effective leaders challenge the status quo both by insisting that the current system cannot

---

[65] Stoller JK. Developing physician-leaders: a call to action. *J Gen Intern Med*. 2009;24(7):876–878. Available at: http://www.ncbi.nlm.nih.gov/pmc/articles/PMC2695517/pdf/11606_2009_Article_1007.pdf.

remain and by offering clear ideas about superior alternatives."[66] Along with implementing change and addressing these challenges, current and future leaders of ACOs must embrace innovation in order to challenge the status quo. With these matters in mind, we should now look at leadership style issues that can accelerate ACO development.

Appropriate leadership styles

In defining the leadership styles that will support ACO development over the next decade, we must identify the underlying skills and traits needed for future physician leaders. Though Figure 11 is not all-inclusive, it does enumerate skills and traits that are inherently important to the style of leadership employed and for the leaders themselves.

Figure 11. Leadership Skills & Traits Needed for ACO Leaders

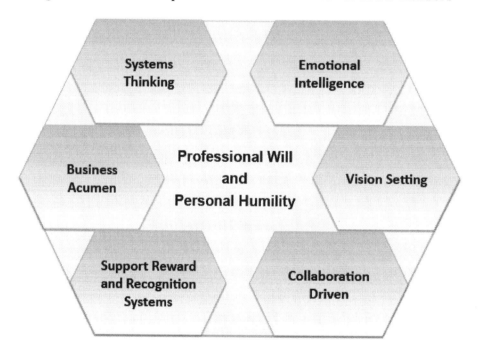

Each physician leader will bring his or her own clinical expertise to the ACO based on their chosen discipline of training, residency, and practice. Nonetheless, Figure 10 illustrates

---

[66] Berwick DM. A primer on leading the improvement of systems. *BMJ*. 1996;312:619-622. Available at: http://www.ncbi.nlm.nih.gov/pmc/articles/PMC2350403/pdf/bmj00532-0035.pdf.

seven key traits and skills that will enable ACO leaders to forge new partnerships and bring about collective and effective improvement of population health across the communities they serve.

1. **Systems thinking**. Originating in the field of engineering, systems thinking pertains to understanding the interrelationships of complex entities and the ways in which individual components affect the functionality of the whole. Systems thinking is part of the foundation of the learning organization theory to be applied in Chapter 7.[67] New systems will emerge as ACOs are formed through new partnerships. Within these systems, a systematic approach to problem solving oriented to people, process, and technology will be a powerful tool for physician leaders to confront these challenges.

2. **Business acumen**. ACO leaders will need core skills derived from the business world to comprehend and manage the spectrum of legal, fiscal, and strategy-related issues that arise daily.

3. **Support reward and recognition systems**. The Institute of Medicine noted in its 2001 report, *Crossing the Quality Chasm*, that physician leaders should have a strong understanding of these systems and the ability to motivate their ACO's administrative, clinical, and technical teams. The shared savings program is an example of an economic stimulus behind the ACO concept that can foster such motivation.

4. **Collaboration-driven**. A passion for effective collaboration across multiple organizations will be a necessity, given the nature of the path toward ACO establishment in markets across the United States. Strong communication skills will help to reinforce this trait along with diplomacy to secure consensus rather than imposing decisions.

---

[67] Pisapia J, Reyes-Guerra D, Coukos-Semmel E. Developing the leader's strategic mindset: establishing the measures. *Leadership Review*. 2005;5:41-68. Available at: http://www.leadershipreview.org/2005spring/PisapiaArticle.pdf; Senge P. *The Fifth Discipline: The Art and Practice of the Learning Organization*. New York, NY: Currency Doubleday; 1994.

5. Vision setting. The ability to describe the future of an organization and convey it in a meaningful way to peer physicians, clinical team members, and others is necessary if they are to have a clear understanding of the tasks before them in establishing and operating the ACO.

6. Emotional intelligence. Beyond the intelligence quotient or IQ, emotional intelligence or EQ is defined as "how leaders handle themselves and their relationships."[68] This trait is considered a must-have in the formation of clinically integrated networks or accountable care organizations. People and their relationships will determine whether an ACO is a success or a failure. Physician leaders must have a firm grip on their own emotions each day along with the awareness and empathy to support and meet the needs of others in their organizations.

7. Professional will and personal humility. Collins identifies these traits as central to what he calls Level 5 Leaders.[69] Physician-executives leading ACOs will have great need for both. Such physicians will surround themselves with team members and other strong leaders, all of whom will have their special expertise and focus. The senior executive tasked with driving negotiations, motivating those around them, and advancing the implementation of health reform agendas will find that these two traits serve them well.

These seven skills and traits may serve as a set of management indicia for present and future ACO leaders today. Within this context, what are some leadership styles to move these organizations forward? We propose three styles in Table 12: situational, transformational, and servant. Each of these is applicable to healthcare organizations—especially those on the way to forming ACOs.

---

[68] Serio CD, Epperly T. Physician leadership: a new model for a new generation. *Fam Pract Manag.* 2006;13(2):51-54. Available at: http://www.aafp.org/fpm/2006/0200/p51.pdf.

[69] Collins J. *Good to Great: Why Some Companies Make the Leap and Others Don't.* New York, NY: Harper Business; 2001.

Table 12. Leadership Styles and Successful ACO Implementation

Situational[70]	Transformational[71]	Servant[72]
Adaptable to specific situations	Influences subordinates to drive toward "ethically inspired goals transcending self interest"	Engages in active listening
Leader assumes one of four roles: coaching, supporting, delegating, or leading		Demonstrates empathy for workers and peers
	Four central components: "idealized influence, inspirational motivation, intellectual stimulation, and individualized consideration"	Strong communicator of concepts
Understands need for workers' empowerment and recognition		Possesses strong persuasive abilities
Leader knows his or her strengths but adjusts when needed	Facilitates team growth through individualized mentoring or coaching relationships	"Exerts a healing influence on individuals and institutions"
Recognizes the need for change		Establishes a community in the workplace

Each of these leadership styles can prove beneficial to an ACO's development. We believe, however, that the transformational style of leadership is best suited to the need to balance the goals of better patient-centered population health management against the needs of the workforce and the greater good of the surrounding community.

---

[70] Chaudry J, Jain A, McKenzie S, Schwartz RW. Physician leadership: the competencies of change. *J Surg Educ*. 2008;65(3):213-220. Available at: http://www.uthscsa.edu/gme/documents/PhysicianLsp-CompetenciesofChange.pdf

[71] Xirasagar S, Samuels ME, Curtin TF. (February 2006). Management training of physician executives, their leadership style, and care management performance: an empirical study. *Am J Manag Care*. 2006;12(2):101-108. Available at: http://www.ajmc.com/media/pdf/AJMC_06febXirasagar101to108.pdf

[72] Schwartz RW, Tumblin TF. The power of servant leadership to transform health care organizations for the 21st-century economy. *Arch Surg*. 2002;137(12):1419-1427. Available at: http://archsurg.ama-assn.org/cgi/reprint/137/12/1419.

Leaders of healthcare organizations must bring dynamic skills and expertise to their positions along with an unwavering commitment to excellence. While each organization and community will have its particular features and requirements that shape its goals and objectives, it can reach a higher level with the help of a leader with clear discernment and vision. For ACOs, the journey involves reintegration of activities that may not have been required in years past. Different leaders will bring their respective talents and backgrounds; however, understanding the importance of transformational leadership will enable them to implement ACOs successfully and reduce risk across clinical, administrative, financial, regulatory, and information technology domains alike.

Who drives the bus?

One of the most important aspects of ACO governance is the element of physician leadership. The criterion of accountability requires ACOs to be led by physicians. The American Medical Association, Institute for Healthcare Improvement, NCQA, MedPAC, and other organizations have all endorsed this stipulation. Ensuring that physicians are the source of medical decisions is critical to patient safety and quality-of-care goals. This insistence on physician leadership is related in part to past experience with HMOs in the 1990s.

In contrast to the HMO model, in which payers primarily used various utilization review methods to control costs, the physician-led ACO model maintains that physicians who are focused on patient care clinical outcomes are far better positioned to help patients achieve or maintain their best state of health and therefore indirectly lower the total cost of care. An associated change is the shift from the utilization review metrics of the past to the quality outcomes measures of the present and future.

In sum, it is important to note that leadership of such healthcare organizations as ACOs is an evolutionary concept that bears further study and analysis.[73] As our health

---

[73] Shortell SM. Challenges and opportunities for population health partnerships. *Prev Chronic Dis.* 2010;7(6):1-2. Available at: http://www.cdc.gov/pcd/issues/2010/nov/10_0110.htm; Shortell SM, Casalino

system evolves in the United States and elsewhere in the world, organizations merge and new relationships lead to new dynamics in the industry. Following our discussion of leadership styles, we must turn to some of the possible organizational configurations for establishing ACOs.

ACO Models

Given the array of possible participants in any given ACO, what are some of the ways these organizations can be combined to operate as a legal entity? Each type of organization has both unique and common characteristics. Two leading types of organizations for facilitating the development of these models are the employed-physician integrated delivery network (IDN) and the clinically integrated (that is. not employed by) network (CIN), in which employed and independent physicians, hospitals, and other care delivery resources come together in various relationships. Employed-physician IDNs are typically large regional health systems with multiple hospitals and ancillary services that have the administrative resources, technology, and a sizable medical staff to support the undertaking of a large-scale initiative—such as ACO formation—in their geographic market. CIN is a broader term, encompassing collections of independent physicians and potentially employed physicians and/or IDNs working together as an integrated unit. The CIN is organized to achieve economies of scale in joint contracting initiatives and to provide opportunities for increasing the quality and coordination of patient care in its geographic region without the need for direct employment relationships.

How to become a CIN with the ability to make joint contracts is in part the subject of Chapter 4, which discusses antitrust legislation and safe harbors. Figure 12[74] provides an

---

LP, Fisher ES. How the center for medicare and medicaid innovation should test accountable care organizations. *Health Aff (Millwood)*. 2010;29(7):1297.

[74] H.R. 3590, Patient Protection and Affordable Care Act, §3022(b)(1)(A-E); Rittenhouse DR, Shortell SM, Fisher ES. Primary care and accountable care—two essential elements of delivery-system reform. *N Engl J Med*. 2009;361(24):2301-2303; Devers K, Berenson R. Can accountable care organizations improve the value of health care by solving the cost and quality quandaries? Robert Wood Johnson policy analysis paper, October 2009. Available at: http://www.rwjf.org/files/research/acobrieffinal.pdf.

illustration of some potential combinations of ACO participants as they have emerged and been analyzed by industry experts in recent years.

Figure 12. Potential Models for ACO Development

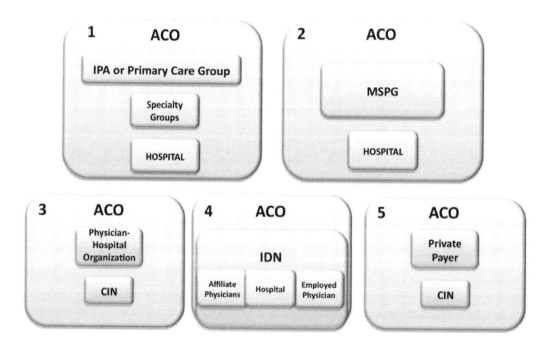

Additional configurations are possible, including academic medical centers in the position of the IDN, and virtual models[75] that combine health systems, physician groups, and payer organizations to provide direct pathways to care coordination. Hence these models are intended as representative examples rather than an inclusive list of the types of arrangements that presently exist or will take shape in the future. Each model has a different partner taking the lead in the formation and management of the ACO. Let us now take a closer look at these five possible configurations and their major characteristics.

---

[75] Blue Shield of California press release. Blue Shield of California, Catholic Healthcare West and Hill Physicians Medical Group to pilot innovative new care model for CalPERS; April 22, 2009. Available at: http://www.hillphysicians.com/Documents/common/press%20releases/press_rel_CalPERS_announce_04220 9.pdf.

1: The IPA-directed ACO. This first model positions the IPA or primary care physician group in the leadership role for the ACO, with specialty groups and hospitals in a subordinate position. This model also brings the PCMH model, already noted as the foundation of the ACO, to the forefront in establishing the newly structured entity. This model allows physicians, both primary care and specialists, flexibility in assigning exclusive or nonexclusive contracting rights. An alternative to this approach is to have primary care physicians operate under exclusive contract rights but allow specialists to work across multiple ACOs within the community.

2: The MSPG-directed ACO. In this second model the multispecialty physician group (such as the Mayo and Cleveland Clinics) directs the ACO with the hospital subordinated to the MSPG. Here physicians (primary care and specialists) work in an ACO with nonexclusive contracting rights, and the ACO will partner with hospitals and ancillary service providers (laboratories, skilled nursing facilities, rehabilitation clinics, and the like) to support clinical integration needs.

3: The PHO-directed ACO. The third model places the physician-hospital organization at the center of the ACO. The PHO will create partnerships with the physician practices that will serve as a collective risk-bearing organization. The PHO will also negotiate the contracting rights of the physician practices (primary or specialty care) when they join the ACO as part of clinical and financial integration. Sutter Health and Scripps Health in California and Advocate Health in Chicago are representative examples of this model.[76] As this third model evolves, the clinically integrated network or PHO (CIN/PHO) has the potential to expand beyond a single ACO.

4: The IDN-directed ACO. The fourth model places the IDN at the forefront of the ACO. In this position the IDN has the option of exclusive or nonexclusive contracting with primary care practices and specialty care groups regardless of whether they are affiliated or unaffiliated with the IDN. In addition, the IDN has control over hospital medical staff

---

[76] Boland P, Polakoff P, Schwab T. Accountable care organizations hold promise, but will they achieve cost and quality targets? *Manag Care*. 2010;19(10):12-6, 19; Shortell SM, Casalino LP, Fisher ES. How the center for medicare and medicaid innovation should test accountable care organizations. *Health Aff* (*Millwood*). 2010;29(7):1293-1298.

organizations, which should be under exclusive contracts to the IDN to support the required level of beneficiaries needed for care under the ACO. Examples of these types of arrangements are Kaiser Permanente, Intermountain Healthcare in Utah and southeastern Idaho, and the Henry Ford Health System in Michigan.

5: The private payer-directed ACO. The fifth model is based on a private payer's forming a direct partnership with physicians, creating a physician-only CIN that would subcontract for hospital or other services. This ACO model could also be formed with IPAs or MSPGs, as it intends the private payer to serve as the partner to provide needed financial support for such infrastructure development of the ACO as health information technology, population data aggregation, and training. As the purpose of the ACO is to improve population health in the communities it serves, it would contract separately with hospitals and ancillary service providers to provide services when needed for inpatient procedures, tests, rehabilitation, and other elements of patient care. Contracting with physicians may be more rigid; that is, the ACO may require more exclusive relationships without flexibility but does so in order to maintain the number of beneficiaries needed to support the ACO model. Even though the payer serves as a principal partner under this model, accountability for patient care would still reside at the local level with a governance board headed by physician leaders.

Many issues will affect ACOs regardless of the model chosen; however, one we wish to highlight at this point is the way in which patients will be assigned to ACOs. According to other observers who have addressed this issue under the CMS ACO scenario,[77] patients may simply be attributed on the basis of the primary care provider who handles the majority of their primary care services. When a single ACO is held accountable for the quality of care and outcomes experienced by a patient, however, attribution becomes complicated when healthcare services are needed outside the ACO. If a patient receives care outside an ACO's geographic market or service area, the ACO may have little or no authority over the orders made for the patient's care, whether the orders are related to inpatient, outpatient, or ancillary care. This possibility may lead to the ACO's being held

---

[77] Luft HS. Becoming accountable—opportunities and obstacles for ACOs. *N Engl J Med.* 2010;363(15):1389-1391.

accountable for the patient's outcomes as he or she is part of the ACO's pool of beneficiaries that the organization is responsible for annually.

A second related issue is that of voluntary as opposed to compulsory beneficiary participation. When beneficiary participation is voluntary, it creates a potential for the loss of numbers necessary to sustain ACO patient volumes. Such challenges may also be a concern for private payer ACOs and others as the industry moves toward more established multipayer ACO models in the future.

Governance

Governance of an ACO is a critical factor in maintaining effective collaboration and competent strategic oversight of operations for the financial, quality and safety, and legal compliance objectives of the ACO. The American Medical Association (AMA) released a set of 13 principles to guide ACO establishment in November 2010; one principle is ACO governance.[78] The AMA identifies four elements necessary to effective governance:

- Medical decisions should be made by physicians.
- The ACO should be governed by a board of directors elected by the ACO professionals.
- ACO physician leadership should be licensed in the state in which the ACO operates and licensed in the active practice of medicine in the ACO's service area.
- When an ACO has a hospital, the ACO's governing board should be separate from and independent of the hospital's board of directors.

These principles have particular relevance to integrated health systems considering entering the ACO arena. The governance of an ACO is such that it will not be business as usual.

---

[78] Interim meeting of the American Medical Association House of Delegates. Accountable care organization (ACO) principles; November 2010; San Diego, CA. Available at: http://op.bna.com/hl.nsf/id/bbrk-8b5szv/$File/ACOandAMA.pdf.

Instead, the ACO board must have contracting oversight of the entire ACO and thus will assume the functions formerly performed by the health system board. Having a physician-led board and governance structure will represent a substantial transition for many health systems. Ensuring that comprehensive clinical transformation is undertaken for the merged organizational activities regardless of the conceptual model or configuration should be the primary oversight activity of the ACO governing body. The healthcare industry has experienced significant changes since the early 2000s with the influx of electronic health record implementation in large- and small-scale organizations alike; and just as strategic governance and oversight have proven to be critical to success in these initiatives, so will it be crucial to have strong governance boards to provide similar strategic oversight over multiyear ACO implementation efforts. Transformation in clinical practice will require effective investment in infrastructure technologies and staff, clinical and administrative process redesign, improved preventive care initiatives and coordination, and better management of chronic disease.[39]

An example of the importance of effective governance in assisting the organizational integration of physician and hospital entities comes from the St. Jude Health System in Fullerton, California. A 2009 article published in *Trustee* summarizes the importance of shared governance in achieving the system's positives results over the years:

> Hospital and health system boards can improve the odds. Our experience with a successful 15-year-old hospital-physician partnership demonstrates the value of shared governance in creating effective integrated systems. It creates opportunities to reconcile competing interests, formulate long-term goals and strategies, and provide the long-term support that such ventures require to succeed.[79]

The authors of the article also cited six principles that were central to the success of the integration spearheaded by their governance. We have illustrated them in Figure 13:

---

[79] Fraschetti R, Sugarman M. Successful hospital-physician integration. *Trustee*. 2009;62(7):11-12, 17-18.

Figure 13. Principles of Successful Integration[53]

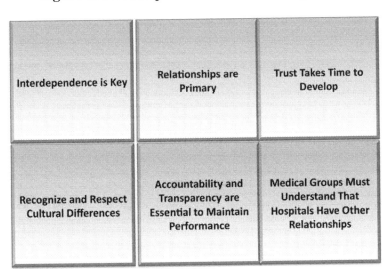

These principles and the necessity for overseeing such multiyear initiatives as ACOs have proven to be lead to the subject of clinical and financial integration.

Clinical and Financial Integration

Achieving clinical integration of the participants in each ACO is one of the major goals that must be accomplished to reach an advanced level of functionality for administrative operations—and most importantly, for clinical processes and operational transformation. In the June 2009 MedPAC Report to Congress, the authors of the report recommended the ACO as a new model to improve clinical and financial integration and accountability for the healthcare of a defined population of Medicare beneficiaries.[80] The MedPAC report went on to describe the elements of two hypothetical ACO models. The first model was based on voluntary participation; in this model, physicians would join with little downside risk but greater potential for upside rewards through a shared savings program similar to that of the CMS Physician Group Demonstration Project. The second model would require mandatory participation (with CMS assignment of physicians to the ACO), and both penalties and rewards would be based on the ACO's performance. As of early 2011 we can

---

[80] MedPAC Report to Congress: Improving Incentives in the Medicare Program (June 2009), Chapter 2: Accountable Care Organizations. Available at: www.medpac.gov/documents/Jun09_EntireReport.pdf, 55.

see the influence of this report in that MedPAC's efforts supported the eventual development of Section 3022 of the PPACA.

There are a number of issues and challenges to be resolved for each ACO in order to achieve this heightened level of functionality. The critical issue of antitrust regulation will be addressed further in Chapter 4. A few of the most important other issues include:

- Ensuring that integrated evidence-based practices are in place;
- Ensuring that an adequate number of primary care professionals are available to provide services;
- Meeting patient-centeredness criteria specified by HHS, which include patient and caregiver assessments or using individualized care plans.[81]

Financial integration of the ACO will be linked to payment/incentive reform (such as P4P, payment bundling, gain sharing or value-based payments) along with tying the financial processes, reward evaluation processes, and risk sharing into the operation and funding of a single new legal entity. These issues will be discussed in more detail in Chapter 7.

Alignment Strategies

Successful alignment of all participants is the lifeblood of the ACO. Moving traditionally competitive organizations in a given community to becoming high-performing collaborators is an important objective requiring tact, diplomacy, and a sense of mission on behalf of each leader as well as the members of the ACO's governance board. This section of the chapter will touch on several topics that leaders should consider in planning for their ACOs regardless of whether they are at an early stage of development or have been operating as an integrated entity for some time.

---

[81] H.R. 3590, Patient Protection and Affordable Care Act, §3022(b)(2)(G). ACO Requirements.

Changes in corporate culture

A major issue for all healthcare organizations involved in establishing ACOs will be the cultural as well as organizational transformation that takes place with the merging of multiple institutions. Two issues we wish to address are first, the importance of cross-function teaming activities in large-scale transformation initiatives; and second, issues related to organizational change management that will be important for ACOs as they move forward. One recent study identified one significant issue, namely "high performing work practices to relational coordination."[82] A key strategic objective for the ACO that was previously noted is improving care coordination. Dr. Jody Gittell and her colleagues presented a model in their study of nine urban hospitals and summarized a number of practices proven to bring about better relational coordination. Figure 14 is taken from their study.

Figure 14. "Relational Model of How High-Performance Work Systems Work"

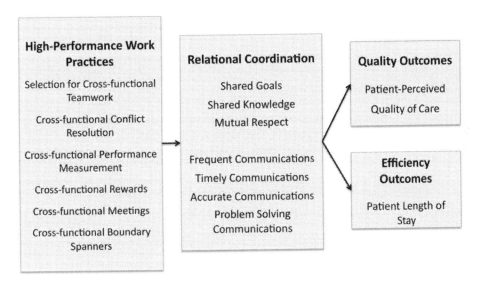

Source: Model from the work of Dr. Jody Gittell on Relational Coordination in Healthcare Organizations. http://www.jodyhoffergittell.info/content/rc2c.html

---

[82] Gittell J, Seidner R, Wimbush J. A relational model of how high-performance work systems work. *Organization Science.* 2010;21(2):490-506; additional material available at: http://www.jodyhoffergittell.info/content/rc2c.html.

So what can we derive from this model? First, with the transitions required for ACOs to integrate previously disparate entities into a cohesive organization, the establishment of multiple cross-functional practices can lead to success. From the present authors' collective experience, the importance of these cross-functional and collaborative practices cannot be overemphasized. It has been demonstrated that utilizing a number of cross-functional multidisciplinary committees and councils to strategically guide EMR implementation for large IDNs can lead to mitigation of risks, highlight successes, and remove long-standing barriers and silos that inhibit collaboration. This approach has the potential to yield similar or greater rewards when applied to ACO development, in view of the transformation that takes place during clinical integration of the ACO participants and the opportunity to improve quality of patient care.

The second important subject is the sharing of goals and knowledge together with the establishment of multiple paths of communication. Increased reliance on and need for health information technology and electronic health records supports the critical nature of these factors as elements that lead to improved efficiency and quality of care for the organizations, as Gittell observed.

Managing organizational change

There are several issues in the field of organizational change management that are critical for successful implementation of an ACO model regardless of the model chosen. The increased importance of clinical integration in the ACO model requires ensuring that physicians are heavily involved in the leadership, formation, and operation of the ACO. For this reason we wish to note some of the factors to be considered and then offer a sample model based on the work of an industry expert on effectively managing cultural and organizational change. To begin, what are some of the factors to consider?

- **Resistance to change**: Virtually all organizational transformations are affected to some degree by resistance to forthcoming changes. This resistance may lower efficiency and effectiveness in operations if not managed appropriately, thereby affecting the quality and cost of care delivered in the ACO's community.

- **Importance of communication**: There are many channels for sending and receiving messages in contemporary healthcare delivery systems. One of the most critical tasks in the management of major organizational change is ensuring that stakeholders receive needed information on a timely and regular basis.

- **Recognizing tolerance for change[83] and having situational awareness**: Physician leaders must pay attention to their team's ability to deal with, accept, and respond to changes that come with ACO implementation. In addition, the leaders themselves must possess a high level of situational awareness that will enable them to foresee both positive and negative developments for participants in their implementation.

- **Participation in decision making and enlisting[84] support**: Involving physicians (whether employed, affiliated, or unaffiliated) and clinicians in the joint decision making process will be critical to ensuring adoption of new policies and new attributes of the ACO as changes are implemented. By enlisting the support of the ACO's physician and clinician population, its physician leaders will secure needed expertise for major decisions as clinical processes are integrated and redesigned across traditionally disparate organizations with the goal of achieving improved population-based health outcomes.

- **Evaluating progress**: Each ACO model will select metrics to evaluate operational performance (discussed further in Chapter 6) in clinical quality and cost of care over time. Ensuring transparency and visibility of these metrics so that all stakeholders understand the pace of progress will be important in diffusing resistance to change and helping the ACO perform on a positive level.

We have developed a model for managing change based on the principles of John Kotter's eight-step change model as presented in his book *Our Iceberg is Melting*.[85] Figure 15 provides a simple three-stage approach to managing change as an ACO moves forward.

---

[83] Kotter J, Schlesinger L. Choosing strategies for change. *Harvard Business Review*. 1979;57(2):106-114.

[84] LeTourneau B. Communicate for change. *J Healthc Manag*. 2004;49(6):354-357.

[85] Kotter J, Rathgeber H. *Our Iceberg Is Melting*. New York, NY: St. Martin's Press; 2005.

Figure 15. ACO Change Management Model

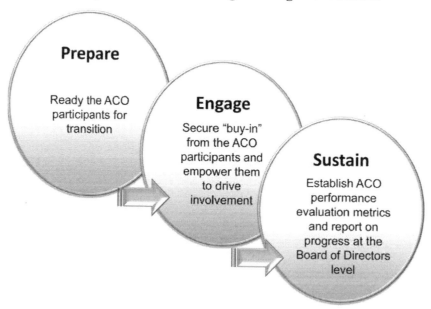

Prepare

Ready the ACO participants for transition

Engage

Secure "buy-in" from the ACO participants and empower them to drive involvement

Sustain

Establish ACO performance evaluation metrics and report on progress at the Board of Directors level

Our three-stage model starts with a **preparation** stage. In this stage physician leaders must set the tone for the organization by defining and communicating a clear vision of the organization's future while acknowledging challenges and risks to confront. Second is the **engagement** stage. Ensuring that clinicians and administrators buy into the ACO at this point is critical, along with empowering physicians and other key personnel to take action in and serve as proponents of redesigning clinical and administrative processes. Last is the **sustenance** stage. In this phase the basic ACO design has been established, cross-functional teams are moving forward, and key resources are in place. Periodic evaluation of progress and reporting at all levels of the organization helps to reinforce gains and support management changes needed for midcourse corrections.

There are many other workable models of change management, including Kurt Lewin's, which consisted of four elements: field theory, group dynamics, action research, and three steps to implement change.[86] Our intention here is to bring the issue to the

---

[86] Suc J, Prokosch HU, Ganslandt T. Applicability of Lewin's change management model in a hospital setting. *Methods Inf Med.* 2009;48(5):419-428.

reader's attention as one to be factored into operational planning to ensure long-term success in implementing an ACO model. Adopting a strategic approach to managing change in any large-scale organizational transformation will help to mitigate risks that can impact quality of care delivered to the patient populations served by ACO participants.

Many Routes, One Goal

An important consideration for those moving toward ACO implementations is to recognize that the ACO is not a one-size-fits-all initiative. With so many different potential organizational combinations, legal structures, models for testing and approaching reimbursement and incentives for physicians and hospitals, as well as the fact that organizations are at different stages in their health information technology and electronic health record integration as of 2011, it is clear that there will be many different routes to achieving the ultimate goals of ACOs.

Figure 16 sketches a generic path for planning and rolling out an ACO. This roadmap is offered here to provide strategic perspective. Other roadmaps are included throughout this book in relation to the topics discussed.

Figure 16. ACO Roadmap 1: Governance and Launching

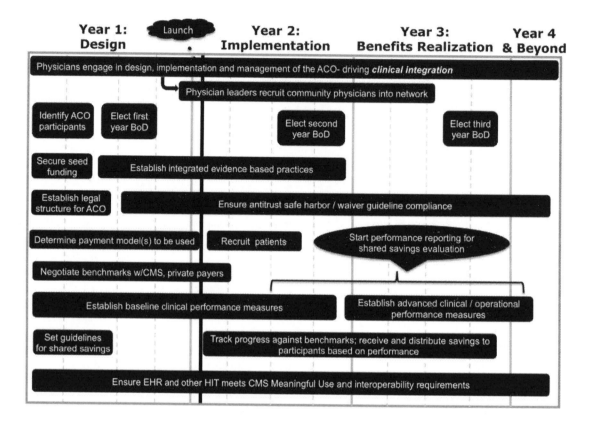

Roadmap 1 shows a number of elements in motion. While many of the components can be drawn in parallel, we show them here separately to help the reader understand the various initiatives requiring attention. That said, the first and perhaps most critical task for an open medical staff IDN is engaging physicians in the design and formation of a clinically integrated network organization. From the outset physicians must not only be involved in but also openly lead the initiative to realize the proposed benefits. With the physicians on board together with administrators and other personnel, the group can turn to designing the functional processes necessary to manage the ACO. After the basics of the design and its functional elements are complete, the ACO's formal governance can be put in place.

Physician recruitment is critical to establishing a successful ACO for independent physicians participating in a CIN. The PPACA Shared Savings Program specifically states, "The ACO shall have in place a leadership and management structure that includes clinical and administrative systems."[87] Having a strong board of directors to provide collaborative governance ensures oversight of all the elements for the clinical and financial integration of the ACO participants. The second step is securing seed funding for any needed infrastructure, training, or development efforts for each ACO. The requirements for funding will vary based on the number of participants, the maturity of the ACO's health information technology, its leadership, and its staffing.

The third step is setting the legal structure in place along with ensuring the establishment of the operation within the parameters of antitrust safe harbor and HHS guidelines. Fourth is the development of a robust quality measurement system and acquisition of the performance improvement resources to achieve the tactical objectives of clinical transformation. These include process redesign, reporting on quality and cost measures, and improvements in care coordination as it is affected by the introduction of such new enabling technologies as telehealth and remote patient monitoring in care delivery.[88]

The fifth step involves determining the payment model(s) to be tested or implemented as well as negotiating benchmarks with CMS and private payer organizations. This determination may be based on geographic regions, the medical claims history of the patient population, and possibly Center for Medicare and Medicaid Innovation grants or other funding mechanisms for testing innovative payment models. It will be important for setting goals to be achieved by the ACO participants. The sixth step is patient recruitment for participation in the ACO. Patients' involvement should be voluntary to allow for flexibility in meeting their healthcare needs.

---

[87] H.R. 3590, Patient Protection and Affordable Care Act, §3022(b)(2)(F). ACO requirements.

[88] H.R. 3590, Patient Protection and Affordable Care Act, §3022(b)(2)(G). ACO requirements.

Last, and one of the most crucial elements of this roadmap, is ensuring that electronic health records and other health information technology meet CMS's meaningful use requirements.[89] Recognizing that many physician practices are on varying schedules and timelines for the adoption of electronic health records, we note that one of the most important measures is establishing health information exchange components with the ability to aggregate data in support of the ACO's population-based health management goals. With aggregated data for analysis the network will have the ability to manage population health on a large scale, perhaps for the first time in history.

Such leading organizations as Geisinger, the Mayo Clinic, and Intermountain Health System already have these capabilities, but they are not widespread across the United States as of early 2011. The exchange of health information and data aggregation are critical to sustaining a large-scale CIN and the success of an ACO. At present, organizations are at stage 1 of the three-stage meaningful use program that runs through 2016. Eligible hospitals and physicians across the country are working to meet those requirements and prepare for stage 2, to be introduced at some point in 2011.

Joint Venture Legal Structures: Options for Formation

There are a number of possible legal structures that ACOs can pursue. For CMS-driven ACOs, the requirement for formal establishment is stated in the PPACA as "The ACO shall have a formal legal structure that would allow the organization to receive and distribute payments for shared savings under subsection (d)(2) to participating providers of services and suppliers."[90] While this issue is related to the following chapter on antitrust issues, this requirement set forth by the PPACA ensures that these organizations will have a mission-oriented focus and legitimate business purpose for clinical and financial integration of their operations. Some types of mergers may include:

1. Horizontal: an IDN merging with another hospital or CIN.

---

[89] Office of the National Coordinator for Health Information Technology. Electronic health records and meaningful use. Available at: http://healthit.hhs.gov/portal/server.pt?open=512&objID=2996&mode=2

[90] H.R. 3590, Patient Protection and Affordable Care Act, §3022(b)(2)(C). ACO requirements.

2. Horizontal: a primary care (PCMH) practice merging with a multispecialty group practice.

3. Vertical: an IDN or CIN merging with one or more PCMHs and multispecialty group practices.

The reader should note two examples of the actual legal structure mandated by the PPACA. First is the *hospital direct employment model,* which would apply to an IDN vertical merger. In this model the physician practice essentially joins the hospital, thus forming an operating division of the IDN. The second model is the *health system parent-subsidiary legal entity model*, in which two or more legal entities are maintained with separate governance boards while the parent health system retains authority in critical issues involving the subsidiary. The parent or the subsidiary may employ physicians, and financial statements are prepared separately for each entity to help ensure financial transparency for stakeholders and regulatory concerns.[91]

In this second model the physicians are not necessarily employed directly by the ACO, although they can be. The clinically integrated network model using an IDN subsidiary corporate structure brings employed and affiliated physicians together in a common CIN provider network. Traditionally, the primary care physicians in the network are exclusive to that network and the specialists are not, or at least not at first. For nonprofit health systems this is one vehicle by which to set up an ACO in an environment with an open medical staff model. When forming these structures and others, ACO participants should adhere to guidance by the Department of Justice and Federal Trade Commission Statements of Antitrust Enforcement Policy in Health Care.[92]

---

[91]Johnson B, Christiansen J. Integrated delivery system legal and organizational structures. MGMA Health Care Consulting Group and Faegre & Benson LLP. Available at: http://www.idsroundtable.com/Resources-Show.aspx?Show=149; http://64.27.92.85/files/IDS%20legal%20and%20organizational%20structures.pdf.

[92] Federal Trade Commission. Guidance on antitrust policy enforcement. Available at: http://www.ftc.gov/bc/healthcare/industryguide/policy/index.htm.

INFOCUS: **Challenges and Risks**

Establishing the appropriate governance structure with so many different possible configurations of physician practices and organizations presents a number of challenges in the early stages of ACO creation. Engaging physicians who are willing to participate in a network offering to a community is a formidable task. We shall consider some of these challenges in concluding this section on governance and joint ventures. Table 13 below provides a set of challenges, risks, and potential mitigation strategies applicable to multiple ACO scenarios.

Table 13. Chapter 3 Challenges and Risks

Challenges	Risks
3a) Engaging physicians to develop and participate in a network initiative.	3f) Hospital systems may develop networks in isolation and thus fail to accrue a sufficient number of providers to adequately manage the patient population.
3b) Who drives the bus (will the ACO be physician practice-led or hospital-led)?	3g) Changes in leadership during the transition period.
3c) Navigating antitrust issues related to clinical and financial integration.	3h) Hospitals that move from a focus on inpatient to outpatient services may lose revenue in the near term.[93]
3d) Securing seed funding for the ACO startup.	3i) Failure to reach agreement with ACO participants on a savings distribution plan.
3e) Securing competent leadership to ensure the success of the ACO and mitigate risk of failure.	3j) Relying on a leadership style that does not fit the local ecosystem, resulting in setbacks for the ACO.

Potential Mitigation Strategies

√ **Engaging Physicians**: Engaging physicians in conversation about the development and management of an ACO is critical to their participation in the network. Early engagement is crucial to success.

√ **Who Drives the Bus:** Regardless of whether the ACO is led by a physician practice or a hospital, ensure that its board of directors is elected by relevant stakeholders from participant organizations and that it maintains its autonomy from the hospital's board. It is also important to ensure that the chair of the board is a licensed physician.[50]

√ **IDNs and CINs**: Engage payers early in planning an ACO startup to ensure alignment with payment model reform and incentives to mitigate loss of revenue during the transition period.

√ **Funding:** Proactively seek grant opportunities for startup funds through the Center for Medicare and Medicaid Innovation and other entities sponsoring ACO demonstration projects.

---

[93] Kocher R, Sahni NR. Physicians versus hospitals as leaders of accountable care organizations. *N Engl J Med.* 2010;363(27):2579-2582.

Chapter 4. Legal Perspectives - Antitrust and Other Critical Issues

Background

Antitrust issues for hospitals and physician organizations over the last several decades have included a number of topics, such as, price fixing, market concentration in specific geographic areas, and non-price competition.[94] To manage the health of a population through collective bargaining with single signature authority over contracting for hospital and physician providers alike would be viewed as anticompetitive and hence of major consideration for the formation of ACOs.

The Federal Trade Commission (FTC) is chartered to ensure that fair pricing of healthcare services are maintained within and across geographic markets and that pro-competitive practices take place in the United States. Congress passed three landmark laws that form the foundation of the FTC's work: the Sherman Act of 1890, the Federal Trade Commission Act of 1914, and the Clayton Act of 1914, as illustrated in Figure 17. The Sherman Act, which was the first U.S. antitrust law, prohibits "every contract, combination, or conspiracy in restraint of trade and any monopolization, attempted monopolization, or conspiracy or combination to monopolize." This law especially pertains to unreasonable restraint of trade.

---

[94] Jacobs P, Rapoport J. Regulation and antitrust policy in health care. In: *The Economics of Health and Medical Care*. 5th ed. Sudbury, MA: Jones and Bartlett Publishers; 2004: Chapter 16.

Figure 17. Framework of Foundational Antitrust Legislation

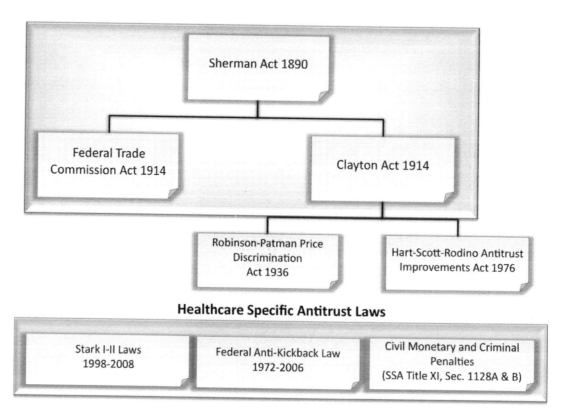

In 1914 Congress created the Federal Trade Commission and the Federal Trade Commission Act, which banned "unfair methods of competition and unfair or deceptive acts or practices." Third, the Clayton Act "prohibits mergers and acquisitions where the effect may be substantially to lessen competition, or to tend to create a monopoly." The Clayton Act was amended twice over the years: first, the Robinson-Patman Act of 1936 that bans "discriminatory pricing and allowances in dealings between merchants"; and second, the Hart-Scott-Rodino Act of 1976 that mandates advance notice of large planned mergers to the FTC. [95]

Antitrust issues are one of the major challenges being addressed jointly by CMS and the FTC through the development of federal rules that will govern ACOs for the public

---

[95] Federal Trade Commission. FTC guide to the antitrust laws. Available at:
http://www.ftc.gov/bc/antitrust/antitrust_laws.shtm

model and also serve as guidance for private insurance payer involvement in ACOs. The formation of ACOs was considered after health management through collective bargaining with single signature authority over contracting for hospital and physician providers alike was viewed as anticompetitive. The three healthcare-specific antitrust laws in the lower portion of Figure 17 are critically important to ACOs and are addressed separately later in this chapter.

As noted at the end of Chapter 3, the FTC issued guidance to the healthcare industry in 1996 with significant amendment in 2009, regarding all types of mergers and joint ventures. This guidance allows physician practices, hospitals, and other provider organizations to take actions with potential anticompetitive effects if they are balanced by pro-competitive efficiency gains in the improvement of quality of care for consumers in specific geographic markets.

While the American Medical Association and others have argued since the 1970s that antitrust laws should not apply to the learned professions, the FTC has ruled many times in opposition, thus stifling what some observers had labeled physician or hospital cartels. To emphasize this point, a 2007 article in a journal of health law stated that

> . . . as early as 1976, the FTC was challenging physician attempts to thwart competition by denying reimbursement to physicians providing services to HMOs, penalizing physicians who accepted salaries or payment on other than a fee-for-service basis or limiting price competition by other means.[96]

By 1996 the FTC had over 50 lawsuits for antitrust violations with half a dozen being brought by the DOJ and a nearly equal number of ongoing cases over the ensuing ten years. Many of these suits, however, have historically not found the kind of substantial clinical and financial integration discussed in Chapter 3 as is deemed necessary to deliver truly improved clinical outcomes and patient care while concurrently lowering the total healthcare spending for a population. Recognizing that such integration is a desirable

---

[96] Greaney T. Thirty years of solicitude: antitrust law and physician cartels. *Houston Journal of Health Law and Policy*. 2007;72:189-226. Accessed online at http://www.law.uh.edu/hjhlp/Issues/Vol_72/Greaney.pdf

endpoint, Federal Trade Commission chair Jon Leibowitz recently commented at an October 2010 workshop regarding ACOs:

> From an antitrust perspective, we want to explore how to develop safe harbors so doctors, hospitals and other medical professionals know when they can collaborate and when they cannot. And we're also considering whether we can put in place an expedited review process for those ACOs that fall outside of safe harbors as some may. And let me assure you, if we can do this we will.[97]

For industry participants, this is an encouraging statement of support as the development of new safe harbors or other mechanisms will allow the process of innovation to speed the evolution of ACOs.

In addition to the core framework of antitrust laws enforced by the FTC, other legislation that is critical to ACO operation includes the Stark Laws (I and II), the Anti-Kickback Law, the Civil Monetary Penalties Law (CMPL),[98] Internal Revenue Service (IRS) tax exemption regulations, and state licensure and insurance regulations of relevance to each ACO dependent on their domicile state. The PPACA granted HHS waiver authority on sections 1128A, 1128B, and Title XVIII of the Social Security Act "as may be necessary to carry out the provisions of this section."[99] This waiver authority is a crucial issue for the entire industry because it will affect the clinical and financial integration of multiple ACO participants and the degree to which innovations can be tested and implemented. Section 1128A [42 U.S.C. 1320a–7a] pertains to civil monetary penalties

---

[97] Leibowitz J. Accountable care organizations and implications regarding antitrust, physician self-referral, anti-kickback, and civil monetary penalty laws. Remarks made at the Centers for Medicare and Medicaid Services workshop; October 5, 2010. Transcript available at: http://www.cms.gov/PhysicianFeeSched/downloads/10-5-10ACO-WorkshopAMSessionTranscript.pdf , 11.

[98] U.S. Department of Health and Human Sserices, Office of Inspector General. Civil monetary penalties. 42 U.S.C. §1320a–1327a. Available at: http://oig.hhs.gov/fraud/enforcement/cmp/index.asp

[99] H.R. 3590, Patient Protection and Affordable Care Act, §3022(b)(2)(G). Section 1128A pertains to civil monetary penalties; available at: http://www.socialsecurity.gov/OP_Home/ssact/title11/1128A.htm. Section 1128B pertains to criminal penalties for acts involving federal health care programs; available at: http://www.socialsecurity.gov/OP_Home/ssact/title11/1128B.htm.

when any person that knowingly presents a claim for medical services or items that they know or should know to be false or fraudulent.[66] Section 1128B [42 U.S.C. 1320a–7b] pertains to criminal acts involving federal healthcare programs in which someone knowingly and willfully makes false statements or misrepresentations to request receipt of any benefit or payment from a federal healthcare program, determine rights to such benefit or payment, and presents a claim, or causes to be presented for a physician's service when they know the individual who provided the service was not a licensed physician.[66]

The October 2010 workshop[100] held by CMS focused on the antitrust issues related to ACO implementation. CMS and the FTC are working together to establish a plan for the waiver authority with collaboration of industry leaders to identify and craft new safe harbors and changes to existing FTC healthcare policies on antitrust enforcement, in order to allow more flexibility in joint venture arrangements, market competition evaluation, and payer/provider contracting.

The remainder of this chapter deals with insights on other important laws and regulations as they affect planning for and operation of ACOs; achieving acceptable clinical integration within the guidelines established by the FTC; and understanding antitrust safety zones (safe harbors) and risk sharing among ACO participants.

Other Critical Laws: Implications for ACOs

Stark Laws I and II

The Stark Law (Section 1877 of the Social Security Act) is also known as the physician self-referral law. The law has emerged in three phases; its general provisions are as follows:

- Prohibits a physician from making referrals for certain designated health services (DHS) payable by Medicare to an entity with which he or she (or an immediate family

---

[100] Centers for Medicare and Medicaid Services workshop. Accountable care organizations and implications regarding antitrust, physician self-referral, anti-kickback, and civil monetary penalty laws; October 5, 2010. Transcript available at: http://www.cms.gov/PhysicianFeeSched/downloads/10-5-10ACO-WorkshopAMSessionTranscript.pdf.

member) has a financial relationship (ownership, investment, or compensation), unless an exception applies.

- Prohibits the entity from presenting or causing to be presented claims to Medicare (or billing another individual, entity, or third party payer) for those referred services.

- Establishes a number of specific exceptions and grants the Secretary the authority to create regulatory exceptions for financial relationships that do not pose a risk of program or patient abuse.[101]

The Stark Law as it has unfolded since the late 1990s has had a significant impact on business relationships in the practice of medicine. The Stark Law must be taken into consideration in ACO implementation regardless of the ACO's specific structure because of the involvement of physicians, hospitals, and ancillary service providers. CMS is the governing body for the rule making process under the Stark Law. It has issued two primary rules (Stark I and II), with two separate phases for Stark II. Some of the highlights of each part are provided in Figure 18.

---

[101] Centers for Medicare and Medicaid Services. Overview of physician self-referral laws. Available at: http://www.cms.gov/PhysicianSelfReferral/.

Figure 18. Stark I-II Summary[102]

Stark I- Phase I	Stark II- Phases II-III
• Chronology- Proposed rule 1998; finalized Jan. 2001.	• Chronology- Phase II proposed March 2004; finalized July 2004. Phase III proposed rule Sept. 2007; final rule Sept. 2008 (with noted proposed revisions)
• Applies only to physicians that refer CMS patients for designated health services to organizations they (or an immediate family member) have a financial relationship.	• (Sept 2007) Phase III- "Stand in Shoes" provision introduced but not finalized. (updated Nov. 2009) noting that physician "titular" ownership does not require the physician to stand in the shoes of the physician organization.
• 20 exceptions are defined.	• This provision impacts the physician's compensation arrangement analysis for determining if one receives direct or indirect compensation in regards to the exception established on this issue.
• Covers 10 designated health services (DHS).	• (Sept 2008) Phase III- Finalized prohibition of unit of service ("per click") payments in lease agreements.
• Exceptions apply only to group practices (2 or more physicians).	• (Mar 2004) Phase II- "safe harbor" added for referring physician that spends at least 20% of their professional time or 8 hours per week providing academic services or clinical teaching services.
• Violations are punishable by up to $15,000 in civil monetary penalties.	

Stark I-Phase I allowed 20 exceptions, including physicians in the same group practice, in-office ancillary services, rental of office space or equipment, prepaid plans (HMOs or Medicare/Medicaid plans), and compensation received in physician recruitment.[103] Stark I-Phase I also specified 10 designated health services that include the following:

- Clinical laboratory services

---

[102] Centers for Medicare and Medicaid Services. Physician self-referral laws: statutory history. Available at: https://www.cms.gov/PhysicianSelfReferral/90_statutory_history.asp#TopOfPage; Gosfield AG. The stark truth about the Stark law. Part I. *Fam Pract Manag.* 2003;10(10):27-33. Available at: http://www.aafp.org/fpm/2003/1100/p27.pdf; Katayama AC, Coyne SE, Moskol KL. Another round of Stark law changes coming your way as early as October 1, 2008. *WMJ* 2008;107(6):305-306. Available at: http://www.wisconsinmedicalsociety.org/_WMS/publications/wmj/issues/wmj_v107n6/107no6_katayama.pdf.

[103] Social Security Act §1877, Limitation on certain physician referrals. [42 U.S.C. 1395]. Available at: http://www.socialsecurity.gov/OP_Home/ssact/title18/1877.htm.

- Physical therapy, occupational therapy, and speech-language pathology services
- Radiology and certain other imaging services
- Radiation therapy services and supplies
- Durable medical equipment and supplies
- Parenteral and enteral nutrients, equipment, and supplies
- Prosthetics, orthotics, and prosthetic devices and supplies
- Home health services
- Outpatient prescription drugs
- Inpatient and outpatient hospital services[104]

Stark II consisted of two phases issued with numerous proposed rules and final versions, the last being for Phase III in September 2008[105]; however, several issues remain open for revision based on health reform needs and statutory changes over time. Figure 14 notes only a few highlights from the Stark rules. These rules are highly complex and should be examined to ensure compliance in all relationships among ACO participants to avoid sanctions that can include civil monetary penalties (such as in the case of claims for a service that a person knows or should know that it may not be made) and potential criminal penalties for arrangements or schemes established with the intent to assure referrals. With the waiver authority granted to HHS, we can anticipate further changes in these rules.

Federal Anti-Kickback Law and Safe Harbors

The federal Anti-Kickback Law was issued in 1972; it provides protection for patients and federal healthcare programs from fraud and abuse through the corrupt influence of monies on healthcare decisions. The law states

> . . . that anyone who knowingly and willfully receives or pays anything of value to influence the referral of federal health care program business, including Medicare

---

[104] Health Care Financing Administration, 42 CFR Parts 411 and 424. *Federal Register*, January 4, 2001. Physician self-referral, final rule (Stark I- Phase I). Vol. 66, No. 3. 856-904.

[105] Physician Self Referral-Final Rule (Stark II- Phase III). *Federal Register. August 19, 2008.* Vol. 73, No. 161. 48688-48732.

and Medicaid, can be held accountable for a felony. Violations of the law are punishable by up to five years in prison, criminal fines up to $25,000, administrative civil money penalties up to $50,000, and exclusion from participation in federal health care programs.[106]

We regularly hear of cases involving Medicare and Medicaid fraud[107]; these laws are enforced by the Department of Justice to protect the sanctity of the medical profession. In this context we provide two examples of violations of the Anti-Kickback Law. First is a landmark case prior to the issuance of safe harbors for the Anti-Kickback Law in the case of *United States v. Greber,* 760 F.2d 68 (3d Cir. Pa. 1985).[108] The defendant, president of Cardio-Med, Inc., argued that payments made to his company for professional services related to tests performed by a laboratory do not constitute Medicare fraud. In the original trial and decision upheld in this appeal, the defendant was convicted on 20 of 23 counts in the original indictment for violations of mail fraud, Medicare fraud, and false statement statutes.

The second case is that of *U.S. v. LaHue*, 261 F.3d 993 (10th Cir. (Kan.) (Aug 17, 2001). In this case the defendants, two principals (physicians) of a specialized medical practice and a chief executive officer of a hospital, had each benefited from fraudulent and kickback activities. The principals of the medical practice received over $1.8M from a medical center, and the medical center received over $39.5M from Medicare for services rendered to the practice's patients as a result of the contracts with the specialized medical

---

[106] Office of Inspector General. Fact sheet, November 1999. Federal anti-kickback law and regulatory safe harbors. Available a:t http://oig.hhs.gov/fraud/docs/safeharborregulations/safefs.htm.

[107] Department of Justice. Press release, June 26, 2003. Largest health fraud case in U.S. history settled. Available at: http://www.justice.gov/opa/pr/2003/June/03_civ_386.htm; Commons J. DOJ indicts 73 in massive Medicare fraud case. *Modern Healthcare*, October 14, 2010. Available at: http://www.healthleadersmedia.com/page-1/FIN-257713/DOJ-Indicts-73-in-Massive-Medicare-Fraud-Case; Clark C. Physician to settle Medicare fraud case for $20M. *HealthLeaders Media*, October 1, 2010. Available at: http://www.healthleadersmedia.com/content/PHY-257184/Physician-to-Settle-Medicare-Fraud-Case-for-20M.html.

[108] *United States v. Greber,* 760 F.2d 68 (3d Cir. Pa. 1985). Available at: http://biotech.law.lsu.edu/cases/FCA/greber.htm.

practice.[109] In this appeal of the original court decision, the Tenth Circuit Court of Appeals affirmed the original decision, which resulted in prison time and monetary penalties for all three defendants. In this case, the court was able to adopt the "one purpose test" (which originated in *Greber*), in which the Anti-Kickback Law is violated if one purpose of a payment in question was to induce future referrals.

Considering the seriousness of penalties resulting from violations of the Anti-Kickback Law, we should discuss the issue of safe harbors, which are provisions made in legislation that reduce or eliminate a party's legal liability, provided that the party acted in good faith. In the 1980s some observers maintained that there is a need for establishing a set of exceptions to the Anti-Kickback Law to provide flexibility for those organizations working to conduct administrative and billing activities in support of the delivery of health services in a lawful manner. There were 10 original safe harbors for the Anti-Kickback Law in 1991; they are enumerated in Table 14:[110]

Table 14. Original Anti-Kickback Law Safe Harbors (1991)

Investment interests	Space Rental	Equipment rental	Personal services and management contracts	Sale of practice
Referral services	Warranties	Discounts	Employees	Group purchasing organizations

While these safe harbors established a baseline of exemptions to the law, more safe harbors were needed as the health system, policies, and practices evolved during the 1990s. In view

---

[109] *U.S. v. LaHue,* 261 F.3d 993 (10th Cir. (Kan.) Aug 17, 2001). The reader is referred to para. 45, note on the financial benefits received by defendants. Available at: http://biotech.law.lsu.edu/cases/FCA/US_v_LaHueII.htm.

[110] U.S. Department of Health and Human Services, Office of Inspector General. Medicare and state health care programs: fraud and abuse; Office of Inspector General anti-kickback provisions, final rule. 42 CFR, Part 1001. July 29, 1991 (56 FR 35952). Available at: http://complianceland.com/aks/fedreg-7-29-91.html.

of changes in the industry, another set of safe harbors was declared by HHS's Office of the Inspector General in 1999. Table 15 provides a summary of those safe harbors:

Table 15. Additional Anti-Kickback Harbors (1999)

Investments in ambulatory surgical centers	Joint ventures in underserved areas	Practitioner recruitment in underserved areas	Sales of physician practices to hospitals in underserved areas
Subsidies for obstetrical malpractice insurance in underserved areas	Investments in group practices	Specialty referral arrangements between providers	Cooperative hospital service organizations

A number of other safe harbors have been created since 1999; however, one rule that is particularly important to ACOs is the August 6, 2008 final rule on safe harbors for "Certain Electronic Prescribing and Electronic Health Records Arrangements Under the Anti-Kickback Statute; Final Rule."[111] With the industry's intensified efforts to accelerate the adoption of EMR technologies and electronic prescribing systems, this rule provides a much-needed set of safe harbors for protection of lawful transactions between hospitals and physician practices. It was originally mandated through the 2003 Medicare Modernization Act. The primary tenets of the electronic health record safe harbor are included in Table 16. One of the key indicia of clinical integration (discussed later in this chapter) is the use of electronic health records to enhance the abilities of physicians and ACO participants to exchange patient data. This safe harbor was also needed to support future industry-wide initiatives to set electronic health record technologies in place and use for healthcare providers throughout the United States per the CMS meaningful use rules.

---

[111] 42 CFR Part 1001 Medicare and state health care programs: fraud and abuse; safe harbors for certain electronic prescribing and electronic health records arrangements under the anti-kickback statute; final rule. *Federal Register*, August 8, 2006. Available at: http://oig.hhs.gov/authorities/docs/06/OIG%20E-Prescribing%20Final%20Rule%20080806.pdf.

Table 16. EMR Safe Harbor Tenets (August 6, 2008)[112]

Topic	Explanation
Covered technology	Software used predominantly to create, maintain, transmit, or receive electronic health records. Software must include an electronic prescribing component. Software packages may also include functions related to patient administration; for example, scheduling, billing, and clinical support. Information technology and training services, which could include Internet connectivity and help desk support services. Does not include hardware.
Compliance standards with donated technology	Electronic health records software that is interoperable. Certified software may be deemed interoperable under certain circumstances. Electronic prescribing capability must comply with final standards for electronic prescribing adopted by the Secretary.
Donors and recipients	Protected donors are (i) individuals and entities that provide covered services and submit claims or requests for payment, either directly or through reassignment, to any federal health care program; and (ii) health plans. Protected recipients are individuals and entities engaged in the delivery of health care.
Selection of recipients	Donors may not select recipients using any method that takes into account directly the volume or value of referrals from the recipient or other business generated between the parties.
Value of protected technology	Recipients must pay 15% of the donor's cost for the donated technology. The donor or any affiliate must not finance the recipient's payment or loan funds to the recipient for use by the recipient to pay for the technology.
Expiration of safe harbor	Safe harbor sunsets December 31, 2013.

---

[112] 42 CFR Part 1001 Medicare and state health care programs: fraud and abuse; safe harbors for certain electronic prescribing and electronic health records arrangements under the anti-kickback statute; final rule. *Federal Register*, August 8, 2006. Available at: http://oig.hhs.gov/authorities/docs/06/OIG%20E-Prescribing%20Final%20Rule%20080806.pdf.

As ACOs evolve along with the joint efforts among the CMS, FTC, and DOJ, these lists of applicable safe harbors are certain to change. Again we recommend further analysis of this topic and enlisting legal counsel for expertise to ensure that as new ACO relationships are structured, all aspects of such relationships fall within the rule of law and existing safe harbors.

Health Insurance Portability and Accountability Act implications for ACOs

The Health Insurance Portability and Accountability Act of 1996 (HIPAA) includes privacy and security rules that effected significant changes in privacy, security, and confidentiality across the healthcare industry. HIPAA will continue to be a major factor in the way in which healthcare providers and organizations manage personal health information (PHI)—especially with the increased industry adoption of EHRs, the focus on improved care coordination, and the move toward state and national interoperability. Currently HHS is working toward several changes to HIPAA through a proposed rule announced in the July 14, 2010, issuance of the *Federal Register*.[113] These changes affect the HITECH Act, the source of the CMS meaningful use rule. The rule has a direct effect on establishing the operations of the HIT and other functions for any given ACO.

Some of the proposed changes that may impact ACOs involve changes to the definition of a business associate; broadening the application of civil monetary penalties (amending the definition of reasonable cause); and adding new provisions for the "permitted and required uses and disclosures of protected health information by business associates." The proposed rule change to HIPAA identifies benefits for covered entities (applicable to future ACOs) that include being responsible to retain and protect the PHI of deceased patients only for 50 years after death, as opposed to protecting the PHI in perpetuity. Given the new approaches to care delivery with the implementation of ACOs and PCMH models, the industry should anticipate future challenges and changes with

---

[113] 45 CFR Parts 160 and 164. Modifications to the HIPAA privacy, security, and enforcement rules under the Health Information Technology for Economic and Clinical Health Act; proposed rule. *Federal Register*. July 14, 2010. Available at: http://edocket.access.gpo.gov/2010/pdf/2010-16718.pdf.

regard to HIPAA.[114] Industry and community health provider leadership, insurance payers, and business associates working on the development of ACOs should monitor the development of this legislation as it will impact relationships and contracting to secure resources for long-term success.

Internal Revenue Service (IRS) implications

Two issues are of key concern with regard to the IRS. First is the issue of the nonprofit status of hospitals, IDNs, and CINs as new horizontal and vertical mergers take place with the formation of ACOs. Will the mergers and subsequent clinical and financial integration initiatives have any impact on their status, or will one participant with nonprofit status be an asset to a newly formed ACO? While the IRS has not yet issued specific guidance on tax treatment of distributions of shared savings received and distributed by ACOs, for ACOs that have participants with federal income tax exemption (Section 501(c)(3)), there will be challenges to address if the tax-exempt entity's involvement in the ACO may generate prohibited "private benefits" or "private inurement"[115] to such nonexempt individuals as physicians.[116] Additional guidance on this issue should be sought in anticipation of future shared savings payments.

A second matter concerns the taxation of the shared savings that will be accrued and paid by CMS and private payers to ACO participants. As these nonprofit and for-profit entities become more tightly integrated in their operating processes and cultures, how will the rules determine who pays federal and state taxes on the gains paid to individual physicians, group practices, IDNs, and CINs? Will the individual physicians be taxed on

---

[114] Steele GD, Haynes JA, Davis DE, et al. How Geisinger's advanced medical home model argues the case for rapid-cycle innovation. *Health Aff (Millwood)*. 2010;29(11):2047-2053.

[115] Internal Revenue Service. Guidance on inurement/private benefit—charitable organizations. Available at: http://www.irs.gov/charities/charitable/article/0,,id=123297,00.html.

[116] Gianni M, Meltebek M, Gordon J. Hospitals and other organizations that are exempt from federal income tax face special challenges. Advisory published by Davis Wright Tremaine LLP, September 1, 2010. Available e at http://www.corpfinblog.com/2010/09/articles/federal-legislation/health-care-reform-accountable-care-organizations-and-exemptorganization-participants/.

their portion of these savings that are realized? Guidance is needed from the IRS, and as the ACO is a relatively new care delivery model, we can expect guidance to come at some point after final rules are issued by CMS on the Shared Savings Program.

State antitrust laws and regulations

State governments have been involved in antitrust and healthcare organization merger activities for many years. State authorities have major responsibilities for regulating health insurance payers; however, responsibility for maintaining fair and open competition in each state's geographic market for health services is shared by federal and state authorities.[117] Certificate of need programs are another issue dealt with by state healthcare regulatory agencies (though not all states have certificate of need programs) in coordination with the DOJ and FTC in regards to regulating volume and capacity of healthcare facilities and services. These programs exist in 36 states as of 2011,[118] so there will be some impact on ACOs either in their formation or operational stages.[119] State regulatory efforts for certificate of need programs are an added mechanism for states that do have the programs focused on managing competition in geographic markets to ensure fair price competition and availability of health services. Given that the programs do not exist in all states, this fact will localize their role in the evolution of the ACOs' nature and governance boards. Administrators involved in ACOs in the early design phase should check with their appropriate state agencies to determine whether any planned actions will create a need for regulatory action.

---

[117] Hellinger FJ. Antitrust enforcement in the healthcare industry: the expanding scope of state activity. *Health Serv Res.* 1998;33 (5 Pt 2): 1477-1494. Available at: http://www.ncbi.nlm.nih.gov/pmc/articles/PMC1070330/pdf/hsresearch00031-0086.pdf.

[118] National Conference of State Legislatures. Certificate of need: state health laws and programs. Available at: http://www.ncsl.org/IssuesResearch/Health/CONCertificateofNeedStateLaws/tabid/14373/Default.aspx.

[119] Varney CA. Remarks prepared for the American Bar Association/American Health Lawyers Association Antitrust in Healthcare Conference, May 24, 2010; Arlington, VA. The reader is referred to Section II, competition advocacy. Available at: http://www.justice.gov/atr/public/speeches/258898.htm; Galloro V. Birth pangs of an ACO: Missouri physician group's plan hits interference from local hospital. *Modern Healthcare*, October 2010. Available at: http://www.modernhealthcare.com/article/20101011/MAGAZINE/310119963#.

Vermont is one example of state involvement. As we noted earlier in Chapter 1, Vermont has taken a very aggressive approach to adoption of PCMH and ACO models. The Vermont state legislature established a task force in 2010 to analyze changes and ongoing initiatives in the state resulting from the PPACA.[120] This task force made some specific recommendations in their report issued on October 13, 2010. Recommendations related to supporting the evolution of ACO models include:

- Continue pursuit of initiatives underway by the Department of Vermont Health Access (DVHA) on publicly funded insurance programs related to PPACA;

- Continue pursuit of initiatives by the Vermont Information Technology Leaders (VITL) focused on supporting CMS meaningful use compliance, electronic prescribing, and health information exchange;

- The Vermont Banking, Insurance, Securities and Health Care Administration (BISHCA) should identify legal barriers and any opportunities for state assistance, such as working toward antitrust exemptions.

Last, states have Medicaid Fraud and Abuse offices[121] to monitor fraudulent activities. Enforcement of the federal civil monetary and criminal penalties for illegal activities that take advantage of state Medicaid resources is an important component to antitrust enforcement at the state level. As Medicaid-focused ACOs are developed, these offices will be engaged at some level to ensure that new healthcare programs and services are operated fairly and within the rule of law. All these state activities will support the growth of fair and competitive health services across geographic markets across the United

---

[120] Report of the Health Care Reform Readiness Taskforce, October 13, 2010. Available at: http://www.vtmd.org/HCRR%20TF%20Report%2010-13-10.pdf; Vermont House of Representatives. An act relating to containing health care costs by decreasing variability in health care spending and utilization. S. 129, 2009. Available at: http://www.leg.state.vt.us/docs/2010/bills/House/S-129.pdf.

[121] Florida Agency for Health Care Administration, Bureau of Medicaid Program Integrity. Available at: http://ahca.myflorida.com/Executive/Inspector_General/medicaid.shtml; State of California, Department of Justice, Bureau of Medi-Cal Fraud and Elder Abuse. Available at: http://ag.ca.gov/bmfea/index.php; Attorney General of Virginia, Medicaid Fraud Control Unit (MFCU). Available at: http://www.oag.state.va.us/CONSUMER/MEDICAID_FRAUD/index.html.

States in which ACOs will operate. The need for oversight by state agencies will persist as new ACO models are tested and implemented.

Clinical Integration: Achieving Operational Excellence within the Rule of Law

The topic of clinical integration was introduced in Chapter 3; however, the FTC's perspective is covered in this section under the purview of antitrust law and the agency's Statements of Antitrust Enforcement Policy in Health Care that originated in 1996.[122]Of particular importance to ACOs are Statements #8 (physician network joint ventures) and #9 (multiprovider network joint ventures). These two statements provide a second framework of rules that the FTC applies to determine whether joint ventures that produce pro-competitive efficiencies and improvements in quality of care for consumers in a geographic market outweigh any anticompetitive effects resulting from such efficiencies.

How does the FTC define clinical integration? In Statement #8 the FTC provides its definition of a clinical integration program:

> Such integration can be evidenced by the network implementing an active and ongoing program to evaluate and modify practice patterns by the network's physician participants and create a high degree of interdependence and cooperation among the physicians to control costs and ensure quality. This program may include:
>> (1) establishing mechanisms to monitor and control utilization of health care services that are designed to control costs and assure quality of care;
>> (2) selectively choosing network physicians who are likely to further these efficiency objectives; and

---

[122] Department of Justice and Federal Trade Commission statements of antitrust enforcement policy in health care. Available at: http://www.ftc.gov/bc/healthcare/industryguide/policy/.

(3) the significant investment of capital, both monetary and human, in the necessary infrastructure and capability to realize the claimed efficiencies.[123]

Achieving advanced levels of clinical integration is a basic goal for every ACO. These programs will test new models to advance care delivery, improve outcomes, eliminate inefficiencies and waste, and reduce the trend toward increasing healthcare costs. The DOJ and FTC jointly issued a healthcare industry report in 2004 that identified four primary indicia of clinical integration. Additional potential indicia were listed within their Statement #8. Figure 19 illustrates these indicia and will be followed by some specific case examples.

Figure 19. FTC Identified Indicia of Clinical Integration[124]

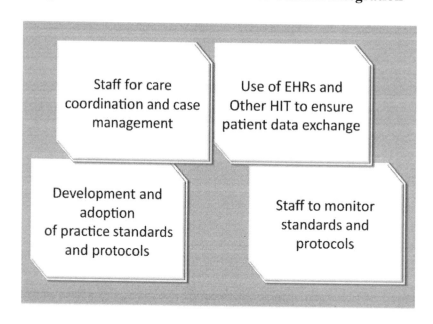

---

[123] Department of Justice and Federal Trade Commission statement on policy enforcement on physician network joint ventures, §8B(1). Available at:
http://www.ftc.gov/bc/healthcare/industryguide/policy/statement8.htm.

[124] Department of Justice and Federal Trade Commission. Improving health care: a dose of competition, July 2004. Available at: http://www.justice.gov/atr/public/health_care/204694/chapter2.htm#4b3. Federal Trade Commission. Statement #8. Paragraph 8(C)1: Examples of clinical integration. Available at:
http://www.ftc.gov/bc/healthcare/industryguide/policy/statement8.htm.

There are some underlying factors related to people, process and technology for the indicia in Figure 19. Let us consider people first. Within an organization's clinical integration program, recruiting and retaining the clinical and administrative staff necessary to meet all four indicia is critical. Physicians as well as clinicians at staff and management levels are needed to meet these requirements.

The second consideration is process. The indicia for standards and protocols are focused on ensuring that clinical workflow processes, prescription medications, and safety procedures adhere to external regulatory and self-developed credentialing guidelines (such as the Joint Commission, CMS, Centers for Disease Control and Prevention (CDC), state health departments, and the like). Moreover, implementing the process redesign of electronic health records is crucial to ensuring adoption by physicians and clinicians. Last is technology. Successfully implementing electronic health records, information sharing tools, and other clinical information systems used across IDNs, CINs, affiliated and unaffiliated physician practices (extended hospital medical staff), and payer organizations is necessary to achieve improved levels of health information exchange and advanced levels of care coordination across the industry. Chapter 8 will address these underlying factors in detail with regard to an ACO's organizational transformation.

The FTC's willingness to redefine safe harbors resulted from a number of cases and opinions built upon historical case law. We wish to reference three FTC rulings for some additional guidance on the indicia of clinical integration. First is the ruling by the FTC in 2007 regarding the Greater Rochester Independent Practice Association (GRIPA) in their evaluation of that entity's clinical integration program. A 2010 Robert Wood Johnson Foundation policy paper summarized the FTC's opinion:

> GRIPA offers an example of a clinically integrated physician arrangement that successfully met the FTC's standard as set forth in the revised 1996 Statements. GRIPA positioned its venture as one offering a new health care product that would combine clinical practice with an integrated clinical improvement program designed to improve the quality of care and create efficiencies in the practice of medicine. GRIPA claimed that this new product would be "intertwined" with its

proposed joint contracting practices with payers (health insurance companies) on behalf of its 500 independent and hospital-affiliated primary care physicians and specialists in practice across 40 separate areas. The FTC agreed that collective bargaining was reasonably necessary to achieve the program's likely efficiencies.[125]

Regarding the above-referenced indicia of clinical integration (FTC Statement #8(B)1), the FTC provided in-depth analysis in the GRIPA opinion on each indicium and validated that GRIPA's proposed clinical improvement services program showed evidence of each and that the program was likely to produce substantial integration among participating physicians.[126] On the subject of physician collaboration, the FTC's opinion indicated that GRIPA presented a number of collaborative initiatives with its physicians that planned to implement or build "from its risk-sharing program as evidencing the physicians' clinical integration through the proposed program." These collaborative activities are summarized in Table 17.

---

[125] Burke T, Rosenbaum S. Accountable care organizations: implications for antitrust policy. Robert Wood Johnson policy analysis paper, March 2010. Available at: http://www.rwjf.org/files/research/57509.pdf; Federal Trade Commission. Advisory opinion, September 17, 2009. Available at: http://www.ftc.gov/bc/healthcare/industryguide/advisory.htm.

[126] Federal Trade Commission. GRIPA advisory opinion, September 17, 2007. Detailed analysis of FTC review of GRIPA evidence for meeting the indicia of clinical integration. Available at: http://www.ftc.gov/bc/adops/gripa.pdf, 11-16.

Table 17. Summary of GRIPA's Collaborative Physician Activities[127]

Topic	Description of Activity
1. Coordination of care	Develop a collaborative, independent network of primary care and specialty care physicians to provide medical care services in a seamless and coordinated manner.
2. Evidence-based practices and performance measurement	Promote physician collaboration in: a) Design, implementation and application of evidence-based practice guidelines or protocols and quality benchmarks; b) Monitoring one another's individual and GRIPA's aggregate performance in applying the guidelines in achieving the network's benchmarks.
3. Use of integrated CIS	Integrate its physicians and ancillary services through a Web-based electronic clinical information system (CIS) that ensures sharing of clinical information.
4. Decrease burdens	Decrease overall administrative/regulatory burden of participating physicians by reducing paperwork and time to process treatment information.

The FTC's plan also included expanding the scope of diseases that GRIPA covered in its disease management services, ensured nonexclusivity options for contracting, and established a clinical integration committee comprising 12 physicians.[128]The FTC recommended in its conclusion that the commission not challenge GRIPA's clinical integration program as its joint negotiation of contracts was "reasonably related to" GRIPA's ability to achieve potential efficiencies from its member physicians integration through the program and in view of the "precompetitive potential of GRIPA's proposed program."[129]

A second opinion rendered by the FTC in the course of approving a clinical integration program was the TriState Health Partners, Inc. (TriState) opinion in April

---

[127] Federal Trade Commission. GRIPA advisory opinion, September 17, 2007, 5. Available at: http://www.ftc.gov/bc/adops/gripa.pdf.

[128] Federal Trade Commission. GRIPA advisory opinion, September 17, 2007, 6. Available at: http://www.ftc.gov/bc/adops/gripa.pdf.

[129] Federal Trade Commission. GRIPA advisory opinion, September 17, 2007, 29. Available at: http://www.ftc.gov/bc/adops/gripa.pdf.

2009.[130] TriState is a physician-hospital organization (PHO) located in Maryland with over 200 physicians engaged in a multiprovider network joint venture. In this case TriState proposed a clinical integration program that would require a joining fee of $2,500 per physician with no additional investment required (which met the financial risk requirement). TriState also proposed joint contracting among all member physicians to maximize the number of patients in the program and the engagement of physicians to maximize the integration of care services within the network. TriState had a similar but slightly more extensive set of indicia of clinical integration than was the case with GRIPA. Looking at TriState's collaborative physician activities in Table 18 we can see that all are aligned with the primary indicia noted in Figure 19 above.

---

[130] Federal Trade Commission. Tristate advisory opinion, April 2009. Available at: www.ftc.gov/os/closings/staff/090413tristateaoletter.pdf.

Table 18. Summary of TriState's Collaborative Physician Activities[131]

Topic	Description of Activity
1. Physician engagement	Requires extensive participation by the clinical integration program's physicians in the program's development, implementation, and continuous operations.
2. Coordination of care	Maintains continuity and care coordination through a within-network referral policy.
3. Evidence-based practices	Establishes a mostly closed panel of providers committed to practicing consistently with evidence-based standards and clinical guidelines created or tailored by the clinical integration program's participants.
4. Performance measurement	Sets up mechanisms to collect and evaluate clinical treatment and performance measurement data, including information on appropriate use of clinical resources.
5. Use of health information technology	Requires the use of health information technology, including electronic health records to coordinate care, foster effective communications with network physicians, collect performance improvement information, and mitigate occurrence of duplicate tests.
6. Governance and peer review	Establishes procedures and mechanisms, including committees with physicians providing feedback on individual and group performance; addressing deficiencies in performance within the network; and when necessary, impose sanctions on physicians whose "performance is chronically deficient regarding program requirements and standards."

TriState went further in demonstrating its clinical integration program with the points made on physician engagement and governance and peer review. These indicia indicate the deeper commitment made by physicians in the network to ensure that continuity and consistency are maintained with the greatest emphasis on improvement in patient care services.

A third opinion to note is that of Advocate Physician Partners (Advocate) and their clinical integration program. In a May 2008 presentation by Advocate's president, Lee B.

---

[131] Federal Trade Commission. Tristate advisory opinion, April 2009, Part B, 3) Infrastructure and program capability for integrating the provision of care and achieving efficiencies, 19-20. Available at: www.ftc.gov/os/closings/staff/090413tristateaoletter.pdf.

Sacks, MD, he indicated that the goal of the program was "to drive targeted improvements in health care quality and efficiency through our relationship with every major insurance plan offered in the Chicago metropolitan area, thus uniting payer, employer, patients, and physicians in a single program to improve outcomes."[132]

The Advocate Clinical Integration Program (CIP) was launched on January 1, 2004. The FTC passed a ruling regarding Advocate's contracting practices in 2006; and in doing so also examined the efforts of the CIP. The FTC did not pass a determination on the legality of the CIP but instead commented that it would continue to monitor the CIP.[133] While the FTC did not provide detailed analysis of the CIP in this case, we can see from the Advocate Health Partners' 2010 Value Report on Clinical Integration a number of benefits derived in 2009 from the program that are shown in Table 19.

---

[132] Sacks LB. Presentation at Federal Trade Commission clinical integration workshop; May 2008; Washington, DC. Available at: http://www.ftc.gov/bc/healthcare/checkup/pdf/Sacks%20Presentation%20-%20Clinical%20Integration%20Workshop.pdf.

[133] Federal Trade Commission. Analysis of agreement containing consent order to aid public comment in the matter of Advocate Health Partners, et al., file No. 031 0021. Available at: http://www.ftc.gov/os/caselist/0310021/061229ana0310021.pdf; Federal Trade Commission. Press release, December 29, 2006. FTC charges Chicago-area doctor groups with price fixing. Available at: http://www.ftc.gov/opa/2006/12/ahp.shtm.

Table 19. Highlights from AHP 2010 Value Report[134]

Clinical Area	Value Generated
Comprehensive asthma outcomes initiative	This initiative produced direct and indirect medical cost savings of $16M annually above national averages. Resulted in an estimated "additional 37,920 days saved annually from absenteeism and lost productivity."
Generic prescribing initiative	The initiative resulted in prescribing rates of 4.6 to 6.4 percentage points higher than those of two large Chicago-area insurers. The initiative generated savings of "$14.8M annually to Chicago- area payers, employers and patients above community performance."
Diabetic care outcomes initiative	This initiative resulted in an additional 12,350 years of life saved, 19,760 years of eyesight preserved and 14,820 years free from kidney disease. Additionally, improvement in poor Hemoglobin A1c levels resulted in nearly $2M annual savings above national averages.
Depression screening	Depression screening and subsequent treatment in patients with diabetes, heart failure or a cardiac event, produced greater than an additional $10.8M annual direct and indirect savings over the standard practice. "Additionally, employers saved more than 8,672 lost work days per year."

Advocate's central concern is demonstrating its economic impact on its community and most importantly its impact on population-based health in the geographic market it serves. Proving the realization of these benefits to the community, consumers, and patients is crucial to having a successful clinical integration program and being compliant within the existing safe harbors of the FTC.

While we have provided examples of three cases in which the FTC approved clinical integration programs, we note that there are other cases in which mergers were not approved. Cases of interest include *Arizona v. Maricopa County Medical Society*,[135] Evanston Northwestern Health System,[136] and North Texas Specialty Physicians.[137] Each

---

[134] Advocate Health Partners. The 2010 value report: benefits of clinical integration. Available at: http://www.advocatehealth.com/documents/app/final_1640_Value%20Report%202010.pdf.

[135] *Arizona v. Maricopa County Medical Soc.*, 457 U.S. 332 (1982). Available at: http://biotech.law.lsu.edu/cases/antitrust/maricopa.htm.

case or administrative opinion has its unique circumstances but ultimately each comes down to the balance of anticompetitive actions engaged in relation to the pro-competitive effects and efficiency improvements in the quality of care and cost of healthcare services on each geographic market and the impact on consumers, patients served, and market competition.

As systems begin to engage physicians around organizing to become ACOs, one compelling truth appears: the primary reason the parties are coming together has to be the delivery of superior quality and value to the consumer. On the other hand, if the discussions focus on joint contracting and economic incentives, the initiative in the minds of many experts will be flawed and at legal risk from the outset.

Antitrust Safety Zones and Networks

One of the most important steps taken by the FTC has been the creation of antitrust safety zones.[138] There are two types, exclusive and nonexclusive, and they are applicable to physician network joint ventures that we shall discuss first. Later we will describe another type of network critically important to ACOs that will involve hospitals, CINs, and IDNs: the multiprovider network. To start our discussion of determining whether the physician network qualifies for one of the antitrust safety zones (and then what happens if it does not qualify), we provide Figure 20.

---

[136] Federal Trade Commission. Press release, August 7, 2007. Commission rules that Evanston Northwestern Healthcare Corp.'s acquisition of Highland Park hospital was anticompetitive. Available at: http://www.ftc.gov/opa/2007/08/evanston.shtm.

[137] *North Texas Specialty Physicians v. FTC,* 528 F.3d 346 (5th Cir. 2008). Federal Trade Commission. Press release, September 12, 2008. FTC issues final order on remand in case of North Texas Specialty Physicians. Available at: http://www.ftc.gov/opa/2008/09/ntsp.shtm.

[138] Department of Justice and Federal Trade Commission. Enforcement policy on physician network joint ventures. Statement #8, Section 8A. Available at: http://www.ftc.gov/bc/healthcare/industryguide/policy/statement8.htm.

Figure 20. Antitrust Safety Zones

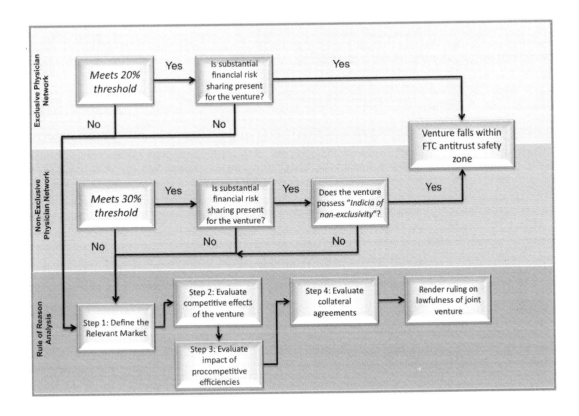

Our model is laid out across three planes that help to determine whether a specific joint venture meets the FTC's criteria. The exclusive physician network and the nonexclusive physician network represent the two antitrust safety zones with the rule of reason analysis providing the mechanism to evaluate relationships that do not meet criteria for these two antitrust safety zones.

There are two key factors for each type of network: market share and determining whether substantial financial risk is shared. First is the exclusive antitrust safety zone. It has the following market share requirements:

1. Network has 20% or fewer of the physicians having active hospital staff privileges in each specialty area within a given geographic market.

2. In a market having less than five physicians in any specific specialty area, "an

exclusive network otherwise qualifying for the antitrust safety zone may include one physician from that specialty, on a nonexclusive basis, even though the inclusion of that physician results in the venture consisting of more than 20 percent of the physicians in that specialty."

Second is the nonexclusive antitrust safety zone. As we can see in Figure 20, if the entity does not meet the criteria for an exclusive network, it defaults to the plane for consideration as a nonexclusive physician network. Its market share requirements are:

1. Network having 30% or less "of the physicians in each physician specialty with active hospital staff privileges who practice in the relevant geographic market."

2. In markets having less than four physicians in any specific specialty area, "a non-exclusive physician network joint venture otherwise qualifying for the antitrust safety zone may include one physician from that specialty, even though the inclusion of that physician results in the venture consisting of more than 30 percent of the physicians in that specialty."

Table 20 provides the indicia identified by the FTC for physician activities that qualify an entity as nonexclusive. The FTC advised physicians to understand these characteristics so as to ensure that if an organization claims to be a nonexclusive network, it is properly structured and operating with regard to its relationships with insurance payers and physicians engaged in the network.

Table 20. Nonexclusive Physicians' Activities: Indicia of Nonexclusivity[139]

No.	Indicia
1	That viable competing networks or managed care plans with adequate physician participation currently exist in the market;
2	That physicians in the network actually individually participate in or contract with other networks or managed care plans; or that there is other evidence of their willingness and incentive to do so;
3	That physicians in the network earn substantial revenue from other networks or through individual contracts with managed care plans;
4	The absence of any indications of significant de-participation from other networks or managed care plans in the market;
5	The absence of any indications of coordination among the physicians in the network regarding price or other competitively significant terms of participation in other networks or managed care plans.

These nonexclusive networks provide a means of keeping contractual relationship opportunities open for providers to engage with both public and private payers allowing them flexibility and keeping their geographic market open to competition for their patient care services.

Once the market share and exclusivity issues are determined, next is the issue of substantial financial risk. When physicians take on financial risk, the tradeoff is typically the degree of clinical integration undertaken by the joint venture to produce intended efficiencies and benefits in terms of improved quality of care and positive economic impact on the patient population and geographic market served. Predictably, the greater the financial risk the greater the degree of clinical integration undertaken. Some of the types of arrangements for the physician joint ventures (either exclusive or nonexclusive) defined by the FTC are presented in Table 21.

---

[139] Department of Justice and Federal Trade Commission. Enforcement policy on physician network joint ventures. Statement #8. Paragraph 8(A)3: Examples of clinical integration. Available at: http://www.ftc.gov/bc/healthcare/industryguide/policy/statement8.htm.

Table 21. Arrangements for Substantial Financial Risk for Physician Network Joint Ventures[140]

No.	Arrangement Description
1	Agreement by participants to provide services at a capitated rate.
2	Agreement by participants to provide designated services or classes of services to a health plan for a predetermined percentage of premium or revenue from the plan.
3	Participants' use of significant financial incentives for its physician participants as a group to achieve specified cost-containment goals. Two methods that the venture can use to accomplish this include: (a) Withhold from all physician participants in the network a substantial amount of the compensation due to them, with distribution of that amount to the physician participants based on group performance in meeting the cost-containment goals of the network as a whole; or (b) Establish overall cost or utilization targets for network physicians in whole, with the network's physician participants subject to subsequent substantial financial rewards or penalties based on group performance in meeting the targets
4	Agreement by participants to provide a complex or extended course of treatment requiring the substantial coordination of care by physicians in different specialties offering a complementary mix of services, for a fixed, predetermined payment, where the costs of that course of treatment for any individual patient can vary greatly due to the individual patient's condition, the choice, complexity, or length of treatment, or other factors.

If it is determined that substantial financial risk has been undertaken and the entity meets the requirements for one of the two safe harbors, then the FTC's analysis is completed. If it does not qualify for either one, then the rule of reason analysis would be initiated.

As Figure 20 indicates, there are four steps in this analysis. Steps 2 and 3 cover the FTC's evaluation of each joint venture's claims to indicia of clinical integration to be weighed against any anticompetitive actions or effects (joint contracting, price fixing, and the like). Statement #8 provides detailed information along with specific hypothetical

---

[140] Department of Justice and Federal Trade Commission. Enforcement policy on multiprovider networks. Statement #8. Paragraph 8(A)4. Available at: http://www.ftc.gov/bc/healthcare/industryguide/policy/statement8.htm.

examples of how the FTC would analyze any given situation.

Multiprovider networks

The network structure applicable to ACOs involving IDNs, CINs, and PHOs in various models and approaches for clinical and financial integration with IPAs is the multiprovider network. The FTC does not provide a safe harbor for multiprovider networks as of early 2011. Because a significant number of ACO programs will be initiated by these types of organizations, the industry is looking to the FTC and CMS for added flexibility in the development and approval of such arrangements. There are several similarities between physician networks and multiprovider networks that include the indicia of clinical integration; rules on substantial financial risk sharing; 20% and 30% rulings; and the rules of reason analysis. In the FTC's evaluation of any multiprovider network, the agency looks at the merger from a horizontal perspective (IPAs with other IPAs or MSPGs) or from a vertical perspective (IDN/CIN with IPAs, MSPGs, or other ancillary care providers). Any of these combinations will be evaluated on the basis of the geographic market they affect, anticompetitive actions taken, and pro-competitive effects and efficiencies resulting from the clinical integration program implemented or proposed for implementation by the parties involved.

With regard to horizontal analysis, there are four factors identified in Statement #9 to be taken into consideration.[141] These factors are:

- Impact of the merger on market share and concentration of physicians/healthcare service providers in the given geographic market

- Competitive effects of joint contracting

- Impact of collateral agreements (do they create unreasonable restrictions on competition among payers for provider services?)

---

[141] Department of Justice and Federal Trade Commission. Enforcement policy on multiprovider networks. Statement #9, section 2(A). Horizontal analysis. Available at: http://www.ftc.gov/bc/healthcare/industryguide/policy/statement9.htm.

- Spillover effects (what is the effect of the horizontal merger on markets for services outside the immediate relevant market?)

For vertical merger analyses, one of the principal concerns is whether the merger will impact markets outside the merging organization's immediate geographic market. These types of mergers are also analyzed for their exclusive vs. nonexclusive traits. In evaluating the effects of a nonexclusive vertical merger, the indicia specified in Table 17 are also used in these multiprovider networks. Other factors evaluated in multiprovider merger analysis include:

- Selective contracting: excluding certain providers for the purposes of cost containment, quality control, and ensuring patient volumes.[142]

- Messenger models: driving contracting between providers and payers while steering clear of price-fixing agreements with competing network providers.[143]

- Potential efficiencies: evaluating potential anticompetitive effects against the potential pro-competitive effects and efficiency gains in lieu of the clinical integration and substantial financial risks undertaken by the network.

As horizontal and vertical consolidation continues across the industry in most geographic markets, cases regarding the lawfulness of mergers involving several of these issues may proliferate. One landmark case in this area is *F.T.C. v. Butterworth Health Corp.*, 946 F. Supp. 1285 (W.D. Mich. 1996).[144] In this particular case the FTC had filed an

---

[142] Department of Justice and Federal Trade Commission. Enforcement policy on multiprovider networks. Statement #9(B)(2)c. Exclusion of particular providers. Available at: http://www.ftc.gov/bc/healthcare/industryguide/policy/statement9.htm.

[143] Department of Justice and Federal Trade Commission. Enforcement policy on multiprovider networks. Statement #9(C). Arrangements that do not involve horizontal agreements on prices or price-related terms. Available at: http://www.ftc.gov/bc/healthcare/industryguide/policy/statement9.htm; Federal Trade Commission. Opinion on Bay Area Preferred Physicians (BAPP) messenger model adoption, September 23, 2003. Available at: http://www.ftc.gov/bc/adops/bapp030923.shtml.

[144] Federal Trade Commission. Press release, November 18, 1996. FTC to appeal district court decision in Butterworth/Blodgett Hospital merger case and to pursue administrative challenge to merger. Available at: http://www.ftc.gov/opa/1996/11/buttblod.shtm.

injunction to block the merger between the hospitals out of concern that it would substantially reduce competition for acute care hospital services in the Grand Rapids, Michigan area and could lead to increased prices for services. While the circuit court concluded that the merger was in violation of Section 7 of the Clayton Act and that it would indeed create substantial market power for the new entity, there was no evidence that the hospitals in the proposed merger would exercise any market power that would cause harm to consumers or patients in the markets they served. Therefore the FTC allowed the merger to move forward. Cases such as this one are important for supporting the developments that take place with ACO models over the years in different forms resulting from clinical and financial integration efforts to strengthen healthcare services and opportunities to improve care coordination through the formation of ACOs.

As we have discussed for ACOs, there is a wide array of potential combinations of organizations through both horizontal (IPAs with IPAs and MSPGs) and vertical (IPAs or MSPGs combining with IDNs or PHOs and possibly additional ancillary healthcare service providers) mergers. ACOs as clinically integrated entities have the potential to serve as enablers of disruptive innovations in care delivery, payment models, and quality or performance measurement as part of a new disruptive value network. Christensen defined disruptive innovation as:

> A process by which a product or service takes root initially in simple applications at the bottom of a market and then relentlessly moves 'up market,' eventually displacing established competitors. [145]

Christensen noted that some organizations, such as Kaiser Permanente, Intermountain Healthcare, Geisinger Health System, and the Veterans Health Administration all have the

---

[145] Christensen C, Grossman J, Hwang J. *The Innovator's Prescription: A Disruptive Solution for Healthcare.* New York, NY: McGraw Hill; 2009. Introduction, xxix, Figure I.2 Existing and disruptive value networks in healthcare; Chapter 1, 3–8, Figure 1.1 Model of disruptive innovation; definition of disruptive innovation. Available at: http://claytonchristensen.com/disruptive_innovation.html.

"scope within themselves to create disruptive value networks."[146] Moreover, as noted earlier in Chapters 2 and 3, these organizations have achieved advanced levels of integration and are operating under the guiding principles of accountable care. Figure 21 is adapted from Christensen's work in *The Innovator's Prescription* (2009) to illustrate the concept of disruptive innovation.

We show the healthcare market (Plane of Competition 1) as it has been driven through managed care and FFS payment systems. As previously stated, that produced a volume-driven system that led to an environment with some anticompetitive actions and fraudulent tactics attempted in the market, requiring the intervention of antitrust laws and policies to maintain fair and pro-competitive balance.

Figure 21. ACOs: Changing the Game

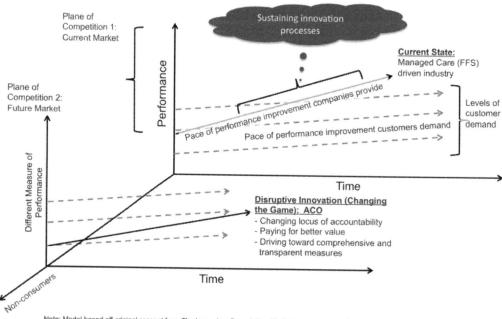

Note: Model based off original concept from The Innovators Prescription (C. Christensen, 2009) Figure 1.1 Model of disruptive innovation

---

[146] Christensen C, Grossman J, Hwang J. *The Innovator's Prescription: A Disruptive Solution for Healthcare.* New York, NY: McGraw Hill; 2009. Introduction, xxix, Figure I.2 Existing and disruptive value networks in healthcare; Chapter 6, 198-207, Figure 6.3 Assessment of candidate entities for managing our healthcare. Available at: http://claytonchristensen.com/disruptive_innovation.html.

The ACO model enters the future market (Plane of Competition 2) as a vehicle for innovative delivery and a disruptive innovation in itself, as seen through CMS pilot projects and demonstrations involving private payers. New performance measures will emerge as market players come together through integration and mergers in the years to come. The core environment for which healthcare services are delivered will evolve as we transition toward more P4P and incentive-driven systems and care delivery organizations.

Consumer expectations and payment reform will fuel this disruptive transformation and drive these changes. These changes in turn may alter the needs and foci of antitrust laws as the DOJ and FTC monitor market responses and functions with new mergers and consolidations among industry participants implementing various forms of ACO models.

As ACOs become more widespread, moving from pilot project and demonstrations to mainstream integrated care delivery models, our nation's framework of antitrust laws at state and federal levels will help guide the efforts within the rule of law. In partnership with ACO stakeholders the FTC should work to develop the flexibility needed in our nation's antitrust statutory framework (Figure 13). These efforts will enhance opportunities for innovation toward a future state in which medical errors are reduced, quality is improved, collaboration and new health information technology improves care coordination, and changes in market competition do not inhibit progress.

As ACO models evolve, the FTC and CMS will likely evaluate the new innovations in care delivery, payment reform, and influx of new indicia of clinical integration resulting from these transformative initiatives that will be tested and implemented across the health system in the United States for years to come.

Future Legislative Impact

As this chapter illustrates, antitrust laws in their current and future forms will have a significant impact on emergent federal health policy. As the Shared Savings Program rules roll out over the coming years along with stages 2 and 3 of the CMS meaningful use rules, modifications to sections of the PPACA, and updates to elements of the core framework of antitrust law described in Figure 15, we can expect changes that will need to be accounted for in the future structuring of ACO models and joint venture relationships. Organizations should also recognize that state government healthcare and insurance organizations also have the potential to issue new rules and regulations that can affect an ACO's operation. Ensuring that resources are in place to monitor these changes at federal and state levels will put ACOs in proactive positions to mitigate unintended consequences, deal with forthcoming changes, and adjust operating or financial plans and clinical integration programs accordingly.

Such initiatives as the Centers for Medicare and Medicaid Innovation will result in the need for new ways of operating by IDNs, CINs, IPAs, MSPGs, related ancillary service providers, and payer organizations as delivery system transformation drives these organizations toward closer integration for the purpose of achieving greater pro-competitive effects and efficiencies that will benefit communities and patient populations. In closing this section we offer ACO Roadmap 2: Navigating the Antitrust Landscape (Figure 22).

Figure 22. ACO Roadmap 2: Navigating the Antitrust Landscape

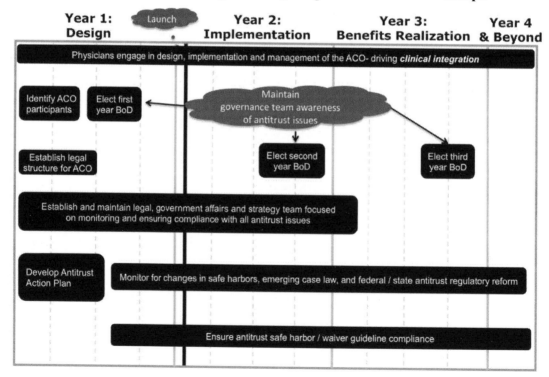

As the reader can see, a central point is establishing a proactive strategy for the ACO around antitrust issues. This strategy will require oversight from the ACO's executive governance board with physician leadership and involvement of all key participants. Second, the participants should develop a comprehensive antitrust action plan for the ACO early in the design period. Planning should involve legal counsel along with select strategy, government affairs, and executive staff from across the ACO entity. Environmental monitoring of changes in the legislative landscape should be made a priority for the government affairs staff. Recognizing that executives from across the ACO will be engaged in various industry associations, organizations may consider establishment of a multidisciplinary executive committee coordinated by government affairs for the purpose of maintaining situational awareness and helping to meet the ACO's need for coordinated industry intelligence for all its ACO participants.

> **DISCLAIMER:** The intent of this chapter is not to provide legal guidance but to raise awareness of many issues, several of which are related to the field of antitrust law. We highly recommend that readers engage legal counsel for themselves and/or their organizations on any specific application of these rules or laws that impact them in the present or future as ACO initiatives evolve. They should also retain counsel for any necessary communication with the FTC regarding obtaining opinions on potential ACO operating models or clinical integration programs.

INFOCUS: **Challenges and Risks to Overcome**

The sphere of antitrust laws will have a significant impact on the evolution of ACOs in both public and private application. Organizations will be striving to achieve and maintain clinical integration programs that will affect their geographic markets along lines of both horizontal and vertical mergers. As mergers are proposed among competitors (horizontal) and across partners throughout the healthcare service supply chain (vertical) in the development of ACOs, federal and state agencies will monitor markets for trends toward oligopolistic competition[147] and the creation of monopolies that may emerge in rural regions as a result of consolidation needed to form ACOs in areas with a limited supply of healthcare services.

As these market changes occur, federal and state regulators should evaluate the implications of allowing the "effects of monopoly extraction"[148] as competition is reduced in some regions and its ability to stimulate innovation for the benefit of all consumers, patients, and industry stakeholders vs. ensuring that the "effects of monopoly extension" do not emerge in any areas. Table 22 offers a set of challenges, risks and potential mitigation strategies applicable to issues from this chapter.

---

[147] Besanko D, Dranove D, Shanley M, Schaefer S. (2004). Competitors and competition. In: *Economics of Strategy*. 3rd ed. Hoboken, NJ; John Wiley and Sons, Inc.; 218–223.

[148] Raskovich A, Miller NH. Cumulative innovation and competition policy. Department of Justice Economic Analysis Group Discussion paper, September 2010. Available at: http://www.justice.gov/atr/public/eag/262643.pdf.

Table 22. Chapter 4 Challenges and Risks

Challenges	Risks
4a) Demonstrating greater value to the consumer with the ability to aggregate, analyze and manage data in significant ways.	4d) If indicia are not met, the FTC or DOJ can rule against the ACO and unwind the makings of the network.
4b) Moving quickly enough to remain competitive in a market while safe harbor requirements remain unclear or are in development.	4e) Moving too quickly or assuming changes that do not come to fruition.
4c) Maintaining the resources to monitor the changing landscape of regulations for the Shared Savings Program, HITECH Act, HIPAA, and antitrust laws.	4f) Losing competitive balance in geographic markets and creating anticompetitive practices that lead to market inefficiencies harming patients, consumers and employers.

Potential Mitigation Strategies
√   Consult legal counsel with expertise in antitrust and anti-kickback statutes.
√   Monitor changes in law as they are released.
√   Develop a strategy for horizontal and vertical relationships needed to form your ACO.
√   Develop an antitrust action plan to ensure compliance across the framework of federal antitrust laws along with state antitrust related laws and regulations.

Chapter 5. Technology Requirements for Managing the ACO

The establishment of health information technology and systems needed for an ACO must meet a number of requirements. With regard to Medicare ACOs, Section 3022 of the PPACA specifies that they must have "clinical and administrative systems" along with the use of telehealth, remote patient monitoring, and other such enabling technologies."[149] These same requirements will apply to Medicaid pediatric ACOs and are also considered part of the infrastructure requirements for private payer-based ACOs. This chapter will touch on some of the core technology requirements, which include electronic medical records (EMRs), forthcoming clinical modifications (CM) of ICD-10, and procedure coding system (PCS) conversion for the U.S. healthcare industry. We will then take an in-depth look at the issue of health information exchange (HIE) and the many factors to be considered by physician leaders and others in ACO implementation when HIE is part of the overall plan.

We will first discuss the importance of EMRs and some factors to consider in mitigating risks associated with their implementation. President George Bush issued a mandate in 2004 for EMRs to be implemented across the nation within 10 years in order to support the establishment of a national health information network (NHIN).[150] This edict was reinforced by the passage of ARRA, the HITECH Act discussed in Chapter 1, and the start of CMS's meaningful use of electronic medical records program in 2010. Many benefits come with the implementation of EMRs, including improved safety through

---

[149] H.R. 3590, Patient Protection and Affordable Care Act, §3022(b)(2)(F) and (G). Requirements for ACOs (2009).

[150] Ford EW, Menachemi N, Peterson LT, Huerta TR. Resistance is futile: but it is slowing the pace of EHR adoption nonetheless. *J Am Med Inform Assoc*. 2009;16(3): 274-281.

elimination of medical errors, reduction of unnecessary procedures and tests, improved care coordination, and the potential to achieve nationwide savings in healthcare costs along with better health outcomes. Healthcare providers across the industry, however, have noted that the adoption of EMRs through 2009 has been slow in light of capital requirements for initial system purchases; difficulty validating projected returns on investments; anticipated maintenance requirements; and resistance on the part of healthcare provider organizations and physicians to make the transition from paper medical records to the EMR environment.[151]

In addition to these issues, the Joint Commission issued a report regarding safety concerns related to implementing health information technology and noted 13 suggested actions to help improve patient safety and mitigate risks associated with the implementation of EMRs.[152] A number of factors were cited in the commission's report; however, the one we wish to emphasize here are the unintended adverse consequences (UACs) identified by Ash, Sittig, and colleagues based on a study of five hospitals and their computerized provider order entry (CPOE) system.[153] The UACs include:

+ More work or new types of work for physicians and other clinicians
+ Workflow complications
+ System demands
+ Communication breakdowns
+ Persistence of paper medical records
+ Emotional repercussions
+ New types of errors

---

[151] Jha AK, DesRoches CM, Campbell EG, et al. Use of electronic health records in U.S. hospitals. *N Engl J Med.* 2009;360(16):1628-1638.

[152] Joint Commission. Sentinel Event Alert, December 11, 2008. Safely implementing health information and converging technologies. Available at: http://www.jointcommission.org/assets/1/18/SEA_42.PDF.

[153] Ash JS, Sittig DF, Poon EG, Guappone K, Campbell E, Dykstra RH. The extent and importance of unintended consequences related to computerized provider order entry. *J Am Med Inform Assoc.* 2007;14(4): 415-423; Campbell EM, Sittig DF, Ash JS, Guappone K, Dykstra RH. Types of unintended consequences related to computerized provider order entry. *J Am Med Inform Assoc* 2006;13(5):547-556.

- Shifts in power in the care environment
- Overdependence on technology

The issue of workflow redesign is crucial to every EMR implementation and requires the engagement of clinicians, physicians, and IT staff along with vendors to ensure that the transition to the new EMR-driven care environment is completed while minimizing the occurrence of UACs, e-iatrogenesis (defined as "patient harm caused at least in part by the application of health information technology"),[154] and other risks that may affect delivery of patient care. With ACOs speeding the work of clinical integration among provider organizations and physician practices through the various models discussed in Chapter 3, ensuring interoperability and interfacing among EMRs from different vendors is a critical issue. It will also be important to ensure accurate and timely data exchange between hospitals and office-based EMRs, as this exchange will support the efficiency of the ACO's coordination and continuity of care.   In light of these issues, CMS's meaningful use of electronic health records incentive program finalized its Stage 1 criteria on July 13, 2010. The criteria provide the set of technical requirements that eligible hospitals and providers must meet in order to receive incentive payments through 2015.[155] Establishing health information exchange, clinical decision support (CDS), and CPOE capabilities are all requirements that will become increasingly stringent in stages 2 and 3, which will be announced in future years. These incentives and the penalties to be imposed in 2016 for entities that do not implement certified EMR technology are intended to accelerate adoption across the industry.

Before discussing health information exchange (HIE), we must also note the importance of the industry-wide conversion from ICD-9 to ICD-10-CM and PCS by 2013. A precursor to this conversion will be a required transition for all certified EMR providers to ensure that administrative systems can adhere to the changes in reporting structure from

---

[154] Weiner JP, Kfuri T, Chan K, Fowles JB. e-Iatrogenesis: the most critical unintended consequence of CPOE and other HIT. *J Am Med Inform Assoc.* 2007;14(3): 387-388.

[155] Blumenthal D, Tavenner M.. The "meaningful use" regulation for electronic health records. *N Engl J Med.* 2010. 363(6): 501-504.

ASC X12 4010a to 5010.[156] Testing and compliance for healthcare providers on this new capability began in 2009; it will continue across the industry through 2012 in preparation for the ICD-10-CM and PCS conversion. This conversion will affect every healthcare organization in the United States that deals with recording, aggregation, or exchanging of patient health information; it will require significant resources and planning in many cases as a parallel to ACO implementation.[157] At the local level for all providers, whether pursuing to become an ACO or not, it will be important to engage health information management (HIM) leaders with physician leaders to ensure that a number of issues are addressed including:[158]

- That adequate training is provided across the ACO for staff members responsible for interpreting and using the vastly expanded coding structures (growing from approximately 17,000 codes under ICD-9 to over 155,000 for ICD-10-CM and PCS[159]);

- That testing of information technology interfaces is conducted to ensure accuracy of health data to support efficient health information exchange across all ACO participants;

- That bidirectional mapping involving medical coding experts is conducted for the transition from ICD-9 to the expanded ICD-10-CM and PCS codes.

As the health care industry strives to implement EMRs and begins to embark upon the ICD-10-CM conversion, achieving interoperability between disparate systems will further

---

[156] CFR Part 162 Health insurance reform; modifications to the Health Insurance Portability and Accountability Act (HIPAA); final rules. *Federal Register* 45; 2009;74:3296-3328.

[157] AHIMA. e-HIM Workgroup on the Transition to ICD-10-CM/PCS. Planning organizational transition to ICD-10-CM/PCS. *Journal of AHIMA.* 2009;80(10):72-77.

[158] Steindel SJ. International classification of diseases, 10th edition, clinical modification and procedure coding system: descriptive overview of the next generation HIPAA code sets. *J Am Med Inform Assoc.* 2010;17(3):274-282.

[159] Raths D. Is ICD-10 a Quality Initiative? Innovators will use ICD-10 to further their business models and clinical capabilities. *Healthc Inform.* 2010;27(9):24-28.

aid in achieving the long term goals of having a more complete and accurate record of the patients health history.

With this background as a starting point, let us move on to some specific details related to the issue of HIE in relation to the IDN.

Virtualizing the Integrated Delivery Network

When asked by David Burda, the editor of *Modern Healthcare*, whether he would want to join an ACO if he were a new physician just starting out, Jay Crosson, the Permanente Medical Group senior adviser for health policy and former chair of the Medicare Payment Advisory Commission, answered, "I absolutely would." [160]

Why such a definitive response? Because Dr. Crosson experienced firsthand the value to both patient and provider when the hospital, physician, and payer are closely aligned during his work as a physician within the Kaiser Permanente system for more than 30 years. Wherever a patient goes within the Kaiser system, be it a hospital or physician's office, each authorized provider—from nurses to primary care physicians to one or more specialists—has an overall understanding of the patient's history and health status based on their ability to review every interaction the patient has had with every member of the care team. This holistic and coherent approach—a 360-degree vision—ensures that care is coordinated and congruent with the protocols and guidelines for that particular patient. In other words, the highest-quality care is delivered at the lowest cost.

Kaiser Permanente has spent billions of dollars over many years on "bricks and mortar" infrastructure to achieve this level of coordination, including buildings, people, and information technology (IT). From an IT perspective alone, Kaiser has spent billions on a hospital and ambulatory information system to ensure that every physician across acute and ambulatory settings is using the same system and that by doing so, he or she has the most

---

[160] Video interview: former MedPAC chairman Jay Crosson on ACOs. *Modern Healthcare*, August 9, 2010. Available at: http://www.modernhealthcare.com/article/20100809/VIDEO/308099999.

recently updated information about every patient.

There is no doubt that the IDN model as exemplified by Kaiser and others has achieved the greatest degree of success in improving care collaboration and reducing the cost of care. On the other hand, a model that requires a single or common ownership and substantial capital resources to build or purchase the infrastructure necessary to replicate an experience like Kaiser's is not realistic for nationwide ACO implementation in that a central goal of an ACO is to lower the cost of care, not increase it. Moreover, as ACOs take shape, many will be joint ventures that include participants and stakeholders who are not part of the same physical or legal organization. The expectation that every provider use the same information system is simply unrealistic, given human behavior, organizational dynamics, cost, and the nature of cross-organizational workflow. Hence the value of the new interoperability standards that will increasingly allow for information exchange at a lower cost of implementation.

Meanwhile integration vendors are working to aid providers in virtualizing the health care record. This integration work is intended to help create the IDN experience and achieve the level of coherence experienced by Kaiser's providers without having to own all the pieces and parts and requiring everyone to be part of the same organization using the same information system. While data standards and interface development are complex and the available information is often limited compared to single source systems, it is however the reality of healthcare today. Because of the episodic nature of an ACO's bundled payment and shared savings model, it presents complex issues of care coordination. All providers involved in a single care episode—hospitals, the primary care physician, specialists, ancillary service providers—become the patient's care team for that episode. While ACOs can be developed with a simple registry, most experts would agree that to achieve a robust and learning network, it will require the leveraging of technology to create an increasingly more complete health care record.

To successfully coordinate care on an episodic basis, distribute funds accurately, and improve on quality benchmarks, community-wide coordination of patient information is essential. HIE technology is the underlying connection of all stakeholders and participants in an ACO across organizational boundaries and disparate information systems. Figure 23 provides a high-level illustration of the range of participants requiring connectivity in an ACO through HIE technology.

Figure 23: Spectrum of Connectivity for ACO Participants

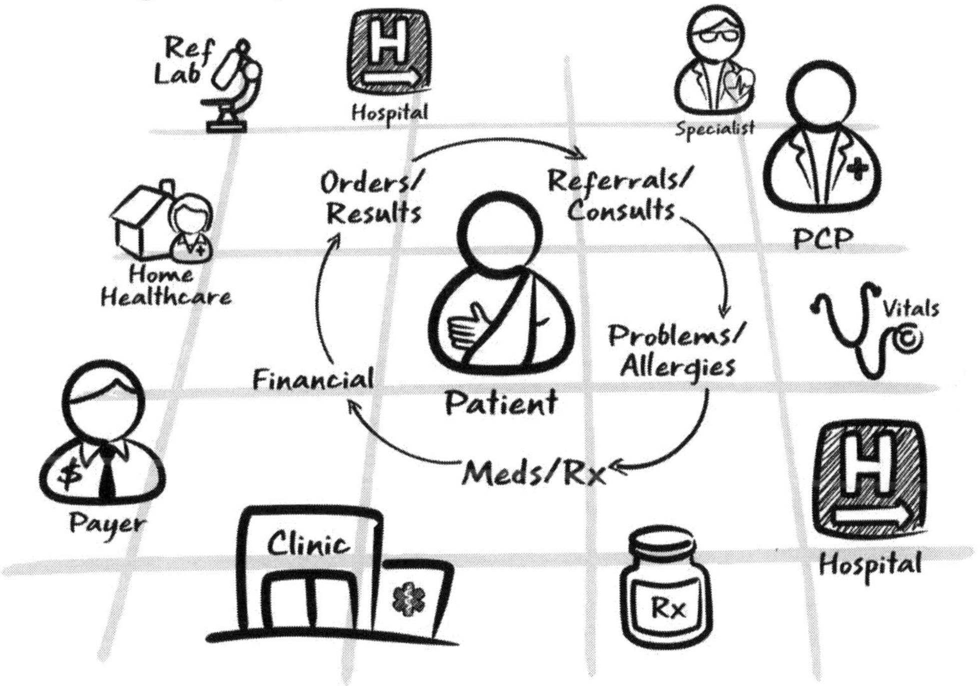

While we are specifically addressing the IDN type of ACO at this point, this spectrum of participants applies to each of the other four ACO models defined in Chapter 3.

Defining HIE: noun or verb?

Before entering too deeply into the technology required to manage a successful ACO, it is important to define "health information exchange" in that users of HIE often use the term in different contexts. HIE as a noun commonly refers to a third-party nonprofit organization formed to enable information sharing among multiple healthcare entities. Examples of this type of HIE are the Regional Health Information Organization (RHIO) and the Health Information Organization (HIO). RHIO, HIO, and HIE are used interchangeably to refer to initiatives serving either a local geographic region or a state.

Some statewide initiatives, such as the Delaware Health Information Network (DHIN), the Pennsylvania Health Information Exchange (PHIX), and the Colorado Regional Health Information Organization (CORHIO) are ARRA-qualified state-designated entities eligible to receive federal funds to support their operations. In the case of such regional initiatives as the Mississippi Coastal Health Information Exchange (MSCHIE), there are a variety of funding mechanisms, both public and private, in place to support business operations. Whether an HIE initiative is statewide or regional, its value hinges to a great extent on the quality and completeness of the data contributed by participating stakeholders.

For a third-party HIE to fully support ACO operations, all providers—not only physicians and hospitals—participating in an ACO must also be participants in that HIE. This participation is usually not the case, however. In a public regional or state HIE, the primary focus in the first few years is connecting hospitals and physician practices. In a mature ACO, *all* stakeholders involved in delivering care to a patient will be connected: hospitals and physician practices as well as long term care facilities, home health agencies, physical therapists, reference labs, imaging centers, and the like. It is therefore less likely that an HIE (in its noun form) will be able to fully support the information exchange needs of an ACO in the near term.

The *verb* sense of HIE commonly refers to the *activity* of exchanging health information across disparate information systems and multiple locations of care, both acute and ambulatory. The third-party HIE introduced above employs the verb sense of the term when it deploys HIE technology to enable the active sharing of information among its participants. Similarly, there are hundreds of private information exchanges in operation nationwide, sponsored by such community hospitals as Hoag Hospital and El Camino Hospital in California, and such health systems or IDNs as Intermountain Healthcare in Utah, Trinity Health in Michigan, and CHRISTUS Health in Texas, Louisiana, and Utah. Each of these self-funded private HIE organizations has deployed HIE technology to actively exchange health information across acute and ambulatory care settings. In the private HIE setting, hospitals and health systems have a much stronger influence over stakeholder participation. As a result, the private HIE has a much higher likelihood of being able to support an ACO comprehensively by engaging all stakeholders beyond its hospitals and physician practices. Figure 24 illustrates this point along with some of the various channels through which information must flow.

Figure 24: HIE as a Verb -- Active HIE Among ACO Participants

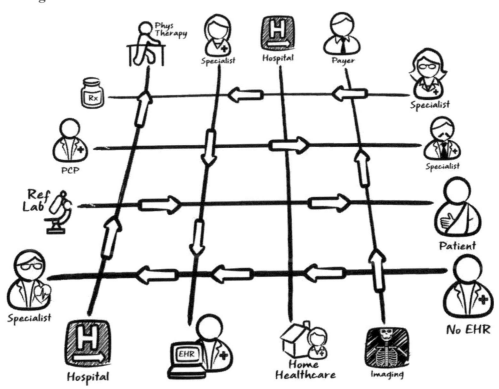

In the end, both the noun and verb forms of HIE are describing the same thing: the exchange of health information. The differences lie in the organizational structures, funding and sustainability mechanisms, and stakeholder participation. The technology required for exchanging health information is essentially the same and in either case is necessary in managing an ACO. Some observers might argue that short-term ACO initiatives could begin with nothing more than stand-alone disease registries; however, the present authors maintain that an ACO would not be sustainable without HIE technology in place.

Successful ACOs must possess an HIE infrastructure with specific competencies to support governance, operations, and clinical goals and objectives. The Vermont Blueprint for Health project discussed in Chapter 2 serves as an example of HIE as a critical component of both PCMH and ACO implementation in that state. HIE technology is critical to coordinate care, bridge the gap across acute and ambulatory settings, track payment distribution, collect data, and facilitate analysis for timely feedback and measuring progress toward quality or outcome goals. In addition to the multiple underlying technologies required to manage an ACO, particularly those at the source that gather, store, assimilate, codify, or process data, there are several HIE-related technologies that are also needed. They are described in Table 23:

Table 23: HIE-Related Technologies: The ACO Technology Framework

HIE Technology Requirement	Benefit to ACO
Real-time data exchange across disparate information systems and care locations	Ensures stakeholders are electronically connected and sharing information bi- and multidirectionally in a patient-centric model; seamless data integration into systems used by providers across the network; information is available at anytime offline, online, or on mobile devices.
Unified view of patients with standardized data and terminology, and accurate patient identification	Ensures providers have comprehensive, accurate, and updated information about all patients across the continuum of care in a longitudinal health record with standardized clinical, financial, and administrative data; information is available to providers any time via any web-enabled device.
Continuous live updates with real-time alerts and clinical decision support	Ensures providers and patients have timely and actionable information to make the best care decisions; enhances patient safety, clinical decision making and cost reduction; information is conveyed dynamically to providers, thereby ensuring proactive care management.
Disease management tools and case-continuity views	Actively engages all members of a patient's care team (including the patient) in the decision-making process with personalized care management; proactive rather than reactive care management and clinical decision-making.
Population management tools	Ensures all members of an ACO population (such as diabetics) are proactively managed with highly coordinated care and patients are engaged in preventive programs for more active health management; reduces costs and improves outcomes for a specific patient subpopulation.
Management consoles, decision support and analytics	Delivers quantitative information regarding costs, quality and process of care across the ACO network of connected providers. Enables the ACO to make better-informed strategic decisions.
Robust security and patient consent framework	Ensures data are secure and that only authorized providers or participants in managing the health of the patient have access to a patient's health information.
Patient/family engagement	Enables patients to take an active role in managing their health, with electronic access to their health information from all participating providers. Enables authorized family members to participate in managing the health of their relatives; enhances the quality of care, improves outcomes and patient satisfaction and reduces costs.

As clinicians migrate to common systems or as EMRs increasingly comply with common language and interoperability standards, information exchange will become easier. Where providers are unwilling or unable to convert to common systems and where health information exchange is implemented those technologies should complement the existing information systems such as electronic medical records used in physician practices, core information systems used in hospitals, information systems in reference laboratories, and physician archiving and communication systems (PACS) in imaging centers.

Nontraditional IT competencies

As noted in the list of technology enablers above, an ACO requires a sophisticated technology infrastructure to facilitate its objectives of improving quality and reducing costs. The most essential feature of this infrastructure is the ability to share information and coordinate care across organizations. In fact, as Glaser and Salzberg noted in *Hospitals and Health Networks*, "While applications such as the EHR and the patient health record are important, data may be the most important ACO information technology asset."[161]

Such traditional healthcare applications as EMRs, hospital information systems, emergency department information systems, office-based practice management systems, laboratory and radiology information systems, and patient administration applications are designed to record patient care information during an episode of care and are limited in scope to that care setting's organizational boundaries. While each discrete solution is important, many of these non office-based technologies were not designed to support the innovative coordination of care model required by ACOs, which extends beyond the four walls of a hospital, an emergency department, an imaging center or a lab for example.

---

[161] Glaser J, Salzberg C. Information technology for accountable care organizations. *Hospitals and Health Networks*, September 2010. Available at:
http://www.hhnmag.com/hhnmag_app/jsp/articledisplay.jsp?dcrpath=HHNMAG/Article/data/09SEP2010/09 0610HHN_Weekly_Glaser2&domain=HHNMAG.

To be successful in the long-term, we believe an ACO will require technology that can seamlessly integrate information and data across organizational boundaries spanning many discrete technologies. Because the participants in the ACO likely will be affiliated with disparate organizations—and unlike Kaiser, not all will be using the same information system—support technology for the ACO will need to facilitate a virtualization of the patient's care team by connecting to disparate systems across multiple care locations and integrating data with local systems and technologies already in use. Figure 25 illustrates the bilateral flow of patient information that is needed to facilitate effective HIE actions:

Figure 25: Electronic Virtual Care Teams

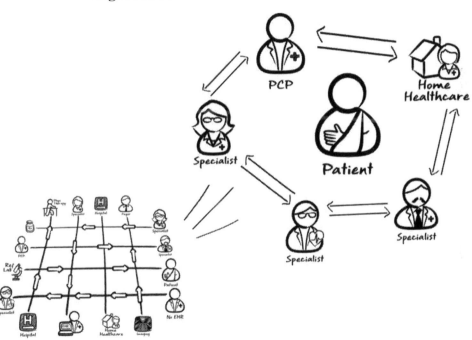

As discussed in Chapter 1, the development and initiation of new community health teams per Section 3502 of the PPACA will be strengthened by HIE capabilities. These teams will support patient-centered medical homes (recognized as part of the foundation of ACOs) with new interdisciplinary team members responsible for specific geographic regions.

Meeting Providers Where They Are

While ARRA and the HITECH Act are focused on enabling physicians to adopt EMRs, the reality is that most physicians rely on paper records and use electronic data mainly for billing purposes.[162] According to the CDC's National Ambulatory Medical Care Survey (NAMCS, 2009), only about 44 percent of physicians answering a mail survey reported using all or partial EMR systems (not including systems solely for billing) in their office-based practices. Of this 44 percent, about 21 percent reported having systems that met the criteria of a basic system, with only 6.3 percent having an extensive and fully functional electronic record system.[163] By definition, this figure means that more than half of all physicians in the United States still maintain paper-based practices. Within those practices, some physicians are comfortable using such electronic technology as e-mail and a Web browser, while others still prefer a paper chart and have no intention of participating in ARRA incentives. Nevertheless, many of these same physicians will need to participate in an ACO. This is especially important to understand as ACO start-ups get underway. Particularly when noting that while the meaningful use incentives discussed at the opening of this chapter will go a long way toward encouraging adoption of EMR technology, it will take years to reach critical mass. Similarly, HIE vendors are emerging daily as the need for this technology has not been lost on opportunists. Integration is and has been done, but it is a long and difficult road that will require sound decisions and implementation methods.

At the same time, the physicians who have adopted EMR technology have done so by selecting a vendor from a universe of hundreds of office-based EMR vendor solutions. While the number of HIE vendors is expanding, certification and interoperability requirements have conversely forced consolidation in the office-based EMR vendor market. Consequently some physicians are finding themselves with unsupported products

---

[162] President's Council of Advisors on Science and Technology. Report to the President realizing the full potential of health IT to improve healthcare for Americans: the path forward. December 8, 2010, 25. Video of full presentation available at: http://www.wellsphere.com/healthcare-industry-policy-article/realizing-the-full-potential-of-health-it-to-improve-healthcare-for-americans-the-path-forward/1299758.

[163] Centers for Disease Control and Prevention. Electronic medical record/electronic health record use by office-based physicians: United States, 2008 and preliminary 2009. Available at: http://www.cdc.gov/nchs/data/hestat/emr_ehr/emr_ehr.htm.

or outdated technologies that need replacements. Others work in markets where a handful of vendors predominate or in environments where local health systems are assisting with single or selected vendor implementations. While the idea of a single-vendor world is appealing, as mentioned earlier it is not contemporary reality. Consequently, any sustainable ACO initiative likely will need to be interoperable with a number of different EMR/EHR solutions.

Of course an ACO could be developed in the absence of such technologies; online registry reporting, for example, would quickly enable large groups of providers to populate a common Web-based system on which limited analytics could be run and from which improved care management could be delivered. We recognize this type of system as a starting point for such an initiative, however, and not the long-term ideal future state of operation. As such, the technology needed to support an integrated ACO would need to be vendor-agnostic and simultaneously support the workflow of the provider wherever he or she stands on the technology adoption curve from a paper-based environment to a fully automated practice.

The HIE technology must be interoperable with paper-based practices in offline modes (autoprint or fax), while offering online tools via the Web or mobile devices. Most important, information should be available to providers and patients at any time and should enable providers and patients to "pull" (search, find, and discover) data, while also enabling data to be "pushed" in real time for proactive notification and alerting. For an ACO to be successful, its participants must recognize that providers are at varying degrees of technology maturity and that they will need help with complex change management initiatives. It will take time for relevant technology to be adopted at all the endpoints of the network; thus having a flexible HIE technology adoption plan will yield high stakeholder participation and the most beneficial results.

Technology and continuity of care

One of the greatest challenges for physicians is being able to see what all the members of the patient's care team are doing, from visits to other practitioners and specialists to trips to emergency rooms and urgent care centers. The following case illustrates the complexities of a typical cross-provider care episode successfully facilitated within an ACO technology framework (Table 20):

Mr. Johnson is a 59-year-old construction worker with a long history of diabetes. He has documented early retinopathy and hypertension but no evidence of other end-organ changes from his chronic diabetes. He presents to his primary care physician, Dr. Clark, with fever, acute shortness of breath, and rales and wheezing in the left lower lobe. Dr. Clark diagnoses Mr. Johnson with acute pneumonia (confirmed on a chest x-ray) and admits him to Metro Community Hospital (MCH).

In the hospital, Mr. Johnson is newly diagnosed with renal disease (elevated serum creatinine, proteinuria, and mild acidosis). At discharge, he is placed in an intensive home care program for strict monitoring of sodium and protein intake along with diabetes monitoring. He is discharged to the MCH home care agency to be seen by a visiting RN. His discharge medications include insulin, an oral antibiotic, and two new medications—a brand-name diuretic and a new ACE inhibitor for renal disease and hypertension.

During the visiting RN's third visit to Mr. Johnson, she becomes concerned by his rising blood pressure, weight gain, and general lethargy. She calls Dr. Clark to order new laboratory tests, which she then draws and delivers to the lab herself. The nurse questions Mr. Johnson, who insists he is compliant with his medication program.

Because MCH, the home care agency, Dr. Clark's practice, the local laboratory, and Bayside Pharmacy, which fills Mr. Johnson's prescriptions, all belong to an ACO, their clinical findings on Mr. Johnson are published in a common electronic community health record powered by HIE technology. This community health record features an innovative patient management "dashboard" displayed electronically to all authenticated members of Mr. Johnson's care team.

The home care nurse consults the dashboard and notices that the list of medications from the MCH discharge summary does not reconcile with the list from Bayside Pharmacy. During further discussions with Mr. Johnson, she learns that he filled the two inexpensive generic prescriptions but not the expensive new diuretic and ACE inhibitor. With the recent decline in the construction business, Mr. Johnson's income has been severely reduced and he admits he cannot afford to take the two medications for his renal disease.

The nurse also receives Mr. Johnson's recent laboratory tests results via the dashboard. The results show a deterioration of renal function with increased serum creatinine levels and electrolytes, suggesting a recurrence of metabolic acidosis. She contacts Dr. Clark, who switches Mr. Johnson to an alternative generic medication for his renal disease. Dr. Clark then sends an electronic referral to a new nephrologist to see Mr. Johnson emergently so he can receive more intensive evaluation of his worsening renal disease.

Because the visiting RN and Dr. Clark were part of an ACO with HIE technology that supports high-quality care and efficient practice, they were able to intervene quickly with use of real-time and accurate patient health data to prevent another admission to the hospital. Without the collaborative capabilities provided by the ACO's technology framework and infrastructure, such a successful outcome would be in doubt and, at the very least, considerably less efficient and more expensive. With this case example in mind, we provide Figure 26 to illustrate the multiple bilateral connections that can exist across organizations and ACO participants.

Figure 26: A Virtual IDN

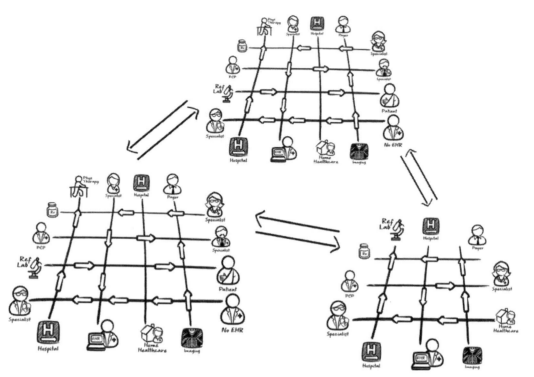

Health data exchange across boundaries leads to improvement in the quality and continuity-of-care information shared in a timely manner among the members of the virtual care team. It enables care collaboration across multiple providers and organizations and is critical for the ACO in achieving optimal levels of clinical integration and population-based health management. Technology to support such continuity of care and enhanced provider collaboration includes:

- Data and workflow integration across disparate information systems and care settings;

- A unified view of the patient across organizations and care locations;

- Continuous live updates from participating entities and alerts of such updates to ensure timely care synchronization across all accountable parties;

- Clinical alerts to ensure adherence to care guidelines and protocols;

- Aggregation of patient information to enable quantitative analysis and business intelligence on patient populations for the purpose of clinical and financial outcomes management.

Semantics of ACO management

Readers familiar with the telephone game or sharing workplace water cooler gossip have likely noted the often-amusing outcomes of miscommunication. In healthcare, however, garbled communication can mean the difference between life and death. How is it possible, then, to share patient data across multiple physician practices, health systems, and allied health providers effectively and efficiently when their IT systems don't even "speak the same language"? Moreover, how do we make those data actionable for managing the ACO?

The ability to create coherence between systems that don't "speak the same language" is an HIE function called semantic interoperability; it is vital to realizing the potential of sharing information across the continuum of care. Semantic interoperability establishes seamless exchange of data between two or more systems or healthcare networks, ensuring that health data are not only understandable within their original context but also capable of supporting clinical decision making, care collaboration, public health reporting, clinical research, health service management, and more.

From Logical Observation Identifiers, Names, and Codes (LOINC) to Systematized Nomenclature of Medicine (SNOMED), ICD-9, ICD-10, National Drug Codes (NDC) and Current Procedural Terminology (CPT) (to name just a few), there are a multitude of code sets and terminologies requiring semantic interoperability in the contemporary ACO environment. Add the subtle nuances of clinician-friendly terminology and free text from physician dictation and one begins to comprehend the semantic challenges of health information exchange.

Consider for example a simple description of an infected tympanic membrane as recorded in the chart of a patient with acute otitis media. Such terms as *erythematous*, *injected*, *inflamed*, or *reddened* all describe essentially the same clinical finding. To enable consistent data sharing across such variations in terminology and disparate code sets, an effective terminology services platform is needed to meet sophisticated mapping process requirements. The result: a unified view of the patient from multiple data contributors, enabling decision support, trending, analytics, and effective care.

In addition to resolving differences in terminology from across the disparate data sources in the care continuum, a similar semantic problem exists with patient identity. A provider in the emergency department who is caring for a patient for the first time needs the most up-to-date information about that patient as a member of the ACO's patient population—particularly in cases in which the patient comes from outside the contracted payer patient population. This type of scenario poses a challenge. In each of the information systems at the endpoints of the network—hospital systems, ambulatory EMRs, practice management systems, and others—the patient has a unique medical record number. In situations in which the physicians or hospitals are using different systems (the far more likely scenario in most locations) data aggregation becomes a complex and limiting problem. Creating interfaces, developing common patient identity management systems, and doing so in a HIPAA-secure environment are only a few of the challenges to aggregating relevant data on behalf of improved patient care.

Further, in the silo-oriented U.S. healthcare system, the multiple encounters are not linked via a unique common patient identifier across organizational boundaries and information systems. This problem does not exist in most developed countries with national health systems because every patient has a single national medical record number, thereby linking together multiple care encounters related to an episode of illness. To effectively manage an ACO, it is essential for HIE technology to correlate, link, and assimilate multiple encounters, so that when a patient presents in the emergency department, the physician can quickly search for all historical data about that specific patient from any previous visit in any care location or from a provider who is a participating stakeholder in the ACO. Ensuring that "John Doe is John Doe" is exceptionally important as we seek to improve the quality of care and enhance patient safety in the United States. Figure 27 illustrates this issue.

Figure 27: Semantic Interoperability and Identity Management Across Organizations and Systems

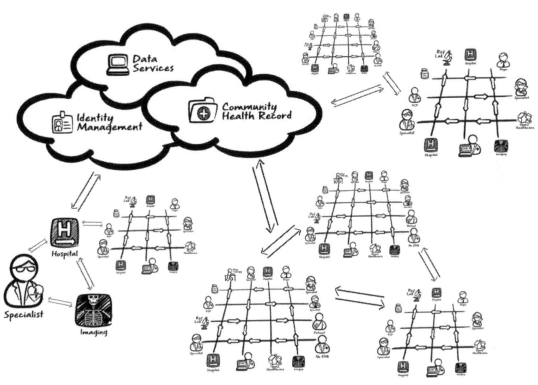

Because semantic interoperability facilitates collaboration, decision support, reporting, and detecting trends—key meaningful uses of actionable data—it will be critical to the success of ACOs.

Creating a Successful HIE Strategy for ACO Management

HIE technology is central to achieving three factors for ACO success: stakeholder collaboration; an end-to-end care delivery network; and a strong technology infrastructure that brings together health records, patient populations, and clinical decision support.

Getting from here to there is a challenge, however. A clear and logical HIE strategy is paramount to effectively building and managing an ACO, yet many organizations do not know where to begin. Funding for such an initiative is going to be one of the limiting factors to having independent physician groups from banding together as Provider Service Organizations and becoming their own ACOs in various markets. Working together with other organizations that can assist in capitalizing the HIE development work is one way in which to mitigate this barrier. In addition to the financial challenges there are operational and technical limitations. The most proven strategy for deploying HIE technology builds a solid exchange on a basic foundation. Additional functions can be layered according to specific needs and timelines, taking into consideration the workflow and technology maturity of the ACO's participants.[164]

An incremental bottom-up approach to deploying HIE is an effective way to produce both immediate and lasting value for the ACO. The bottom-up approach involves first connecting hospitals, physician practices, and such ancillary service providers as reference laboratories and imaging centers and "liquefying" transactions at a local level. This approach is in contrast to a traditional top-down RHIO approach to HIE that attempts to connect all possible stakeholders at once and aggregate all data simultaneously.

The first step is to engage healthcare providers where care is delivered, connecting disparate information systems and automating clinical messaging and workflow to create a solid and well-adopted HIE foundation. The HIE can then build upon that foundation and provide greater value over time by adding other functions and services. An important aspect of this first step is automating core healthcare transactions: ordering tests, referring patients among providers, and coordinating information among care teams. In accomplishing this critical step, the basic HIE connects core hospital systems (that is, the laboratory, radiology, transcription, ADT, emergency department), EMRs, practice management systems, and other entities in such a way that information flows securely across the HIE infrastructure.

---

[164] Agency for Healthcare Research and Quality, National Resource Center for Health Information Technology. Webinar, May 14, 2010. Building and maintaining a sustainable health information exchange (HIE): experience from diverse are settings.

Automating core transactions yields the following benefits:

- Creates immediate value for providers: improved information quality as well as savings in time and money, leading to user satisfaction and high early-adoption rates.

- Enables a lower-cost and more rapidly deployable approach than common methods of building an HIE, which require extensive and expensive infrastructure to accomplish the same goal.

- Establishes connections to all stakeholders participating in the ACO and fosters rapid coordination of care and collaboration.

As more and more connections come online and the HIE grows from the bottom up, its additional functions may include:

- Aggregating patient records and health information from all connected stakeholders to create a longitudinal record of care.

- Applying identity management services to ensure identification of a patient's correct longitudinal health record.

- Applying terminology services to ensure data are semantically correct across all data sources connected to the ACO via HIE technology.

- Establishing registries and applying disease management and population management tools for information retrieval, proactive and personalized care management, and analytics.

- Deploying gateway services to exchange information with such external networks as the NHIN, other HIEs, and public health agencies.

The bottom-up approach, which focuses first on system integration and exchange at a local level with local systems presently used by providers, has proven successful in a wide range of environments. It delivers significant value in a short time frame and at a lower cost than traditional "build it and they shall come" models of HIE deployment. Certainly efforts to standardize and aggregate normalized data in a centralized manner are the ideal; however, they are also time-consuming and complex endeavors. Rather than compete with such systematic approaches, bottom-up HIE leverages those initiatives and will better position ACO development and management activities.

Thus a good HIE strategy is based upon established standards while simultaneously ensuring flexibility and adaptability over time. The rapidly evolving contemporary environment does not adhere to any one specific standard or approach. Many methods are used, and even such common "standards" as HL7 come in several flavors. The HIE solution must be "future-proof," complying with all current privacy, security, and communication standards while still being open and adaptable to future standards as they evolve. The definitive piece in the strategy is selecting technology that enables providers to always keep the patient in focus and empowers all authorized providers to actively participate, collaborate, and proactively coordinate care.

The road to interconnectivity and data exchange

What follows is a high-level conceptual roadmap for HIE implementation. Figure 28 illustrates some of the key elements necessary for engaging appropriate stakeholders and support for HIE requirements within an ACO and across multiple ACOs. As the present chapter focused on the virtual IDN model, we have noted that many of the concepts can be applied to any of the five ACO models and our roadmap is intended to be universal in nature as well.

Figure 28. ACO Roadmap 3: Establishing the ACO Technology Framework

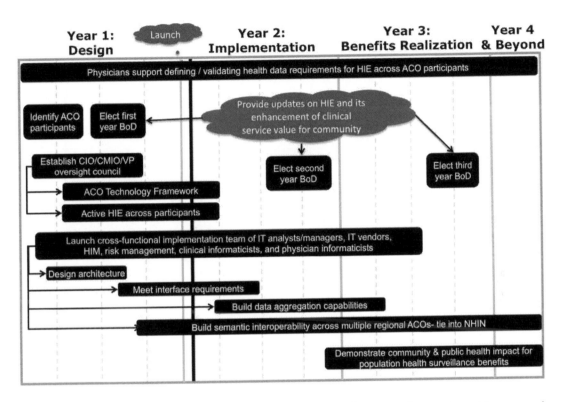

Our roadmap for establishing the ACO technology framework starts with engaging physicians from the ACO in process design for ensuring that information needed to support population-based health management for the ACO's patient population and the broader community is taken into account. Here we focus on some of the high-level activities needed to ensure successful HIE is achieved, assuming for purposes of illustration that EMR/EHR implementation for the ACO provider facilities and physician practices is either in place or in the process of establishment to meet CMS meaningful use criteria and requirements. Next comes establishment of the ACO's board of directors and keeping board level executives apprised of developments in which HIE is proving to enhance clinical service value to the communities served by the ACO. Establishment of an oversight council focused on all elements of HIE is identified as a C-level responsibility. These high-level teams will provide leadership and guidance to the cross-functional implementation team and set the strategic objectives for long-term success of the ACO's HIE initiative.

Forming and launching a cross-functional team to drive the implementation is crucial. This team should consist of subject matter experts and talent from such areas as IT, nursing, EMR/IT vendors, risk management, health information management, and employed or affiliated physicians to ensure that risks are mitigated through all phases of the implementation, including but not limited to architectural design, interface development, and data aggregation capabilities. As the healthcare industry braces for the conversion to ICD-10 in 2013, vendors, insurers, and all ACO participant organizations will need to concentrate on ensuring that semantic interoperability is secured for the ACO and to meet care coordination and HIE requirements both regionally and nationally through the NHIN.

The last element of our roadmap concerns strategic benefits realization for the ACO at the community level. Implementation of effective HIE will accelerate the ACO's ability to support requirements for data needed by physician or clinician leaders in population health surveillance. Ultimately, each ACO's roadmap will vary to some degree depending on the participants involved and the model being implemented.

INFOCUS: Challenges and Risks to Overcome

ACOs depend on the ability to share and synchronize information about specific patients through peer-to-peer communications in a highly secure network. As discussed throughout this chapter, authorized providers involved in delivering care to a patient need a complete picture of a patient's past and current care, thereby reducing the potential for medical errors, eliminating redundant tests and procedures, improving provider-to-provider coordination, streamlining workflow, improving patient and provider satisfaction, cutting down on administrative inefficiencies, and reducing costs. This level of patient-centered care collaboration and coordination among providers who have established relationships with the patient is the key to truly meaningful health information exchange and effectively managing an ACO.

What makes good provider collaboration and care coordination possible in the real world of healthcare is coherence: connecting information, services, and people in a significant way to work together and arrive at a complete view of patient health—

effectively virtualizing the IDN experience.

An additional challenge lies in the area of continuing to strengthen CDS and analytical tools for both hospital and physician practice settings. CDS is known to be a critical problem across the industry, and as vendors continue to improve the robustness of these tools the capabilities for ACOs will strengthen. As the field of analytics continues to build momentum, these tools will enhance an ACO's situational awareness and monitoring capabilities for population-level health management along with continued strengthening of modeling and simulation capabilities. One study has noted the importance of such tools in the field of pharmacotherapy to reinforce a hospital pharmacy staff's ability to predict potential drug interactions and reduce adverse events.[165] As the healthcare industry has traditionally lagged behind other industries in this field, we are catching up rapidly with dedicated research and development efforts that will yield benefits for ACOs and other care delivery organizations; however, challenges remain in analytics and CDS capabilities continue to mature.

Advances in technology are making the virtual IDN model and others possible by bridging systems, networks, and people to create a coherent care model that keeps the patient in focus at all times, connecting cloud services; bricks-and-mortar clinical, administrative, and financial networks; such local applications as patient management systems (PMSs) and EMRs; and the community of people that care for the patient. These advances enable organizations, affiliated providers, and other allied caregivers who work together, but are not part of the same entity to collaborate on a platform and create a high level of coordinated care, much like what happens in the top IDNs across the United States. ACO success will hinge on selecting HIE technology that extends beyond legal and physician organizational boundaries to create that end-to-end virtual IDN. Table 24 provides a set of challenges and risks to consider for this aspect of ACO implementation along with a few proposed high-level mitigation strategies.

---

[165] Barrett JS, Mondick JT, Narayan M, Vijayakumar K, Vijayakumar S. Integration of modeling and simulation into hospital-based decision support systems guiding pediatric pharmacotherapy. *BMC Med Inform Decis Mak.* 2008;8(6). Available at: http://www.ncbi.nlm.nih.gov/pmc/articles/PMC2254609/pdf/1472-6947-8-6.pdf.

Table 24. Chapter 5 Challenges and Risks

Challenges	Risks
5a) Data aggregation across disparate systems at different levels of maturity.	5d) Not ensuring fully functioning IT interfaces across ACO participants (potential for patient data corruption, inaccuracies, or delays in transmission).
5b) Enabling a common or interoperable ACO technology framework across all participants and ensuring accessibility for providers outside the ACO.	5e) Allowing terminology conversions to create delays that impact continuity of care.
5c) Meeting stage 2 and 3 criteria for CMS meaningful use of EMR requirements for effective HIE as they will be defined in the future.	5f) Not achieving continuity of care and care coordination goals due to inadequate interface development.

Potential Mitigation Strategies

√ Ensure effective project implementation on semantic terminology and conversions.

√ Establish cross-functional committees to manage HIE implementation and track progress.

√ Engage clinicians and physicians jointly with IT professionals and vendors to ensure that all health data elements and disparate systems are accounted for in HIE required interfaces.

Chapter 6. Quality Reporting- Performance Measurement

Landscape of Issues

Setting the performance measurement systems in place for evaluating ACOs is a critical issue for the success of the CMS Shared Savings Program along with private payer ACO initiatives and Medicaid pediatric ACOs that will emerge over the coming years. We noted in Figure 7 at the beginning of Chapter 2 that the IOM's Redesign Challenge #6 is "Performance and Outcome Measurement for Quality Improvement and Accountability." Measurement is related to two of the three major tenets of ACOs: improved accountability and performance improvement systems.

As of early 2011 there are a number of organizations involved in determining the identification of measures and cost or spending targets to be used in evaluating ACOs. These measurement issues are summarized in Figure 29.

Figure 29. Measurement Areas for ACOs

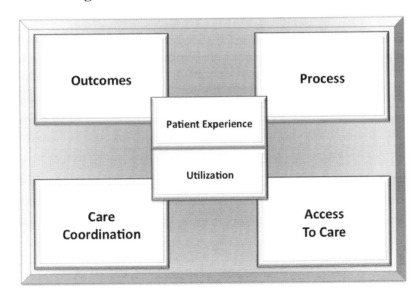

Some of the challenges that affect many measures across these different areas include 1) regional variations in procedures and conditions treated; 2) cost and time required for development and testing of new measures; 3) different rules of attribution based on payers or demographics (such as geriatric vs. pediatric); 4) risk adjustment factors; 5) setting appropriate spending targets;[166] and 6) process measures linkage to outcomes.[167] An additional challenge discussed in Chapter 5 is the transition in 2013 to ICD-10 coded data for the entire health system in the United States. Quality measures that involve the use of coded health data will need to be examined for necessary retooling and mapping of ICD-9 codes to ICD-10 code structures.[168]Maintaining the integrity and accuracy of these quality measures will be important to ACO performance evaluation in detecting trends in health outcomes across time periods involving both old and new codes.

In view of these challenges and others to industry workgroups and government agencies concerning ACOs, a considerable amount of information will most certainly emerge after the release of this book. This chapter offers a summary of the most recent information regarding:

- Legislative guidance regarding measures (PPACA);
- Stakeholders involved in the development of measures and testing processes;
- Current industry reporting initiatives of quality measures to be synthesized with ACO measures;
- Current workgroups and collaboration initiatives across the industry;
- Results from past and current ACO demonstrations and pilot projects;
- Future paths and convergence of activities together with a proposed roadmap for individual ACOs.

---

[166] Berenson R. Shared savings program for accountable care organizations: a bridge to nowhere? *Am J Manag Care*. 2010;16(10): 721-726. Available at: http://www.ajmc.com/issue/managed-care/2010/2010-10-vol16-n10/AJMC_10oct_Berenson_721to726.

[167] Kerr EA, Krein SL, Vijan S, Hofer TP, Hayward RA. Avoiding pitfalls in chronic disease quality measurement: a case for the next generation of technical quality measures. *Am J Manag Care*. 2001;7(11): 1033-1043. Accessed online at http://www.ajmc.com/media/pdf/AJMC2001novKERR1033-1043.pdf.

[168] Giannangelo K, Hyde L. Retooling quality measures for ICD-10. *Journal of AHIMA*. 2010;81(6):56-57.

Legislative Guidance: PPACA

PPACA Section 3022[169] contains limited guidance regarding the quality measures to be reported, in that Congress and CMS recognized that significant work remains to be done in this area. What we do know is that measures will cover clinical processes and outcomes, patient and caregiver experience, and utilization rates. The details of these services will emerge as federal rules for ACOs are clarified; as major stakeholder groups develop and test outcome measures; and most importantly as new data accumulate from the operation of the first ACOs in various geographic markets.

There are three other sections of the PPACA that should be noted here: Section 3013 on quality measures development; Section 3014 on quality measurement; and Section 3015 on data collection and public reporting.

Section 3013

This section of the PPACA appropriates $75,000,000 for fiscal years 2010–2014 for the development of new measures at a minimal three-year interval for new and expanded programs under the PPACA. Major high-level factors that will be considered in the identification of measures include: 1) gaps requiring new quality measures; 2) improvement of existing measures; 3) pediatric quality measures identified in Section 1139A of the Social Security Act; and 4) measures identified in Section 1139B of the Social Security Act in the Medicaid Quality Measurement Program.[170] In addition to these, section 3013 identifies several priorities that are summarized in Table 25.

---

[169] H.R. 3590, Patient Protection and Affordable Care Act, §3022(b)(3)(A)(i-iii) Shared savings program quality measures criteria.

[170] H.R. 3590, Patient Protection and Affordable Care Act, §3013(b) Identification of quality measures.

Table 25. Priorities for Quality Measure Development[171]

No.	Description
1	Health outcomes and functional status of patients;
2	Management and coordination of healthcare across episodes of care and care transitions for patients across the continuum of providers, health care settings, and health plans;
3	Experience, quality, and use of information provided to and used by patients, caregivers, and authorized representatives to inform decision making about treatment options, including the use of shared decision making tools and preference-sensitive care;
4	Meaningful use of health information technology;
5	Safety, effectiveness, patient-centeredness, appropriateness, and timeliness of care;
6	Efficiency of care;
7	Equity of health services and health disparities across health disparity populations and geographic areas;
8	Patient experience and satisfaction;
9	Use of innovative strategies and methodologies;
10	Other areas identified by HHS.

Table 25 prompts a number of observations and questions. First, it is apparent that this section of the PPACA now funds the industry's formation of authoritative organizations to cover the costly development of measures needed to evaluate not only ACOs but also many other new and expanded programs established under the PPACA. The results from these newly developed measures will support comparative effectiveness research that at some point in time should involve evaluating the effectiveness of ACOs as new models of care delivery.

As healthcare moves away from individual episodes of care in the direction of care across the continuum, evaluating and measuring patient-centeredness in light of care

---

[171] H.R. 3590, Patient Protection and Affordable Care Act, §3013(c)(2). Prioritization in the development of quality measures.

provided by multidisciplinary teams, care across multiple settings,[172] and continued increases in ambulatory care will no doubt directly affect the evaluation of ACO models. Furthermore, as innovations are developed and tested through the Center for Medicare and Medicaid Innovation from 2011 onward, new ways of measuring the effectiveness of those innovations will be needed as they yield new processes and means of delivering care. Each priority presents unique challenges but it can be identified due to present inability to provide effective evaluation of initiatives and startup or currently operating programs.

The setting of quality measure benchmarks for each ACO is related to the development and selection of measures for ACOs. Regional variation, risk adjustments, applicability across care settings, and characteristics of patient subpopulations will have to be taken into account with Medicare, Medicaid, and private payer ACOs.[173] Definitions of CMS quality benchmarks will unfold through the federal rule making process, cover the measurement areas identified in Figure 25, and include input from across the industry.

Sections 3014 and 3015

Section 3014 of the PPACA calls for the establishment of regional multi-stakeholder groups involving voluntary participation and public nominations.[174] The purpose of each group will be to provide input to the selection of quality measures through compilation and submission of an annual report to HHS by February 1 of each year, starting in 2012.

---

[172] American Medical Association. Response to the Centers for Medicare and Medicaid Services regarding request for information on accountable care organizations and the Medicare shared savings program (75 *Fed. Reg.* 70,165; November 17, 2010), December 2, 2010. Available at: http://www.ama-assn.org/ama1/pub/upload/mm/399/cms-aco-comment-letter-2dec2010.pdf, 8.

[173] American Hospital Association, Committee on Research. Accountable care organizations: research synthesis report, June 2010, 10-11. Available at: http://www.aha.org/aha/research-and-trends/cor.html.

[174] H.R. 3590, Patient Protection and Affordable Care Act, §3014(a). New duties for consensus-based entity.

This annual report will address gaps in quality measures based on priority areas and national strategy for quality measures to be taken into account by HHS in the maintenance and phasing out of measures.[175] The sum of $20,000,000 was designated for transfer to the Centers for Medicare and Medicaid Services Program Management Account for each fiscal year between 2010 and 2014 to fund these activities.[176]

Section 3015 identifies grant funding for these multi-stakeholder groups—along with Federal Indian Health Service programs and other qualified organizations—to provide services for the collection and aggregation of measures for quality and resource use. This section also accounts for the funding and development of websites between the years 2010 and 2014 for public reporting of information on quality and performance measures.

Organizations and Collaborative Efforts Related to ACO Quality Measures

There are many organizations involved in the development and selection of quality measures for the healthcare industry. Each brings specific expertise to participate in and encourage collaborative efforts across the industry. Some of the national organizations and their work in relation to quality measures and future measures for ACOs include:

- **Centers for Medicare and Medicaid Services (CMS)**: CMS leads efforts in the industry with numerous pilot projects and demonstrations that support the advancement of healthcare delivery. CMS's Measures Management System[177] provides a standardized process for ensuring "that CMS will have a coherent, transparent system for measuring quality of care delivered to its beneficiaries." This system has been developed in coordination with the other organizations mentioned in this section.

- **Agency for Healthcare Research and Quality (AHRQ):** AHRQ is the agency within the Department of Health and Human Services that provides a clearinghouse for quality

---

[175] H.R. 3590, Patient Protection and Affordable Care Act, §3014(b). Multi-stakeholder group input into selection of quality measures.

[176] H.R. 3590, Patient Protection and Affordable Care Act, §3014(c). Funding.

[177] Centers for Medicare and Medicaid Services. Measures management system. Available at: http://www.cms.gov/MMS/Downloads/QualityMeasuresDevelopmentOverview103009.pdf.

measures and annual national reporting of clinical quality measures. It also manages the Consumer Assessment of Healthcare Providers and Systems (CAHPS).

- **National Committee for Quality Assurance (NCQA):** The NCQA is one of the primary certification and accreditation organizations for Patient-Centered Medical Home (PCMH) initiatives, health plan accreditations, and other healthcare provider certification and recognition programs. The NCQA provides and governs the development of the Healthcare Effectiveness Data and Information Set (HEDIS) that we shall discuss in the next section. In the fall of 2010 the NCQA issued an extensive document for public comment regarding measures and analysis of measures for ACOs[178] in support of the rule making process to govern ACOs.

- **National Quality Forum (NQF):** The NQF focuses on building consensus on national healthcare priorities and goals for performance improvement. It is the leading endorsement organization in the industry for approval of quality measures. As new quality measures are developed and tested for new ACO models and changes in care coordination across settings, the NQF will play a vital role in validating these measures before their official use and application by industry stakeholders and ACO teams.

- **American Medical Association (AMA):** The leading national association for physicians, the AMA convened the Physician Consortium for Performance Improvement® (PCPI). Started in the year 2000, the PCPI has grown to include participants from over 130 organizations and has identified 270 measures across 43 measure sets. With regard to ACOs, the PCPI is working to develop measures on patient-centeredness that will cover a range of disciplines and multiple chronic conditions.[179]

---

[178] National Committee for Quality Assurance. Appendix A: ACO measure grid. Available at: http://www.ncqa.org/portals/0/publiccomment/ACO/Appendix%20A_ACO_Measure_Table.pdf.

[179] American Medical Association. Response to the Centers for Medicare and Medicaid Services regarding request for information on accountable care organizations and the Medicare shared savings program (75 *Fed. Reg.* 70,165; November 17, 2010), December 2, 2010. Available at: http://www.ama-assn.org/ama1/pub/upload/mm/399/cms-aco-comment-letter-2dec2010.pdf, 8.

Collaborative efforts

CMS issued a request for information through the *Federal Register* on a number of issues on November 17, 2010. This request included input on measures to evaluate and the ways in which patient and caregiver experiences should be evaluated.[180]While many organizations across the industry replied to this request, the NCQA brought together a collective of recognized experts from various healthcare organizations in June 2010.[181] This group will concentrate on defining qualification criteria and measures for all types of ACOs, given its involvement with private payers, CMS, and the PCMH program.

Current Industry Quality Measure Reporting Initiatives

There are a number of quality measure initiatives in the industry; while we cannot discuss all of them, we have addressed the initiatives identified in Figure 30.

Figure 30. Select Industry Quality Measure Initiatives Related to Future ACOs

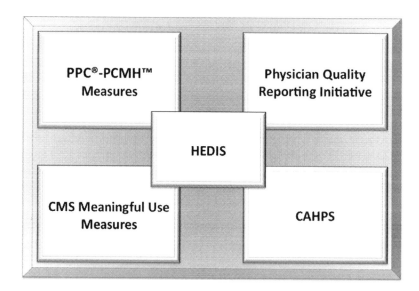

---

[180] Centers for Medicare and Medicaid Services. Request for information on accountable care organizations and Medicare shared savings program. *Federal Reg*ister Vol. 75, No. 221. 70165-70166. November 17, 2010.

[181] National Committee for Quality Assurance. Press release, June 2, 2010. NCQA convenes experts to define criteria for accountable care organizations. Available at: http://www.ncqa.org/tabid/1200/Default.aspx.

These five initiatives include measures across all six of the measurement areas identified in Figure 28.

HEDIS

HEDIS, which stands for Healthcare Effectiveness Data and Information Set, "is a tool used by more than 90 percent of America's health plans to measure performance on important dimensions of care and service."[182] The NCQA governs the development of HEDIS quality measures, which undergo a process that may take as long as 28 months.[183] HEDIS measures are used by CMS to provide quality rankings for health plans based on their performance achieved in partnership with provider organizations and physicians. There are 71[184] HEDIS performance measures identified across eight domains, as denoted in Table 26.

Table 26. HEDIS Domains of Care

Number	Title
1	Effectiveness of care
2	Access to / availability of care
3	Satisfaction with the experience of care
4	Use of services
5	Cost of care
6	Health plan descriptive information
7	Health plan stability
8	Informed health care choices

HEDIS measures are one area of concern for ACOs as new guidance and measures are issued each year. With industry movement toward multipayer ACO models, both HEDIS

---

[182] National Committee for Quality Assurance. HEDIS and quality measurement. Available at: http://www.ncqa.org/tabid/59/Default.aspx.

[183] National Committee for Quality Assurance. HEDIS measures development process. Available at: http://www.ncqa.org/Portals/0/HEDISQM/Measure_Development.pdf.

[184] National Committee for Quality Assurance. What is HEDIS? Available at: http://www.ncqa.org/tabid/187/default.aspx.

measures and others developed for other Medicare- and Medicaid-focused programs will be needed to meet the evaluation needs of public and private shared savings programs.

PPC®-PCMH™ Measures

As discussed in Chapter 2, the NCQA has established ten requirements for patient-centered medical homes. While there are several reporting topics, Requirement #8 calls for reporting of standardized measures. These measures may be derived from any number of NQF-endorsed quality measures (either outcome or process-related), or HEDIS measures from the NCQA.

CMS Meaningful Use Measures

The Meaningful Use program is a three-stage program to increase electronic measurement reporting requirements through 2015. Starting in 2016, eligible providers and hospitals[185] that do not meet the requirements will be assessed a penalty against Medicare or Medicaid claims submitted to CMS for payment. Measures for Stage 1 were finalized and announced in July 2010; they include a set of core measures and clinical quality measures[186] that are illustrated in Figure 31.

---

[185] Centers for Medicare and Medicaid Services. Overview of eligibility criteria for providers and hospitals. Available at: http://www.cms.gov/EHRIncentivePrograms/15_Eligibility.asp#TopOfPage.

[186] Centers for Medicare and Medicaid Services. Overview of the CMS meaningful use program. Available at: http://www.cms.gov/EHRIncentivePrograms/01_Overview.asp#TopOfPage.

Figure 31. Measures for Stage 1 Meaningful Use Reporting to CMS

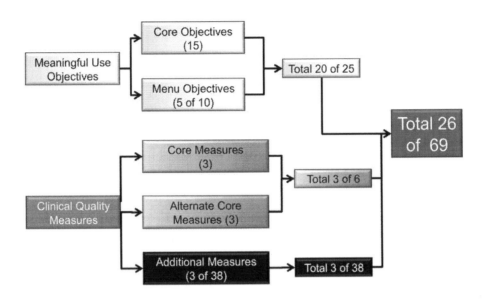

These measures cover a spectrum of clinical quality issues. Core and menu objective measures can be found at http://www.cms.gov/EHRIncentivePrograms/Downloads/EP-MU-TOC-Core-and-MenuSet-Objectives.pdf. These 25 measures consist of a number of outcome and process topics, such as patient demographics, vital signs, problem lists, clinical decision support, health information exchange, and the like.

Details of the 44 clinical quality measures can be found at http://www.cms.gov/QualityMeasures/03_ElectronicSpecifications.asp. Initially only a handful of these measures will be required for stage 1 incentives; however, as the program continues, one can expect that relevant optional indicators will become increasingly required for continued participation. Given that the Department of Health and Human Services is providing $19 billion in incentive funds to eligible providers and hospitals meeting Stages 1 through 3 reporting requirements, it is widely anticipated that these measures—some of which are still unknown as only Stage 1 measures have been identified and released—will be integrated with ACO quality measure requirements for the shared savings program reporting requirements.

Consumer Assessment of Healthcare Providers and Systems (CAHPS)-

CAHPS is a growing set of surveys from CMS for obtaining consumer and patient feedback on services across the domains of 1) fee-for-service; 2) hospitals; 3) in-center hemodialysis; 4) Medicare Advantage; and 5) nursing homes. As indicated in the American Medical Association's December 2, 2010 response to CMS on its request for information about the ACO program, these surveys could provide a foundation for gaining the patient experience feedback needed by ACOs. The surveys are not, however, currently designed to utilize any electronic record systems. This may be an area in which the country's regional health improvement collaboratives may be employed to implement such a feedback program, to obtain the data needed by ACOs and support the quality measurement of patient experience in new and existing ACO organizations.[187]

Physician Quality Reporting Initiative (PQRI)[188]

The PQRI reporting program was launched in 2007 after being enacted through the 2006 Tax Relief and Health Care Act. This program allows individual eligible providers to report individual quality measures or measure groups to CMS on Part B Medicare claims, or to a qualified PQRI registry, or through use of a qualified EHR system. Group practices that meet the reporting requirements have the opportunity to capture an incentive payment of up to "2% of their estimated Medicare Part B PFS allowed charges." The PQRI measures are also endorsed by the NQF, with some having been developed by the NCQA.

---

[187] American Medical Association. Response to the Centers for Medicare and Medicaid Services regarding request for information on accountable care organizations and the Medicare shared savings program (75 *Fed. Reg.* 70,165; November 17, 2010), December 2, 2010. Available at: http://www.ama-assn.org/ama1/pub/upload/mm/399/cms-aco-comment-letter-2dec2010.pdf, 7.

[188] Centers for Medicare and Medicaid Services. Physician Quality Reporting Initiative (PQRI). Available at: http://www.cms.gov/PQRI/01_Overview.asp#TopOfPage.

One can thus begin to see how these national measure-reporting initiatives are interrelated across the industry. Even so, there remain gaps and large areas of as-yet-undefined measures. Over time these will continue to be defined in order to fully evaluate the effectiveness of ACOs.

Quality Measurement from Demonstrations and Pilots

As was discussed in Chapter 1, CMS's Physician Group Practice Demonstration Project had a well-defined set of measures used to monitor and evaluate the impact of changes made in the participating physician group practices' operations and the way they delivered care. Since that program began in 2000, other healthcare organizations have started forming private payer-based ACOs in order to verify their impact on quality improvement in care provided and their economic impact on cost reduction. While the present authors were not able to identify publicly reported quality or cost savings results for any of the private payer-based ACOs, we can summarize the recently updated results for CMS's Physician Group Practice Demonstration project. Those results are summarized in Table 27.

Table 27. Results of Physician Group Practice Demonstration (Through 12/2010)[189]

Performance Year	Type of Results	Description
1	Clinical quality	All 10 physician groups improved clinical management of diabetes patients achieving benchmarks for at least 7 of 10 diabetes clinical quality measures.
1	Shared savings	Two physician groups shared $7.3M in savings (out of $9.5M total for Medicare).
2	Clinical quality	All 10 physician groups achieved benchmarks at least 25 of 27 quality measures for patients with diabetes, coronary artery disease and congestive heart failure. Five groups achieved benchmark on all 27 quality measures.
2	Shared savings	Four physician groups shared $13.8M in savings (out of $17.4M total for Medicare).
3	Clinical quality	All 10 physician groups continued to improve quality of care and achieved benchmarks on at least 28 of 32 quality measures for patients with diabetes, coronary artery disease, congestive heart failure, hypertension, and cancer screening. Two groups achieved benchmark performance on all 32 measures.
3	Shared savings	Five physician groups shared $25.3M in savings (out of $32.3M total for Medicare).
4	Clinical quality	All 10 physician groups continued to improve quality of care and achieved benchmarks on at least 29 of 32 quality measures for patients with diabetes, coronary artery disease, congestive heart failure, hypertension, and cancer screening. Three groups achieved benchmark performance on all 32 measures.
4	Shared savings	Five physician groups shared $31.7M in savings (out of $38.7M total for Medicare Trust Fund).

---

[189] Centers for Medicare and Medicaid Services. Physician group practice demonstration project fact sheet, updated December 2010. Available at:
https://www.cms.gov/DemoProjectsEvalRpts/downloads/PGP_Fact_Sheet.pdf.

Methods to Effect Performance Improvement

ACO performance improvement teams will need to employ new tools and methods to identify opportunities that will help reach the six aims of higher quality healthcare as identified in Chapter 1, Figure 1. Healthcare organizations ranging across the spectrum of provider organizations, physician groups, and private and public payer organizations have been employing quality improvement tools and techniques for several decades.[190] One of the industry's pioneers in healthcare quality improvement, Avedis Donabedian, MD, MPH, gave us his quality framework, which analyzes quality improvement in the three areas depicted in Figure 32.

Figure 32. Donabedian's Quality Framework[191]

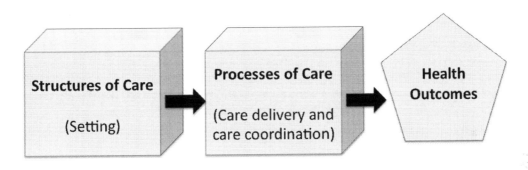

We can see that this basic model sets the foundation for much of what is evaluated in healthcare quality as of 2011, with the guiding work of the IOM and other organizations leading to the core principles of the ACO. Of course, a number of quality improvement

---

[190] McIntyre D, Rogers L, Heier E. Overview, history, and objectives of performance measurement. *Healthcare Finance Review.* 2001;22(3):7-21. Available at: http://www.cms.gov/HealthCareFinancingReview/Downloads/01springpg7.pdf.

[191] McDonald KM, Sundaram V, Bravat DM, et al. *Closing the Quality Gap: A Critical Analysis of Quality Improvement Strategies.* Rockville, MD: Agency for Healthcare Research and Quality; 2007. AHRQ Technical Review 9, §5b. Methodological approach, model 2: Donabedian's quality framework. Available at: http://www.ncbi.nlm.nih.gov/bookshelf/br.fcgi?book=hstechrev&part=A25445; Donabedian A. Evaluating the quality of medical care. *Milbank Quarterly* 2005;83(4):691-729. Reprinted from *Milbank Memorial Fund Quarterly* 1966;44(3):166–203. Available at: http://www.milbank.org/quarterly/830416donabedian.pdf.

tools and methods have emerged since the work of Dr. Donabedian. One that we wish to highlight is Six Sigma. This method of improvement has demonstrated value in facilitating necessary innovations and continuous improvement efforts needed for the implementation and ongoing management of ACOs.

Performance improvement teams have traditionally focused on rigorous analysis of clinical and administrative processes to identify waste and areas for improvement along with and most importantly opportunities to improve health outcomes. At its core Six Sigma is "an organized and systematic method for strategic process improvements and new product and service development that relies on statistical methods and the scientific method to make dramatic reductions in customer defined defect rates."[192] The Six Sigma approach includes a toolbox of various methods for process improvement. From "work outs" to "DMADV" and "DMAIC," an entire workforce of black belts, yellow belts, and subject matter experts have emerged to assist working groups with the use of these tools. One tool that many projects rely on is the application of the core DMAIC roadmap.[193] The five DMAIC steps are as follows:

1. **Define**: Establish the performance improvement project's goals and the customer's requirements.

2. **Measure**: Evaluate the current level of performance.

3. **Analyze**: Determine the root cause of poor performance.

4. **Improve**: Eliminate defects to improve efficiency, reduce waste, and achieve cost savings or increase revenue.

5. **Control**: Establish new procedures, policies, and use of new tools to monitor and maintain performance.

---

[192] Vest J, Gamm L. A critical review of the research literature on Six Sigma, Lean and StuderGroup's Hardwiring Excellence in the United States: the need to demonstrate and communicate the effectiveness of transformation strategies in healthcare. *Implementation Science*. 2009;4(35):1-9. Available at: http://www.implementationscience.com/content/pdf/1748-5908-4-35.pdf

[193] Six Sigma. DMAIC roadmap. Available at: http://healthcare.isixsigma.com/index.php?option=com_k2&view=item&layout=item&id=1477&Itemid=372

Projects are conducted throughout all areas of healthcare operations (such as finance, risk management, surgery, pharmacy, radiology, rehabilitation, and the like), and have produced strong results in many cases in terms of improving patient safety, increasing revenue cycle performance, and achieving cost savings. In some cases projects have been combined with Lean Thinking methodology, which focuses on waste elimination and the application of value stream mapping[194] to illustrate the current state of processes, establish the amount of time or resources required for various steps, and provide quality improvement teams and stakeholders with a roadmap to better understand where they can make changes to create a stronger organization.

Applying these methods in the formative design stage of ACOs will be one key to the successful development of ACOs.

Future Path

As has been noted, a number of organizations are actively involved nationally in determining the path for quality measures needed. ACOs will take shape with the implementation of different models in different care delivery settings and markets; with different patient populations and demographics; and with stakeholder organizations at different stages of development. Given these varying factors, we can expect a number of new measures to be required for evaluating ACOs in the future. Our next ACO Roadmap is illustrated in Figure 33 for quality measurement activity at the local level.

---

[194] Schroeder R. Just-in-time systems and lean thinking. In: *Operations Management: Contemporary Concepts and Cases*. 3rd ed. New York, NY: McGraw-Hill Irwin; 2007; 408-411.

Figure 33. ACO Roadmap 4: Quality Measure Activity At the Local Level

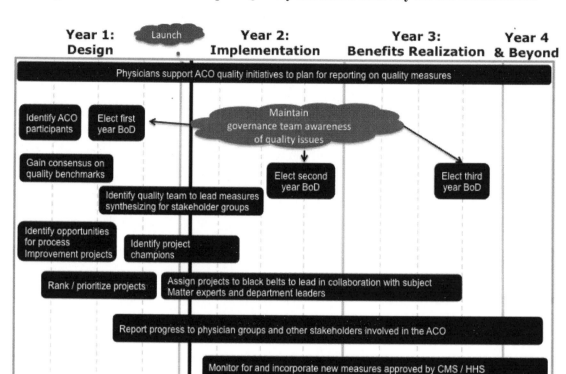

Let us address a few points in ACO Roadmap 4. First, as previously illustrated, physician involvement in the early design stage will be important. As leaders of ACO organizations, physicians can help set the stage for identification and selection of measures that the ACO will monitor and report, together with supporting the prioritization and selection of process improvement projects. Second, as ACOs will involve mergers of organizations, there will be new opportunities for collaboration, and this area will lend itself to great opportunities for these types of teams to be formed and engaged to make use of performance improvement methods to advance ACO development.

Third, many issues will go through future federal rule making processes. Therefore, continued monitoring and engagement with government affairs personnel in the ACO should be a priority for those in leadership to ensure that as issues emerge (such as changes to required quality measures, changes to beneficiary attribution rules, and changes to shared savings program formulae), they remain a priority for environmental scanning and monitoring activities.

INFOCUS: Challenges and Risks to Overcome

Many challenges lie ahead in the field of quality measures development and performance evaluation for ACOs. With pilot programs and demonstrations that have produced documented results and others that are ongoing in the public and private sectors, there are data and past performances to build upon. As new ACOs emerge and new organizational structures take shape across the country, new ways of measuring and validating performances and their processes will be needed. Table 28 summarizes some of the challenges, risks, and potential mitigation strategies.

Table 28. Chapter 6: Challenges and Risks

Challenges	Risks
6a) Factoring in regional variation in patient conditions and service utilization.	6e) Cost and time to develop and test new measures may impede efforts to evaluate ACOs efficiency and performance improvement.
6b) Maintaining flexibility in quality benchmarks.	6f) Setting quality benchmarks may be unattainable for the some ACOs if volume of physician participation fluctuates (i.e. exclusive vs. nonexclusive contracting effect) or if beneficiary attribution changes due to voluntary participation.
6c) Identifying new innovations in care delivery processes to help ACOs reach quality benchmarks and spending targets.	6g) Not synthesizing Meaningful Use, HEDIS, PQRI measures could create duplicated work for overburdened and stressed physician practice groups if they are not merged with larger ACO support staff.
6d) Evaluating patient and care giver experience in an effective and timely manner that also clearly delineates responses and who the positive or negative feedback is applicable to for any given episode of care.	6h) Not factoring in ICD-10 transition to quality measure trends post 2013 may result in inaccuracies for evaluating ACO performance on health outcomes.

Potential Mitigation Strategies

√ Support requests for input to federal rule making processes with meaningful and well-constructed ideas to assist legislators in crafting best approaches for the industry.

√ Support industry stakeholder group nominations (i.e. PPACA Section 3014) with viable candidates that can aid efforts in performance evaluation, rule making, and gap identification.

√ Engage physicians with performance improvement teams early to identify new opportunities to improve processes, reduce waste, and achieve cost savings to effect transformation around the structure of care, process of care, and health outcomes at the population level.

Chapter 7. Financial Perspectives

Thus far we have covered a number of issues for ACO development, including the basic elements of organization; quality measurement and evaluation; antitrust law and institutional mergers; healthcare-related information technology; and the historical background of the American health system. The financial issues related to health services, such as providing reimbursement and incentives for healthcare providers while simultaneously lowering utilization costs for specific population-based chronic conditions within each geographic region or market are central concerns for the industry during the transition to ACOs. This chapter will examine the PPACA parameters regarding the CMS shared savings program for ACOs; P4P strategies and models implemented in pilots and demonstrations with private payers and CMS-focused ACOs; and other complexities of fiscal management related to ACO design and maintenance.

First, however, let us consider some mounting challenges at the local and regional levels posed to our nation's primary care, multispecialty care, and hospitals over the last decade.

Landscape of ACO Financial Issues

☐ Several fiscal issues have driven the development of ACOs and other reform initiatives, as was discussed in the historical section of Chapter 1. Some of the most pressing concerns include:

- Unresolved sustainable growth rate (SGR) adjustments in Medicare payments to physicians and their practices;[195]

- CMS meaningful use penalties to be assessed starting in 2016 for providers who have not achieved compliance with Phases 1 through 3 of the finalized rules;[196]

- Expansion of the CMS recovery audit contractor (RAC) program to all institutional providers and adoption of the RAC program concept by private payers;[197]

- Rising costs of malpractice insurance;

- Costs of healthcare for the uninsured and underinsured patient population;

- Capital outlay requirements for new facilities and enterprise-level HIT implementation.

Health systems and physician groups across the United States have faced considerable challenges in financial management, given the decrements by CMS and private payers in reimbursement rates for healthcare services (such as inpatient hospitalizations) and formulary changes affecting prescription drug coverage—particularly for treatment of chronic conditions.[198] These issues and others have driven many independent physician practices to either close or join larger medical groups. In addition these same economic pressures have prompted some medical groups to consider joining or affiliating with large IDN organizations. Chief financial officers across the country have had to confront these challenges, which are further complicated by federal and state

---

[195] Simmons J. Medicare payments face another 6.1% cut under SGR. *HealthLeaders Media*, June 28, 2010. Available at: http://www.healthleadersmedia.com/print/FIN-253111/Medicare-Payments-Face-Another-61-Cut-Under-SGR.

[196] Centers for Medicare and Medicaid Services. Meaningful use program overview. Available at: http://www.cms.gov/EHRIncentivePrograms/.

[197] Centers for Medicare and Medicaid Services. Recovery audit contractor, recent updates. CMS expands FY 2010 RAC ADR limits to all institutional providers, January 29, 2010. Available at: http://www.cms.gov/RAC/03_RecentUpdates.asp#TopOfPage.

[198] Center for Healthcare Research and Transformation. Issue brief, July 2010, Health care cost drivers: chronic disease, comorbidity, and health risk factors in the U.S. and Michigan. Available at: http://www.chrt.org/assets/price-of-care/CHRT-Issue-Brief-August-2010.pdf.

regulations, tax requirements, investment management, accounting for uncompensated care, nonprofit exemptions, and revenue cycle issues, together with the broader economic downturn experienced from 2008 to the present.

As the ACO is the focus of this book, this chapter will concentrate on the financial implications of the public, private, and eventual multipayer ACO models, illustrated by a high-level timeline for the last three decades. The timeline depicts the current slate of financial health reform initiatives leading up to the emergence of the ACO and other current reform models. Though not a comprehensive timeline of the entire industry, Figure 34 identifies some of the key programs, systems, and methodologies implemented during the period from 1980 onward.

Figure 34. 30 Years of Health Services Payment Reform Models & Programs

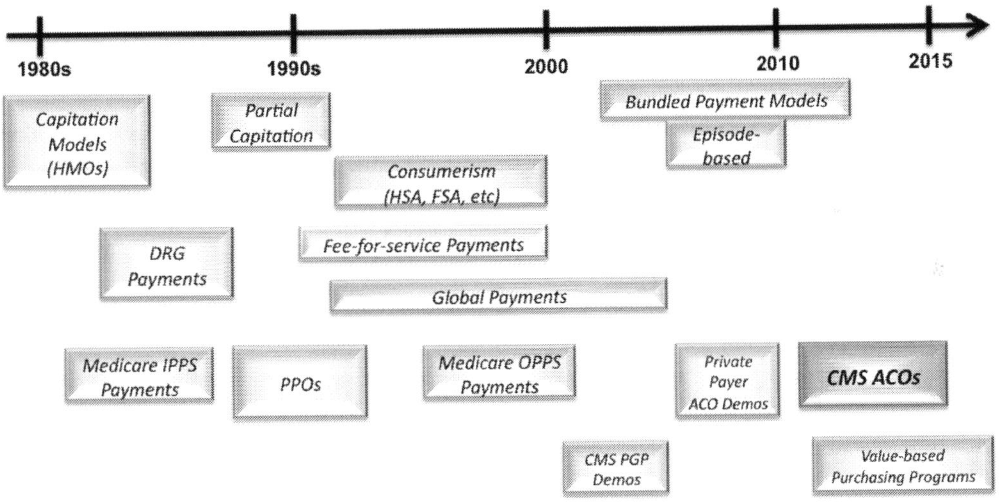

Note: boxes are only to indicate an approximate market entry point in time for each program / model

There are many concepts underlying the transition in payment reform over the last three decades. Two in particular include:

- *Risk bearing*: This concept has to do with identifying those who bear the risk in the cost and quality of care delivered.[199] As the managed care industry came into being and grew through the 1970s and 1980s, HMOs and capitated payment models became its mainstay. In these models physicians received set amounts based on the conditions for which patients were treated. The potential for "under-prescribing" needed services was a significant risk to the quality of care delivered. With the advent of fee-for-service (FFS) systems, the risk of lowered quality of care shifted as providers were (and are) rewarded for the volume of services prescribed—not necessarily the quality of services. As the industry recognized the advantages and disadvantages to patients and consumers with these models of reimbursement, partial capitation entered the market. With partial capitation, the burden of risk began to shift again as providers received less in capitated payments in exchange for performance rewards with the start of P4P initiatives. Consumer-oriented products (such as health savings accounts and flexible spending accounts) shifted the burden of care to the consumer; however, as noted in Chapter 1, these products achieve monetary savings at the expense of not having a qualified medical professional engaged in the patient's healthcare decisions. These products and models brought us to the environment of 2011, which is more heavily focused on P4P, placing risk with the organization or professional accountable for ensuring that quality care is delivered, and paying for value in the quality of care and services delivered on the individual as well as the population-based level.

- *Productivity and reward*: A second concept underlying the present transition is that of firm productivity. One of the key drivers for companies across all industries is the implementation of compensation systems that reward participants for strong performance and high-quality goods and services of greater value.[200] As the healthcare industry was confronted with the poor quality of care documented in such reports as the IOM's *To Err Is Human*, consumer awareness of problems in

---

[199] Goldsmith J. Analyzing Shifts In Economic Risks To Providers In Proposed Payment And Delivery System Reforms. *Health Aff (Millwood)*. 2010;29(7): 1299-1304.

[200] Cutler D. How Health Care Reform Must Bend The Cost Curve. *Health Aff (Millwood)*. 2010;29(6): 1131-1135.

the healthcare system grew rapidly. It led to the need for change—specifically, demand for and movement to stronger P4P-related systems.

Financial risk sharing and integration

Every ACO must contend with multiple issues in financial risk sharing and strategy. Assuming a certain degree of financial risk is a basic requirement for the hospitals and physician practice organizations in the ACO. As we discussed the proposed qualification criteria in Chapter 2 (Table 5), ACOs will be able to take on greater degrees of risk on the basis of the level of controls and complexity they have implemented along with risk sharing agreements in place among participants (that is, IPAs and MSPGs). These agreements are often linked to participation in clinical integration programs as discussed in Chapter 4, when the increased levels of risk assumed are offset by higher potential incentives for improving quality of care and population health for certain disease conditions targeted for improvement under the ACO and its clinical integration program when applicable. HHS will monitor risk sharing to ensure that ACOs do not exclude or avoid providing care for at-risk patients. If an ACO is found to be taking these steps it will not only be placed under sanctions but will also be terminated from participation in the CMS shared savings program.

Legislative Scope and Impact

The PPACA, presently the subject of intense debate across the country, will have a profound financial impact. Different organizations estimate the long-term financial impact of the PPACA and various programs in the bill differently; however, the Congressional Budget Office (CBO) provided its final preauthorization assessment of the bill's long-term overall financial impact on the nation's budget on March 20, 2010. "CBO and JCT estimate that enacting both pieces of legislation—H.R. 3590 and the reconciliation proposal—would produce a net reduction in federal deficits of $143 billion over the 2010–2019 period as result of changes in direct spending and revenues."[201]

---

[201] Congressional Budget Office. Letter to Nancy Pelosi, March 20, 2010. Estimated budgetary impact of the legislation, 2. Available at: http://www.cbo.gov/ftpdocs/113xx/doc11379/AmendReconProp.pdf.

The CMS ACO is one model that is anticipated to generate savings over the long term. A number of parameters were provided in PPACA Section 3022 that are being shaped further along with the interim and final rules to be issued on the shared savings program. Chief financial officers and financial teams across ACO participant organizations will need to collaborate to ensure integration of financial planning along with maintaining the transparency and integrity of their organizations. Figure 35 provides an overview of a CMS ACO compensation model.

Figure 35. CMS ACO Compensation Model Overview

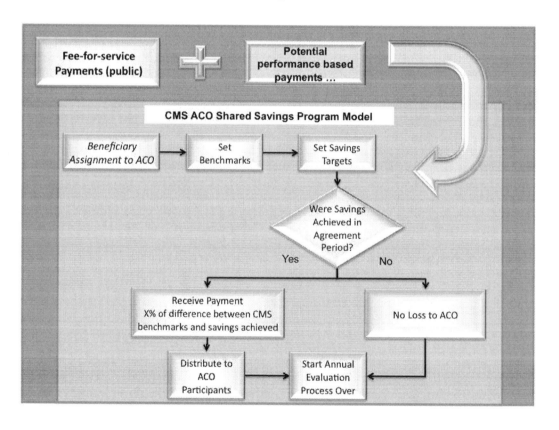

This model focuses on the CMS version of an ACO. It starts with recognizing that part of the overall compensation received for health services provided by the ACO are the FFS payments for claims received from CMS—albeit at the prevailing or decremented rates of 2011 and predicted for the future. The second part of the model is the ACO shared savings program process. The steps of the process defined in Section 3022 are illustrated above. Now let us take a closer look at the implications of each step.

Organizations exempt from participation

The PPACA specifies that there are two situations in a "provider of services or supplies" would not be allowed to participate in an ACO:[202]

1) Those participating in a model tested under the CMMI that involves shared savings or any other programs or demonstrations that involve shared savings;

2) Those participating in the "independence at home medical practice pilot program" under Section 1866-E of the Social Security Act;

The Center for Medicare and Medicaid Innovation noted in Chapter 1 has designated 20 types of models it will request organizations to test. These models are focused on reform of both delivery and payment systems.[203] As the CMMI is a new center established within CMS in November 2010 that will fund over $10B in projects through 2019, organizations should ensure that any possible involvement with future CMMI projects does not affect their ability to participate in the ACO program. The "independence at home medical practice pilot program" involves a team of healthcare professionals receiving shared savings for achieving goals to reduce preventable hospitalizations and readmissions as well as improving health outcomes and efficiency of care.

Determination of shared savings

As all readers of this book are aware, interim and final rules will provide additional detailed guidance on the methods to be used to determine shared savings payable to each ACO; in general, however, the details of the process are illustrated in Table 29:

---

[202] H.R. 3590, Patient Protection and Affordable Care Act, §3022(b)(4). No duplication in participation in shared savings (2009).

[203] Guterman S, Davis K, Stremikis K, Drake H. Innovation in Medicare and Medicaid will be central to health reform's success. *Health Aff* (*Millwood*). 2010;29(6):1188-1193.

Table 29. Details for Elements of ACO Shared Savings Program Process

Element	Key Points
Each ACO is evaluated in each year of the agreement period	a. Minimum 3-year agreement between ACO and HHS. Each ACO is evaluated in each year of the agreement period.
Beneficiary assignment	a. CMS stated in the PPACA that it would establish a method for assigning patients (beneficiaries) to ACOs based on their utilization of primary care services.[204]
Setting benchmarks[205]	a. Estimate a benchmark for every agreement period for each ACO, making use of its most recent three years of FFS data for Medicare Parts A and B beneficiaries. b. Benchmark to be updated on the basis of beneficiary characteristics and projected absolute amount of growth in national per capita expenditures for Parts A and B of the original FFS program. c. Benchmarks to be reset at start of each agreement period.
1) Determine savings[206]	a. Determine if the ACO's FFS Parts A and B beneficiaries (adjusted for beneficiary characteristics) estimated average per capita Medicare expenditures are at least the percent designated by HHS below the specified benchmark. b. HHS will set the above percentage accounting for normal variation in expenditures based on the quantity of Medicare FFS beneficiaries assigned to an ACO.
Payments for savings to ACOs[207]	a. When ACO meets requirements, a percentage (determined by HHS) of the difference between the benchmark and the "estimated average per capita Medicare expenditures adjusted for beneficiary characteristics" for the agreement period will be paid to the ACO and remainder goes to CMS. b. HHS will set a limit on the total shared savings that can be paid to any ACO.

---

[204] H.R. 3590, Patient Protection and Affordable Care Act, §3022(c). Assignment of Medicare fee-for-service beneficiaries (2009).

[205] H.R. 3590, Patient Protection and Affordable Care Act, §3022(d)(1)(B)(ii). Determining benchmarks (2009).

[206] H.R. 3590, Patient Protection and Affordable Care Act, §3022(d)(1)(B)(i). Determining savings (2009).

[207] H.R. 3590, Patient Protection and Affordable Care Act, §3022(d)(2). Payments for shared savings (2009).

Now let us examine the elements in the table.

Beneficiary assignment: CMS will establish a method of assigning beneficiaries to ACOs.[208] Because that method is a critical element to identify and secure a critical mass of patients for each ACO, however, CMS sought industry input for determining the best approach in their November 17, 2010 request for information as posted in the *Federal Register*.[209] Moreover, there will be challenges in determining which primary care physician or specialist claims a beneficiary for purposes of filling their ACO beneficiary threshold for situations in which patients are treated for multiple chronic conditions.

Setting ACO benchmarks (spending targets): MedPAC noted in 2009 that CMS would have to account for geographic variations across the United States in spending at the beneficiary level. It also noted that the targets should be developed on the basis of "changes in spending" rather than the "level of spending," while accounting for the amount of resources used by any given ACO. These changes would also be tied to geographic variations and opportunities to achieve economies of scale in population-based health management. This adjustment would benefit larger practices and health systems more than smaller provider organizations.[210]

Determining achievement of savings: Making annual comparison of the benchmarks set in comparison to the actual costs incurred, the evaluation would be based on per capita Medicare expenditures and adjusted for beneficiary characteristics. As discussed in Chapter 6, performance improvement systems must move toward providing real-time analysis to keep ACO executives aware of efficiency gains, improvements in outcomes, or challenges

---

[208] H.R. 3590, Patient Protection and Affordable Care Act, §3022(c). Assignment of Medicare fee-for-service beneficiaries (2009).

[209] Centers for Medicare and Medicaid Services. Request for information on accountable care organizations and Medicare shared savings program. *Federal. Register Vol. 75, No. 221:* 70165-70166. November 17, 2010. Section II. Solicitation of comments.

[210] MedPAC Report to Congress: Improving Incentives in the Medicare Program. (June 2009). Chapter 2: Accountable Care Organizations. Accessed online at http://www.medpac.gov/chapters/Jun09_Ch02.pdf.

experienced across the ACO. With effective tools and systems in place, organizations will be able to provide predictive modeling to support ACO budgeting and forecasting requirements as well as provide leaders with early recognition of savings to be realized through the shared savings program for distribution to ACO participants.

Payments for realized savings: Qualifying ACOs will receive FFS payments accordingly, and shared savings distributions will be received from CMS if the ACO meets quality standards (surpassing benchmarks) established by HHS and the qualifications noted previously in Table 2.

At the time of publication, CMS is finalizing the rules on the ACO model. These rules will be disseminated for public comment and eventually published for implementation by health systems across the country.

Payment Reform Models Associated with ACOs

Shared savings programs are one of a number of payment reform initiatives undergoing testing and implementation in various organizations and at different stages across the United States and especially in ACOs. As noted in Chapter 1, Table 2, payment model reform starts with the industry's recognizing the need to move away from FFS systems. Due to the complex nature of these systems, transition across the industry is occurring gradually in that some models have been tested since the 1990s while others are more recent. In addition to the ACO model, what are some of the other payment reforms being tested and implemented? We shall discuss three: bundled payment approaches, global payment approaches, and value-based purchasing programs.

Bundled payments

One of the frequently discussed payment reform models is bundled payment. The premise for bundled payments is that the payer provides a set amount for a particular episode of care, starting from the point of hospital admission for a specified procedure through discharge or possibly post-acute care requirements based on the terms set for the payment bundle (including an adjustment factor for severity of the case). The payment bundle is determined by the physician and provider organization (such as hospital organizations), agreeing to a package of services for treating specific conditions that yields a single payment received and allotted on the basis of the agreement.[211] A number of organizations have tested and used payment bundling.

While we have not discussed academic medical centers (AMC) in detail up to this point, other observers have noted that these organizations may benefit greatly from ACO implementation and moving to a bundled payment approach in both care delivery and the education of future physicians.[212] In Griner's article in the November 2010 issue of the *New England Journal of Medicine*, he pointed to a number of benefits and challenges for academic medical centers implementing bundled payment systems in the future:

- Benefit: "Bundled payment is more consistent with AMCs' core values than is fee for service, and their teaching and service missions can benefit from its successful implementation — in part because it would encourage trainees to hone their physical exam skills."

- Benefit: "Bundled payment will be an incentive for hospital leaders to help their medical and nursing staffs reduce these inefficiencies by integrating their work more effectively. Among the results should be an improved learning environment for students of all the health professions."

- Challenge: " [The AMC] will need to address income disparities between primary care physicians and subspecialists";

- Challenge: "[It] will need to develop more centralized financial systems and management philosophies, recognizing the cultural transformation that may be required at some medical schools."

---

[211] Evans J. Current state of bundled payments. *American Health and Drug Benefits*, August 2010. Available at: http://www.ahdbonline.com/sites/default/files/Evans_JulyAug2010.pdf.

[212] Griner P. Payment reform and the mission of academic medical centers. *N Engl J Med*. 2010;363(19): 1784-1786.

In addition, MedPAC recommended in 2009 that academic medical centers take a proactive stance for educating both students and residents on payment reform models and approaches.[213] Ensuring that medical students and residents obtain the skills necessary for leadership and financial acumen on these transformative issues is crucial for their future careers. Being equipped to operate in performance-based compensation environments will be vital to help them quickly grow into their roles—not only to provide excellent direct patient care but also to navigate and serve in multidisciplinary and cross-functional teams tackling the administrative and financial challenges faced by healthcare provider organizations.

Some noteworthy examples of projects involving bundled payment approaches include an ongoing CMS demonstration project and the Prometheus Payment Model. First is a current CMS project ongoing to test bundling payments called the Acute Care Episode (ACE) Demonstration. The demonstration began in 2009 and involves four health systems in Texas, Oklahoma, New Mexico, and Colorado.[214] The demonstration with each entity will last three years and test the bundling of Medicare Part A and B payments into a single payment for an episode of care on specific cardiovascular or orthopedic procedures meeting volume thresholds. In addition to the competitively bid payment arrangements, providers (physicians, clinician care teams, and hospitals) are eligible for shared savings remuneration based on the cost savings achieved on a specified episode of care. For this program CMS also provides patients with a 50% share of the savings realized by CMS for patients who have procedures at the participating sites. Participating organizations include:

- Hillcrest Medical Center, Tulsa, Oklahoma
- Baptist Health System, San Antonio, Texas
- Oklahoma Heart Hospital LLC, Oklahoma City, Oklahoma

---

[213] Medicare Payment Advisory Commission. Report to Congress: Improving incentives in the Medicare program, June 2009. Chapter 1: Medical education. Available at: www.medpac.gov/documents/Jun09_EntireReport.pdf, 18-19.

[214] Centers for Medicare and Medicaid Services. Acute care episode (ACE) demonstration fact sheets. Available at: http://www.cms.gov/DemoProjectsEvalRpts/downloads/ACEFactSheet.pdf, http://www.cms.gov/DemoProjectsEvalRpts/downloads/ACE_web_page.pdf.

- Lovelace Health System, Albuquerque, New Mexico

Each organization has a different focus to its program in terms of procedures covered. In addition, transparency for viewing the actual savings achieved at the episode-of-care level can be seen for each facility on all procedures conducted in the program by drilling down on the results linked at the following CMS webpage: http://www.cms.gov/DemoProjectsEvalRpts/downloads/ACE_web_page.pdf

Second is the Prometheus Payment Model developed in 2006 by a project funded by the Robert Wood Johnson Foundation (RWJF).[215] The Prometheus model was set up to compensate provider organizations of care in two ways. First, the model calculated an evidence-informed case rate (ECR®)—that is, a patient-specific budget adjusted for the severity and complexity of the case. The ECR was translated into a bundled budget for all necessary interventions, accounting for the entire episode of care and services provided by the physicians, hospitals, laboratories, pharmacies, and post-acute care facilities and services. The Prometheus model also provides an allowance in addition to the ECR® to compensate for typically known potentially avoidable costs (PACs).

When care provider teams manage a full episode of care in an efficient and high-quality manner and avoid the occurrence of PACs, they are rewarded by keeping any portion of the PAC allowance unused in the patient's episode. This bundled budget concept differs slightly from bundled payments in that providers are still reimbursed on the basis of fee-for-service claims from payers; however, the budgets for the bundled services for specific types of episodes of care are compared to actual costs on a quarterly basis that includes a review of PACs that were avoided. When savings are achieved they result in bonuses for the provider teams and organizations involved. Four organizations are involved in piloting the Prometheus Model;[216] they include:

---

[215] de Brantes F, Rosenthal MB, Painter M. Building a bridge from fragmentation to accountability—the Prometheus Payment model. *N Engl J Med*. 2009;361(11): 1033-1036.

[216] Robert Wood Johnson Foundation, Health Care Incentives Improvement Institute. Prometheus payment: On the frontlines of health care payment reform, July 2010. Available at: http://www.rwjf.org/files/research/66748.pdf.

- ♦ Health Partners of Minneapolis, MN
- ♦ Krozer-Keystone Health System, Philadelphia, PA
- ♦ Employers Coalition on Health, Rockford, IL
- ♦ Spectrum Health, Grand Rapids, MI

Global payments

Global payment models are similar to the bundled payment model. They are already being used by a number of organizations, including IDNs, IPAs, and MSPGs. The key distinction is that whereas a bundled payment is set for a specific episode of care, such payments do not manage or influence the number of episodes treated by a physician or provider organization. The global payment model provides a physician or provider organization a single payment to cover all the costs of care for a patient's treatment requirements during a specific period of time regardless of the number of inpatient episodes they experience.[217] In a study done by the Commonwealth Fund published in February 2010, the authors noted the complex challenges in describing global payment systems. They did, however, define global payments as "holding providers financially accountable, to a greater or lesser degree, for the total cost of care provided to the patient population assigned to them."[218] An excerpt from the report is provided in Appendix E, in which the authors also discuss the varying levels of risk that can be assumed under global payment models.

Global payments can also be considered a form of capitation payments, which have fallen out of favor as HMO enrollment has declined in recent years.[219] Some organizations

---

[217] Miller H. Pathways for physician success under healthcare payment and delivery reforms. Report for the American Medical Association, part C, June 2010. Comprehensive care payment, 26. Executive summary available at: http://www.ama-assn.org/ama1/pub/upload/mm/399/payment-pathways-summary.pdf.

[218] Robinow A. Commonwealth Fund Report, February 2010. The potential of global payment: insights from the field. Available at: http://www.commonwealthfund.org/~/media/Files/Publications/Fund%20Report/2010/Feb/1373_Robinow_p otential_global_payment.pdf , 3-5, 13-14.

[219] Zuvekas SH, Cohen JW. Paying physicians by capitation: is the past now prologue? *Health Aff (Millwood)*. 2010;29(9):1661-1666.

using these models include Kaiser Permanente, MassHealth (Massachusetts Medicaid Program[220]), the Veterans Health Administration, and Blue Cross/Blue Shield of Massachusetts (BCBSMA). Another organization, Northeast Health Systems Physician Hospital Organization, established a five-year alternative quality contract (AQC) program in 2010 (referenced at the end of Chapter 1) that will use a global payment model as the basis of its reimbursement strategy.[221]

Value-based purchasing programs

Chapter 1 referred to Section 3001 of the PPACA as the new hospital value-based purchasing program. What was the legislative genesis of this new program? In addition to the recent acts (HITECH and PPACA) already discussed, Congress passed the Deficit Reduction Act of 2005 (DRA) in 2006. The DRA contains Section 5001(b), which calls for HHS to develop a plan for a hospital value-based purchasing program.[222] This piece of legislation as well as other efforts led to a broader set of value-based purchasing programs. In 2009 CMS released a paper titled "Roadmap for Implementing Value Driven Healthcare."[223] This report presented the CMS roadmap as a three- to five-year plan for multiple value-based purchasing program initiatives that would work in concert with ACOs and other incentive-oriented programs.

---

[220] Heit M, Piper K. Global payments to improve quality and efficiency in Medicaid: concepts and considerations. Boston, MA: Massachusetts Medicaid Policy Institute; November 2009. Available at: http://www.massmedicaid.org/~/media/MMPI/Files/20091116_GlobalPayments.pdf.

[221] *Becker's Hospital Review*, May 26, 2010. BCBS of Massachusetts, Northeast Health Systems sign 5-year global payment deal. Available at: http://www.beckershospitalreview.com/hospital-financial-and-business-news/bcbs-of-massachusetts-northeast-health-systems-sign-5-year-global-payment-deal.html.

[222] Public Law 109–171, February 8, 2006. 2005 Deficit Reduction Act (DRA), §5001(b). Available at: http://www.gpo.gov:80/fdsys/pkg/PLAW-109publ171/pdf/PLAW-109publ171.pdf; Centers for Medicare and Medicaid Services. Issues paper, January 17, 2007. HHS Medicare hospital value-based purchasing plan development. http://www.cms.gov/AcuteInpatientPPS/downloads/hospital_VBP_plan_issues_paper.pdf.

[223] Centers for Medicare and Medicaid Services. Roadmap for implementing value driven healthcare in the traditional Medicare fee-for-service program, January 2009. Available at: https://www.cms.gov/QualityInitiativesGenInfo/downloads/VBPRoadmap_OEA_1-16_508.pdf, 2.

How do we define value-based payments? Following the legislative definition per PPACA Section 3001, these types of payments would be incentive payments to hospitals that meet performance standards based on a minimum number of cases at the hospital for specific conditions and procedures noted in Chapter 1 within a given fiscal year. In addition to the hospital value-based purchasing program, the CMS roadmap provides plans for starting value-based purchasing programs for nursing homes,[224] home health care, and physician services related to the PQRI program described in Chapter 6.

With regard to physician services and value-based purchasing, the PPACA also contains Section 3007: Value-Based Payment Modifier under the Physician Fee Schedule.[225] This section requires the establishment of a value-based payment modifier that physicians or groups of physicians will be eligible for during specific performance periods. These payments will be based on performance measured against specific quality standards to be released by January 1, 2012. The rule making will take place in 2013 and reporting will begin in 2015.

Payment reform summary

The impact of payment reform on provider organizations, physicians, and payers will be significant over the years ahead. From the physician's perspective, an important factor in determining which payment reforms and models to implement will be risk tolerance or identifying who bears the greatest burden of risk between physician and payer. Figure 36 is a basic diagram ordering payment models on the basis of their acceptance of financial risk.

---

[224] Centers for Medicare and Medicaid Services. Medicare demonstrations. Nursing home value-based purchasing program (2009). Available at:
http://www.cms.gov/DemoProjectsEvalRpts/MD/itemdetail.asp?filterType=none&filterByDID=-99&sortByDID=3&sortOrder=descending&itemID=CMS1198946&intNumPerPage=10.

[225] H.R. 3590, Patient Protection and Affordable Care Act, §3007. Value-based payment modifier under the physician fee schedule (2009).

Figure 36. Payment Model Reforms and Risk[226]

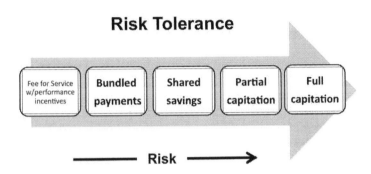

From this illustration we can see that the ACO's shared savings program lies at the center of the risk tolerance continuum. Chapter 1 discussed the declining use of health maintenance organizations and full capitation contracts that were the prevalent model of physician compensation by insurers in the 1980s and 1990s. Physicians bore the greatest burden of risk[227] with these contracts. At the other end of the continuum we have the FFS system, also discussed in Chapter 1 as the volume-driven model that our industry is moving away from. A significant aspect of bundled payments on this continuum is the issue of managing episodes of care and the movement toward managing inter-episodes of care associated with the evolution of the ACO. Chapter 2 discussed an instructive example of this type of program in Geisinger Health System's ProvenCare® program.[228] We illustrate here a three-level payment model in Figure 37 with the issue of risk tolerance in mind.

---

[226] BDC Advisors presentation slide, January 2011.

[227] Welch P, Welch G. Fee-for-data: a strategy to open the HMO black box. *Health Aff* (*Millwood*). 1995;14(4):104-116.

[228] Goldsmith J. Analyzing shifts in economic risks to providers in proposed payment and delivery system reforms. *Health Aff* (*Millwood*). 2010;29(7):1299-1304.

Figure 37. ACO Payment Models[229]

Level 1 Asymmetric shared savings	Level 2 Symmetric Model	Level 3 Partial Capitation Model
• Continue operating under current insurance contracts / coverage models (e.g. FFS)	• Payments can still be tied to current payment system, although ACO could receive revenue from payers and distribute funds to members (depending on ACO contracts)	• ACO receives mix of FFS and prospective fixed payment
• No risk of losses if spending exceeds targets	• At risk for losses if spending exceeds targets	• If successful at meeting budget and performance targets, greater financial benefits
• Most incremental approach with least barriers for entry	• Increased incentive for providers to decrease costs due to risk of losses	• If ACO exceeds budget, more risk means greater financial downside
• Attractive to new entities, risk-adverse providers, or entities with limited organizational capacity, range of covered services, or experience working with other providers	• Attractive to providers with some infrastructure or care coordination capability and demonstrated track record	• Only appropriate for providers with robust infrastructure, demonstrated track record in finances and quality and providing relatively full range of services

There are a number of issues implied in this illustration; we will address a few of them at each level. Level 1 aligns with an ACO at a lower level of readiness for acceptance of risk. Level 2, the symmetric model, would afford ACO participant physicians opportunities for greater percentages of shared savings because it has a stronger infrastructure and capabilities in place to accept greater accountability for care of a specific patient population. Level 3 represents an ACO at a high level of capabilities with more advanced indicia of clinical integration.

Each ACO will ultimately determine its own level on the basis of the amount of risk that it as an organization is willing to accept as the pace of its infrastructure and capabilities advances. As the industry as a whole continues to move toward the various P4P models,

---

[229] McClellan M, McKethan AN, Lewis JL, Roski J, Fisher ES. A national strategy to put accountable care into practice. *Health Aff (Millwood)*. 2010;29 (5):982-990: BDC Advisors presentation slide, January 2011.

physicians will continue to lose more of their FFS payments (continuously under pressure for reduction), but they will have increasing opportunities to earn back compensation through P4P models based on good quality outcomes as demonstrated in performance measures reported to payer organizations.

Starting with policy reform and testing of these new models and approaches as the industry has done over the last decade, financial management operations for physicians and providers will continue to evolve. Academic medical centers will help to prepare future physicians for the new world of compensation models they will confront in the various fields of medical practice that they enter.[230]

Other Financial Topics

Two other subjects we wish to discuss are 1) medical loss ratios as they will affect ACOs in the future; and 2) funding opportunities to support ACO development.

Medical loss ratio (MLR) and its implications

As noted in Chapter 1, Table 2, Section 2718 of the PPACA imposed new regulations affecting the operations of insurance companies. The section mandates that companies ensure that 80–85% of the premium revenues they collect from consumers (individuals, small companies, and large companies) go toward payment for clinical services and direct patient care to increase the value for consumers. The rule will hold insurance companies accountable and require them to better manage administrative costs. The National Association of Insurance Commissioners was required to collaborate with HHS in providing recommendations for changes to the method of calculating the medical loss ratio (MLR) because such calculation is a highly complex issue and requires substantial vetting by industry stakeholders to arrive at a consensus. The final rule on MLR was approved and released by HHS on November 22, 2010; it took effect on January 1, 2011.

A few highlights of the new rule include:

---

[230] Griner P. Payment Reform and the Mission of Academic Medical Centers. *N Engl J Med.*. 2010;363(19): 1784-1786.

- Establishing greater transparency and accountability: Beginning in 2011, the law requires that insurance companies publicly report their spending of premium dollars. This information will provide consumers with meaningful information, clearly accounting for the amount that goes toward actual medical care and activities to improve health care quality versus the amount spent on administrative expenses like marketing, advertising, underwriting, and executive salaries and bonuses.

- Ensuring that Americans receive value for their premium dollars: Beginning in 2011, the law requires insurance companies in the individual and small group markets to spend at least 80 percent of the premium dollars they collect on medical care and quality improvement activities. Insurance companies in the large group market must spend at least 85 percent of premium dollars on medical care and quality improvement activities.

- Providing consumer rebates: Insurance companies that do not meet the medical loss ratio standard will be required to provide rebates to their consumers. Insurers will be required to make the first round of rebates to consumers in 2012. Regardless of whether the rebate is provided to enrollees directly or indirectly through their employers, each enrollee must receive a rebate proportional to the premium amount paid by that enrollee.[231]

ACO and PCMH initiatives will need to ensure that as the delivery system is reformed through various models and efforts to change practices across the country that reimbursement policy or rules by private insurance payers remain flexible and provide appropriate incentives to support transformation. The MLR rule will encourage the industry to move away from the FFS system and toward the P4P, bundled payments, shared savings, and VBP models for reimbursing PCMHs and ACOs. Thus it will be important for

---

[231] Healthcare.gov. News release, November 22, 2010. Medical loss ratio: getting your money's worth on health insurance. Available at: http://www.healthcare.gov/news/factsheets/medical_loss_ratio.html.

providers to be able to receive reimbursement for innovative initiatives that may include fees for care coordination, incentives for quality improvement, and reimbursement for investments in health information technology needed to help drive these initiatives for both the ACO and primary care's PCMH transformation.

That said, one should recognize that areas of the country where the fee structure remains largely FFS and commercial payment have an economic incentive to remain as they are. It is only in highly competitive markets or highly penetrated managed care markets where systems have already moved to some degree of at-risk contracts that participants have an incentive to change. In the other areas, however, and as mentioned earlier, to move too quickly means to put oneself at a financial disadvantage.

More specifically, if the economic engine that runs the hospital's bottom line is acute care inpatient revenues, then reducing a large segment of that business without a different funding vehicle could in fact lead to the extinction of the parent entity. Christensen makes this point in a variety of ways. To survive in this new world means to have new funding sources. Engaging payers early in the process to assure funding resources to approximate high-acuity losses will be important during a payment transition period.

Funding opportunities for ACO development

As both physician practices and provider organizations grapple with the capital requirements for covering the multiyear expenditures needed to establish the clinical and cultural transformations associated with establishing ACOs, many are seeking new sources of funding and determining who bears the burden of these costs. Part of the answer to this challenge may lie with the initial determination of the type of organization positioned at the head of the ACO. For instance, in the case of the CMS ACOs, the PPACA did not provide for any grant funding to support their development and implementation.

In preparation for releasing the interim and final rules on ACOs, however, CMS issued a request for information from the industry in the *Federal Register* on November 17, 2010. In its request, CMS specifically asked for input regarding the financing models and mechanisms it should put in place to support the financial needs of small physician practices involved in ACO development.[232] Organizations working on ACOs with private payers may find that the challenge may lie more in deciding whether the infrastructure requirements are to be funded by the larger IDNs who have larger resource pools in place in terms of technology, staff, and finances, or by private payer organizations who also have the financial resources to provide support for the infrastructure development needed by small physician groups and CINs. As partnerships are negotiated and organizations form alignments across the industry, they will make decisions that will drive financing. In sum, this issue reinforces the importance of collaboration between public and private payers in the industry.

The incentives, compensation systems, and financial support of needed infrastructure are all reasons for payers to work together closely and carefully to ensure uniformity in setting spending targets for ACOs and that the incentives are sufficiently large enough to engage stakeholders and offset decremented FFS payments. Examples of positive results from coordination and teamwork are already being realized in cases like the demonstration projects noted in Chapter 1 with the Dartmouth-Brookings Collaborative, Premier ACO Collaborative, and the BCBSMA AQC project, along with the Prometheus Model project noted earlier in this chapter.

Next-Generation Payment Reform: The Road Ahead

We wish to provide two conceptual maps in concluding this chapter. The first focuses on the industry level, approaching industry evolution from a learning system or learning organization perspective for the advancement of the complex issue of payment system reform. The second map is a continuation of our ACO Roadmap series.

---

[232] Centers for Medicare and Medicaid Services. Request for information on accountable care organizations and Medicare shared savings program. *Federal Register. Vol.75, No. 221.* 70165-70166. November 17, 2010.

Learning organizations

The concept of a learning organization has great applicability here for the industry, especially in the area of payment reform where we have seen an abundance of new payment models and incentive programs piloted and demonstrated since 2000, with results providing needed feedback to leaders and policy decision makers.

The IOM's 2001 *Crossing the Quality Chasm* report[233] discussed this concept. In 2007 the institute held a Learning Healthcare System Workshop,[234] which engaged some of the principles introduced in its 2001 report. Given the complexity of the financial issues and time needed to analyze incentive programs along with P4P programs, the learning system concept provides a philosophy as well as a structure to visualize the maturity of the healthcare industry in order to uncover the best path to strengthen cost performance in concert with improvements in quality of care. To this end we provide Figure 38 to illustrate a possible path—which could have many variations—for the evolution of an ACO on the basis of this concept.

---

[233] Institute of Medicine, Committee on Quality of Health Care in America. Building organizational support for change: stages of organizational development. In: *Crossing the Quality Chasm: A New Health System for the 21st Century*. Washington, DC: National Academies Press; 2001: 112–117.

[234] Institute of Medicine roundtable on evidence-based medicine. Workshop on the learning healthcare system, October 2007. Available at: http://books.nap.edu/openbook.php?record_id=11903&page=R1.

Figure 38. The Learning System: ACOs and Payment Reform Progression

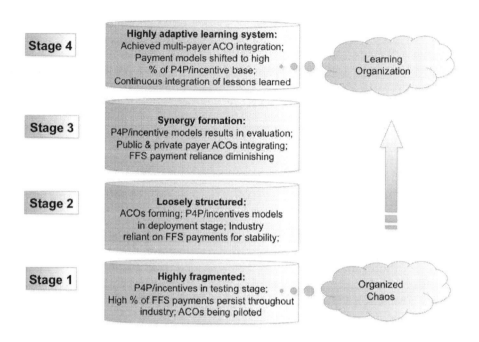

Our four-stage model is based on the "Stages of Evolution of the Design of Health Organizations" provided by the IOM in 2001. Any number of factors could be presented or applied to the various stages along with application of the ACO qualification criteria from Fisher and colleagues discussed in Chapter 2. Our perspective here focuses on the transition away from FFS payments toward a higher percentage of incentive and P4P payments for physician and provider compensation across the industry, along with the evolution of ACOs toward fully functional and clinically integrated multipayer models. Such organizations as the IOM, the CMS Center for Medicare and Medicaid Innovation, and others are collectively providing leadership for the industry. One can anticipate that focused initiatives for review of the results as ACOs are formed across the industry, together with results from payment reform approaches (that is, improvements in care and financial savings realized from shared savings, bundled payments, global payments, and value-based purchasing initiatives) begin to translate into lessons learned and emergence of best practices, the industry will continue to advance toward Stage 4 in functioning as a highly adaptive learning system.

Pathways for ACO financial issues

As we have done in previous chapters, we continue with our ACO Roadmap series presented at the individual ACO level. Here we focus on some key issues to address questions of financial and payment reform as presented in Figure 39.

Figure 39. ACO Roadmap 5: Navigating the Financial Issues for Your ACO

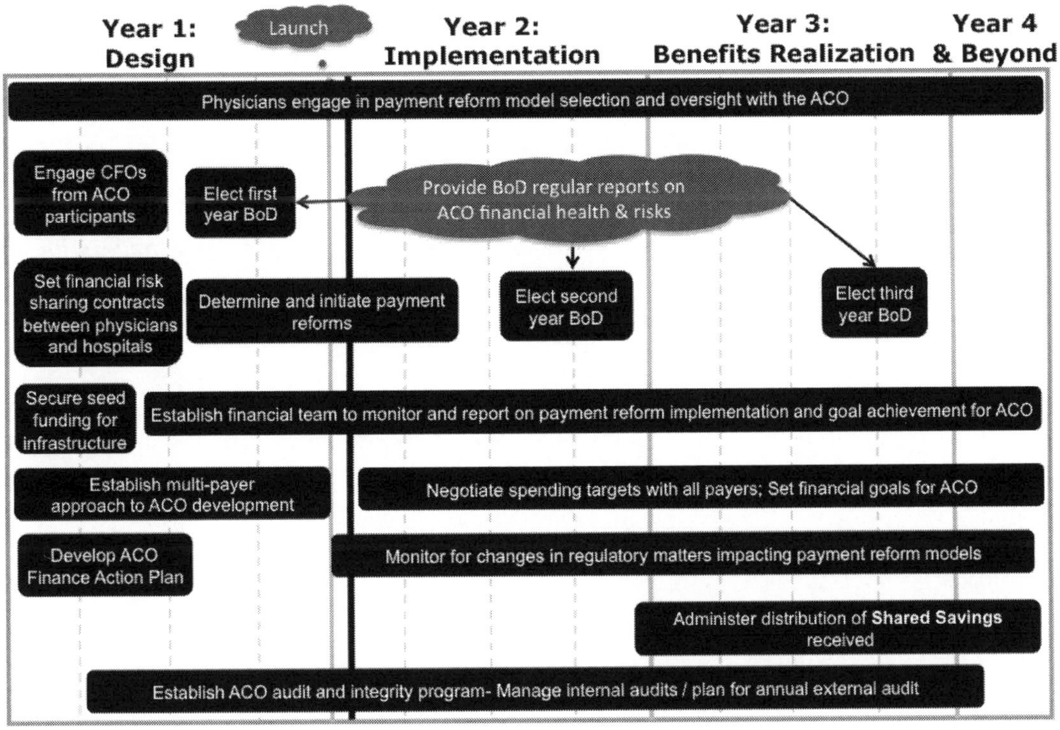

Dissecting a few elements of this roadmap, we wish to point out first that in the beginning physician leaders should partner with senior financial leaders, including CFOs, practice administrators and others, depending on the ACO's targeted configuration and participants. This partnering is an important move for setting the strategic agenda for future tactics and addressing antitrust issues that will affect financial and contracting relationships for all participants. The second point involves securing needed finances for infrastructure development, changes, and training that will be needed throughout the transformation process. Third, ACO participants should put in place a number of plans in order to a) work toward a multipayer level of functionality to serve as an attractive vehicle for engendering payment model reform for all payers; b) generate multi-stakeholder reporting on the financial health of the ACO and audits to ensure transparency for all parties involved; and c) as noted in our first ACO Roadmap, negotiating benchmarks and spending targets with the payer community.

INFOCUS: Challenges and Risks to Overcome

The financial challenges and risks for ACOs are high. Many can be mitigated, however, by engagement of appropriate stakeholders and careful planning activities. Unintended consequences may occur throughout ACO startups that impact their financial performance; but organizations that embrace a collaborative governance approach and establish strong financial metrics early will be better positioned to report progress to their leadership and to take corrective actions that influence population-based care management as it ties into financial reforms.

Seeking to balance setting benchmarks with realistic and attainable spending targets that are consistent with goals for improvement in the ACO's quality of care at the population level will be critical. Table 30 offers a set of challenges, risks, and potential mitigation strategies applicable to issues from the chapter.

Table 30. Chapter 7: Challenges and Risks

Challenges	Risks
7a) Developing a transition plan to begin to assume risk while working in a largely indemnity market.	7e) Moving too early without new funding sources to underwrite the loss of inpatient revenues.
7b) Developing total cost of care accounting metrics.	7f) Inadequate tracking systems to manage clinical/financial risk meaningfully.
7c) Securing funding needed for infrastructure expenditures.	7g) Inadequate changes to physician training curricula to keep future physicians apprised of forthcoming changes that will impact their compensation arrangements in the future.
7d) Tracking, capturing, and distributing incentives and value-based payments to appropriate stakeholders.	7h) Unintended consequences that may arise from initiating shared savings program in relationship to impact on quality of patient care and services provided to a specific patient population.

Potential Mitigation Strategies
√ Begin to pilot shared risk initiatives to develop cores competencies.
√ Begin to explore total cost of care accounting vehicles.
√ Engage financial modeling expertise to forecast financial impact to all stakeholders based on changes to be made with clinical integration programs.
√ Plan for early launch of payer relationship strategy discussions to move toward multi-payer ACO model at an accelerated pace.

Chapter 8.   Conclusion- The Road Ahead

Where We Stand

The advancement of the health system in the United States will require many changes, for which ACOs are only one significant option. Many other questions exist, including insurance market reform and expanded coverage for 40 to 45 million Americans.[235] How will we accommodate the predicted dramatic increase in patient volume in a system that is already stressed? Efforts have been made to improve the American health system since the IOM's *To Err Is Human* was published in 1999, with implementation of new technologies, improvement in quality management, the transformation of primary care, and formation of clinical integration programs that have led to better population-based health outcomes. As an industry, however, we still have room for improvement in reducing the rate of medical errors and adverse events[236] coupled with managing the expected increase in the size of the patient population.

These issues and others have led to a paradigm shift in healthcare, giving rise to ACOs along with other innovations in the reform of the delivery system, such as strengthening public health services as well as preventive health and wellness programs, increased funding for training of new healthcare workers, and improving the nation's Indian Health Services programs as outlined in Title X of the PPACA will help us meet these needs along with others that will emerge in the future. With these changes will come new ways to measure performance and greater emphasis on comparative effectiveness

---

[235] Holahan J. The 2007–09 Recession And Health Insurance Coverage. *Health Aff (Millwood) 2010;*30(1):1-8.

[236] Landrigan CP, Parry GJ, Bones CB, Hackbarth AD, Goldmann DA, Sharek PJ. Temporal Trends in Rates of Patient Harm Resulting from Medical Care. *N Engl J Med.* 2010; 363(22): 2124-2134; Wilson D. Mistakes Chronicled on Medicare Patients. *New York Times.* November 11, 2010. .Available at: http://www.nytimes.com/2010/11/16/business/16medicare.html; Adverse Events in Hospitals: National Incidence Among Medicare Beneficiaries..*Department of Health and Human Services Office of Inspector General Report.* November 2010. Available at: http://oig.hhs.gov/oei/reports/oei-06-09-00090.pdf.

research on the patient population, consumers, physicians, and other healthcare workers and stakeholders.

We have covered a range of issues, starting with the current history of the industry, providing evidence of the reasons that change is needed for the general good. Then, recognizing ACOs as a vehicle for the next stage of delivery system reform, we discussed their formation with the Patient-Centered Medical Home as the foundation of the ACO model. The importance of this transition cannot be overstated as we improve the quality of healthcare in the United States. We then explored the issue of governance, importance of physician leadership, and clinical integration as a foundational element of every ACO. This chapter then led to discussion of antitrust law and the many issues that ACOs must deal with on the legal frontier. We also discussed health information technology, quality reporting and performance measurement, financial perspectives, and organizational change, as they are all critical issues for the development of new ACO models within the U.S. health system.

There are many separate ACO initiatives that have already started across the country involving private and public payer shared savings programs. Building on these efforts, ACOs should eventually transition to a multipayer focus, as we have noted and as has been recommended by other industry experts. The opportunity to capitalize on the benefits of clinical integration efforts, changes in administrative processes, new physician leaders, and new technologies to benefit multiple payers and multiple patient populations should be expedited to maximize returns on investments—and most importantly to close the healthcare quality gap in the communities we serve.

Future economic impact

The Congressional Budget Office's March 2010 final estimate regarding estimated impacts on budget deficit and revenue for the PPACA projected a total $143B reduction in spending and decreased budget deficit over the ten-year period from 2010 to 2019.[237]

---

[237] Congressional Budget Office (CBO) Letter to the Honorable Nancy Pelosi regarding the CBO and Joint Committee on Taxation estimate of the direct spending and revenue effects of an amendment in the nature of

Figure 40 shows the forecasted impact on spending that will result from the first 10 years of the Medicare Shared Savings Program.

Figure 40. Estimated Effects of the Medicare ACO Program
(Effects on direct spending and revenues in billions of dollars by fiscal year)

PPACA SECTION	2010	2011	2012	2013	2014	2015	2016	2017	2018	2019	2010-14	2010-19
3022 Medicare Shared Savings Program	0	0	0	-.1	-.3	-.6	-.7	-.9	-1	-1.2	-0.5	-4.9
Note 1	Estimated effects on direct spending and revenues in billions of dollars, by fiscal year											
Note 2	Source: http://www.cbo.gov/ftpdocs/113xx/doc11379/AmendReconProp.pdf											

Thus we can see that an increasing amount of savings is expected starting in year two of the program. This projection tracks with the results realized from the CMS Physician Practice Demonstration Program. Appendix C (December 2010) shows an increasing trend in shared savings for the 10 physician practices that started at $7.3M in year 1 and most recently concluded with $31.7M in savings distributed back to the physician practices for distribution after year 4 ended in March 2010.

As these shared savings programs are implemented, the behavioral effects of participating organizations should be evaluated against the other financial incentive programs discussed in Chapter 7 for their comparative effectiveness and broader economic impact. While the transition will not be easy and there are numerous factors to manage, there is a clear path to success through innovative programs that focus on achieving improved health outcomes for targeted chronic diseases across a population.

Strategic focus

With all the issues to be analyzed and managed, we can now see the importance of strategic planning for the individual ACO. In addition to having a roadmap for the near and long term, the reader should consider an environmental scan of critical issues currently affecting

---

a substitute to H.R. 4872, the Reconciliation Act of 2010. March 20, 2010. Available at: http://www.cbo.gov/ftpdocs/113xx/doc11379/AmendReconProp.pdf.

the organization. One can view the scanning process through a set of lenses as illustrated in Figure 41.

Figure 41. Strategic Lenses for ACO Strategy Review

| Economic | Societal | Political | Clinical |

Economic Perspectives	Societal Perspectives	Political Perspectives	Clinical Perspectives
Supply drivers-healthcare workers	Cultural Considerations	Pending reform legislation	Population health
Public demand for services	Uninsured care	Congressional allies	Emergent conditions
Antitrust issues	Aging population care	Election impact	New interventions
Market influencers	Pediatric care	Grassroots movements	Delivery system reform

Analysis of Emerging Trends and Innovations Under Each Lens

Information and insights gained from this scanning process should serve as background for development planning as well as due diligence considerations for physician leaders and other members of the governance team. Each of these four lenses provides a different but interrelated perspective for leaders to consider in setting and correcting course for the ACOs that they lead.

Under the **Economic Perspectives:** An increase in the demand for services given the reduction of the uninsured population will have a profound impact on the healthcare delivery system. This change alone will create a demand to increase the number of physicians needed to provide care and expand the care delivery capacity of the U.S. health system.

Societal Perspectives should be considered by leaders of ACOs in order to manage the health of a population and the many factors that impact a specific group. Examining each issue under this lens relates to health disparities that should be reduced and eventually eliminated in the ACO's geographic market.

There are certain to be new market influences as changes occur in the **Political Perspectives** in the decade to come. Health policy at local, state, and federal levels will be affected as ACOs mature and new interventions drive changes in care delivery.

Last but certainly not least is the **Clinical Perspective.** This is the lens through which each physician leader should look most closely especially as they relate to delivering quality care. Taking into account new interventions resulting from technological innovation or reform of the care delivery process will provide insights for setting strategic and tactical objectives for improving population health and lessening the impact of emergent clinical issues.

These perspectives can be part of any strategic planning process for any ACO. The insights and knowledge gained will support the need for information in evaluating strengths, weaknesses, opportunities, and threats; provide direction in political affairs; identify market forces acting on the ACO; and establish a perspective on the world surrounding the ACO.

Planning on the community level

As ACOs begin to form, it will be imperative for their leaders to collaborate with government agencies at the local and state levels to further improve population-based health management. Many physicians and clinical leaders are already engaged at this level in collaborating with cross-functional teams and workgroups focused on public health matters. These groups examine health disparities, changes in outcomes, patient safety, and other issues in light of the populations they serve as influenced by the factors identified under the strategic lenses in Figure 41. Other matters to be taken into account at the community level that will affect ACO implementations will include:

- New interventions and innovations tested and implemented under the Center for Medicare and Medicaid Innovation programs;

- The introduction of ICD-10 (discussed in Chapter 5 and referenced in Chapter 6) that will improve collection of healthcare data for clinical decisions and research;

- New programs launched on national and local levels from the PPACA.

Given the many levels of strategy for ACOs, collaborating within the community system will be a vital part of working toward local long-term goals. One planning model originally introduced in 2000 and redesigned and published in 2010 offers a "framework for community health action planning."[238] Figure 42 illustrates several factors and elements in which ACO leaders can help drive improvements in regional population-based health management.

---

[238] Fawcett S, Schultz J, Watson-Thompson J, Fox M, Bremby R. Building multisectoral partnerships for population health and health equity. *Prev Chronic Dis*. 2010;7(6). Available at: http://www.cdc.gov/pcd/issues/2010/nov/10_0079.htm ; Institute of Medicine. *The Future of the Public's Health in the 21st Century.* Chapter 4. Community, Figure 4-1 Framework for Collaborative Community Action On Health. Washington, DC. National Academies Press; 2002. Available at: http://books.nap.edu/openbook.php?record_id=10548&page=186.

Figure 42. Framework for Community / Population Health Planning and Management

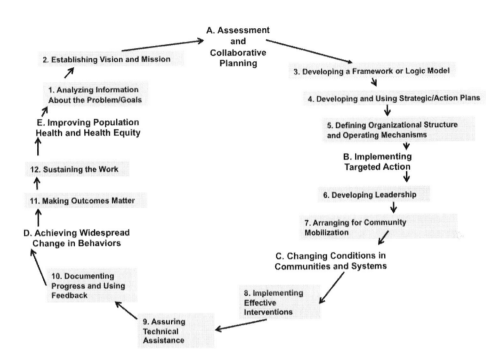

Elements A through E are the original facets of the framework. In our transition from a volume-driven compensation system for healthcare providers and physicians to one that rewards value and performance, engagement at this level of planning by ACO physician leaders will support strategic objectives for improving health outcomes for local citizens and stakeholder groups. The implementation and evolution of community-level planning models in which ACOs serve as part of larger systems will help to achieve true population-based health management and support organizational transformation in delivery of care.

Elements 1 through 12 provide an added layer of actions to consider for incorporation into the planning framework as proposed by Fawcett and colleagues. While the actions are sequentially numbered, the reader will note that each action can be taken independently for the benefit of the ACO and its community stakeholders. Highlighting a few of these actions, we start with "Analyzing Information about Problems and Goals." The strategic lenses identified in Figure 41 can channel analysis, problem solving, and goal identification to establish parameters for mission and vision creation for the ACO and its broader role in public health service. "Developing Leadership" takes us back to our discussion of physician leadership in Chapter 3 and its importance for the maturation of the ACO in itself and within its community. Last is "Sustaining the Work." An important element of any change management approach, evaluating how well an organization sustains its work helps in analyzing the effectiveness of implementation.[239] It ensures that better programs, policies, and processes are adopted and allows for the organization to measure its effectiveness over the long term. When sustaining the work is recognized as part of organizational transformation, our value is demonstrated incrementally in terms of our economic impact on our communities and improvement in quality of care and health outcomes for citizens and patients.

The potential benefits for communities and ACOs alike from initiating a community-wide planning process include early identification of health risks for patient populations in their geographic region; recruitment and development of clinical leaders; and implementation of systems for evaluating performance and providing feedback to leaders of ACOs and other community stakeholders in support of critical decisions. Whether this model or another is engaged, the reader should recognize the importance of collaboration. As ACOs are formed across the country, new clinical integration programs will be started in order to meet the indicia discussed in Chapter 4 for the benefit of patients served in the organization's geographic market. These efforts will result in new mergers and joint ventures enabled by support from the FTC in antitrust regulations, and ultimately to deliver higher-quality care across communities as a whole.

Learning system approach

As was discussed in Chapter 7, a learning system approach may be helpful from a strategic perspective in governing the evolution of ACOs. This concept, while not new and having been proposed by other industry experts,[240] lends itself to implementing structured as well

---

[239] Weiner B. A theory of organizational readiness for change. *Implementation Science.* 2009;4(67).

[240] Shortell SM, Casalino LP, Fisher ES. How the center for medicare and medicaid innovation should test accountable care organizations. *Health Aff (Millwood).* 2010;29(7):1293-1298.

as unstructured feedback at both local and national levels to advance the care delivery model and mitigate risk of failure by later-stage adopters across the industry. To this end we offer Figure 43 as a conceptual roadmap for ACOs from the perspective of the learning system in order to achieve a higher level of functionality.

Figure 43. ACO Reform Progression: Evolving as a Learning System

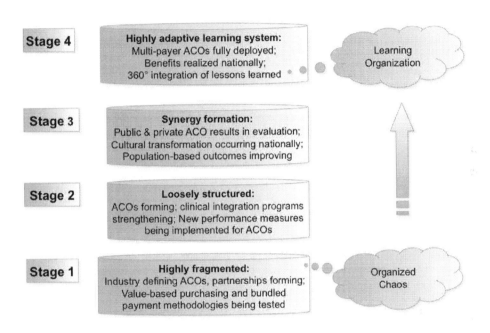

This particular model incorporates our own thoughts on some of the issues through the four stages. Each stage can be refined for individual ACOs, regional conglomerates of ACOs, or on the national level based on the needs of any particular audience. A few points to make from our perspective include the following:

1. We have incorporated ideas from all topics previously discussed.

2. Evidence-based medicine practices should be included throughout and factored in as part of the foundation starting at stage 1.[241]

---

[241] H.R. 3590, Patient Protection and Affordable Care Act, §3022(b)(2)(G). ACO requirements.

3. There are inherent risks and challenges in advancing toward Stage 4, as noted throughout our book, that must be addressed across the industry as different organizations will be at different stages over time.

4. **Stage 1:** The beginning of the journey for many in the industry while others are further down the path. Testing new ways of paying for healthcare will help to move the nation's health system away from the traditional FFS system at this stage. An important element at the local level in Stage 1 is implementation of specific learning organization systems and frameworks[242] in addition to tools that assist clinicians with adhering to evidence-based practices in making medical decisions[243] at the individual patient and population level.

5. **Stage 2:** This is a key issue that will help to evaluate the effectiveness of new ACO models implemented in differing configurations with different targeted areas for improvement. As clinical integration programs continue to strengthen, the industry will also begin to realize new levels of care coordination and improved clinical outcomes. Continued evolution and advancement of evidence-based medicine practices with advanced application of CDS to improve evidence usage with further integration of learning organization systems to support clinician and physician workforces across ACO participants.

6. **Stage 3:** The cultural transformation that will take place across the industry with development and evolution of the ACO models will tear down long-standing barriers and silos. With this transformation will come the shift toward stronger population-based health management related to the *Healthy People 2020*[244] goals, which includes improvement in health services as a major determinant of achieving those goals.

---

[242] Crites GE, McNamara MC, Akl EA, Richardson SW, Umscheid CA, Nishikawa J. Evidence in the learning organization. *Health Research Policy and Systems*. 2009;7(4).

[243] Kilicoglu H, Demner-Fushman D, Rindflesch TC, Wilczynski NL, Haynes RB. Towards Automatic Recognition of Scientifically Rigorous Clinical Research Evidence. *JAMA*. 2009;16(1): 25-31. Available at: http://www.ncbi.nlm.nih.gov/pmc/articles/PMC2605595/pdf/25.S1067502708001874.main.pdf.

[244] Healthy People 2020 Initiative's Framework. Available at: http://www.healthypeople.gov/2020/Consortium/HP2020Framework.pdf.

7. **Stage 4:** We see the ultimate goal of ACOs as the ability to leverage multipayer functionality to maximize shared savings and achieve economies of scale in improving quality of care and lowering its cost across the country.

Legislative Outlook

The legislative landscape will help shape ACO initiatives in the future. As new ACOs start to produce results for specific patient populations and communities over the coming years, those results will be returned to federal (CMS, FTC, and CDC) and state agencies for analysis and determination of value delivered in terms of improvement in both cost and quality of care. With these results we can expect new legislation and reform in the future to build on the foundation set by the PPACA and other previously enacted legislation. We have discussed key sections of the PPACA along with payment reforms that will continue to see policy changes as P4P models yield new results in the area of reimbursement and compensation for physicians and care provider organizations.

Another area of current and future national health policy attention related to ACOs should be the advancement of patient-centered care. While "patient-centeredness"[245] is a recognized requirement for ACOs, the topic has been identified in recent literature[246] as a policy area that may directly contribute directly to the effectiveness of both patient-centered medical home initiatives (noted as part of the foundation of ACOs in Chapter 2) and ACOs themselves:

- *Communications*: support for education of clinicians on best practices and communication techniques that mitigate health disparities, and support for technology enablers that improve health communications in order to advance ACOs in their community mission;

---

[245] H.R. 3590, Patient Protection and Affordable Care Act, §30222(b)(2)(H). Requirements for ACOs.

[246] Epstein RM, Fiscella K, Lesser CS, Stange KC. Why The Nation Needs A Policy Push On Patient-Centered Health Care. *Health Affairs (Millwood)*. 2010;29(8):1489-1495.

- *Measures of effectiveness*: evaluating new interventions, technologies, clinical processes, and interactions among clinicians, patients, and families that directly impact patient relationships, recognized as a critical element of patient-centered care;

Last, the field of comparative effectiveness research will certainly examine key issues with the evolution of ACOs. With the PPACA having established the Patient-Centered Outcomes Research Institute (PCORI),[247] efforts to assess the effectiveness of ACOs in comparison to other models of care may have future policy implications. New legislation regarding performance reporting, payment reforms, and other topics will emerge that will influence the advancement and refinement of ACOs.

In Conclusion

ACOs will evolve under different models in each community over the years following 2011. We leave you with some points for future consideration beyond the material and concepts provided in this book. First, in Chapter 3 we identified five ACO models, and we recognize the need for and suggest comparative evaluations as industry results emerge in the coming years. Second, we suggest exploring the issue of introducing innovations (processes, technologies, or other interventions) into new ACOs. See whether specific paths for introduction are emerging or whether physician leaders and industry participants are able to accelerate the pace of change, improve the quality, and lower the cost of care. Third, given the rapid adoption of health information technology across our industry, we suggest further assessment of this trend's effects on improvement in care coordination, care delivery, and quality of care provided by all models of ACOs. Fourth, policy changes that occur beyond the publication of this book require continuous monitoring by industry stakeholders and ACO participants based on their specific needs and interests. Other issues will come to the surface as changes in health policy take effect on national and state levels and people's satisfaction with the quality of their care undergoes further assessment.

---

[247] H.R. 3590, Patient Protection and Affordable Care Act, §6301(b). Establishment of Patient-Centered Outcomes Research Institute.

We have provided a collection of models throughout the book as well as roadmaps at the end of several chapters. They are intended as a high-level guide to stimulate executive thinking about activities to launch or engage and participants to include or recruit. We know that these roadmaps and models should and will be reexamined over time in light of new legislation, emerging best practices, and evidence from the field. Depending on the ACO model employed and the stakeholders involved, each roadmap may require any number of alternative paths and courses. We recognized that we could not cover every issue in depth nor was that the intention of this book. It is our hope nonetheless that regardless of an ACO's stage of development or level of involvement that the roadmaps, illustrations, and concepts presented here help strengthen organizational readiness for your own organization's journey through healthcare reform and ACO implementation.

Hospitals and hospital systems must redefine themselves as they increasingly function as cost centers of ever-larger community health systems. Medical specialists will find themselves assisting their primary care colleagues in keeping patients healthy, and primary care physicians will look to their specialist colleagues for definitive therapies that make the most clinical and financial sense for their patients. Hospitalizations will become more often regarded as outpatient treatment failures and quality measures will define performance standards. By knowing the facts, keeping patient-centered quality as the guiding standard, and enabling physicians to lead, we are on the cusp of real change.

Bibliography

2010 Physician Survey on Impact of Healthcare Reform administered by Merritt Hawkins for the Physicians Foundation.

AAFP Accountable Care Organization Task Force Report October 2009.

Accountable Care Organizations: Research Synthesis Report. American Hospital Association. June 2010.

Adverse Events in Hospitals: National Incidence Among Medicare Beneficiaries. *Department of Health and Human Services Office of Inspector General Report*. November 2010.

AHIMA. e-HIM Workgroup on the Transition to ICD-10-CM/PCS. Planning organizational transition to ICD-10-CM/PCS. *Journal of AHIMA*. 2009;80(10):72-77.

Ash JS, Sittig DF, Poon EG, Guappone K, Campbell E, Dykstra RH. The extent and importance of unintended consequences related to computerized provider order entry. *J Am Med Inform Assoc*. 2007;14(4): 415-423.

Barrett JS, Mondick JT, Narayan M, Vijayakumar K, Vijayakumar S. Integration of modeling and simulation into hospital-based decision support systems guiding pediatric pharmacotherapy. *BMC Med Inform Decis Mak*. 2008;8(6).

Berenson R. Shared savings program for accountable care organizations: a bridge to nowhere? *Am J Manag Care*. 2010;16(10): 721-726.

Berwick DM. A primer on leading the improvement of systems. *BMJ*. 1996;312:619-622.

Besanko D, Dranove D, Shanley M, Schaefer S. (2004). Competitors and competition. In: *Economics of Strategy*. 3rd ed. Hoboken, NJ; John Wiley and Sons, Inc.; 218–223.

Blumenthal D, Tavenner M. The "meaningful use" regulation for electronic health records. *N Engl J Med*. 2010;363(6): 501-504.

BodenheimerT, Wagner EH, Grumbach K. Improving primary care for patients with chronic illness: the chronic care model, Part 2. *JAMA*. 2002;288:1909-1914.

Boland P, Polakoff P, Schwab T. Accountable care organizations hold promise, but will they achieve cost and quality targets? *Manag Care*. 2010;19(10):12-6.

Burke T, Rosenbaum S. Accountable care organizations: implications for antitrust policy. Robert Wood Johnson policy analysis paper, March 2010.

Campbell EM, Sittig DF, Ash JS, Guappone K, Dykstra RH. Types of unintended consequences related to computerized provider order entry. *J Am Med Inform Assoc* 2006;13(5):547-556.

Casalino LA, Devers KJ, Lake TK, Reed M, Stoddard JJ. Benefits of and barriers to large medical group practice in the United States. *Arch Intern Med*. 2003;163: 1958-64.

Chaudry J, Jain A, McKenzie S, Schwartz RW. Physician leadership: the competencies of change. *J Surg Educ*. 2008;65(3):213-220.

Christensen C, Grossman J, Hwang J. *The Innovator's Prescription: A Disruptive Solution for Healthcare*. New York, NY: McGraw Hill; 2009.

Closing the Quality Gap: A Critical Analysis of Quality Improvement Strategies. Stanford University. (June 2007). *AHRQ Technical Review Number 9.*

Collins J. *Good to Great: Why Some Companies Make the Leap and Others Don't.* New York, NY: Harper Business; 2001.

Crites GE, McNamara MC, Akl EA, Richardson SW, Umscheid CA, Nishikawa J. Evidence in the learning organization. *Health Research Policy and Systems.* 2009;7(4).

Cutler D. How Health Care Reform Must Bend The Cost Curve. *Health Affairs (Millwood).* 2010;29(6): 1131-1135.

de Brantes F, Rosenthal MB, Painter M. Building a bridge from fragmentation to accountability—the Prometheus Payment model. *N Engl J Med.* 2009;361(11): 1033-1036.

Devers K, Berenson R. Can accountable care organizations improve the value of health care by solving the cost and quality quandaries? Robert Wood Johnson policy analysis paper, October 2009.

Donabedian A. Evaluating the quality of medical care. *Milbank Quarterly* 2005;83(4):691-729. Reprinted from *Milbank Memorial Fund Quarterly* 1966;44(3):166–203.

Epstein RM, Fiscella K, Lesser CS, Stange KC. Why The Nation Needs A Policy Push On Patient-Centered Health Care. *Health Affairs (Millwood).* 2010;29(8):1489-1495.

Glasser J. and Salzberg C., (September 2010). "Information Technology for Accountable Care Organizations," *Hospitals & Health Networks.*

Falk I, Rorem R, Ring M. A summary of the findings. In: *The Costs of Medical Care: A Summary of Investigations on the Economic Aspects of the Prevention and Care of Illness.* Chicago, IL: University of Chicago Press; 1933.

Fawcett S, Schultz J, Watson-Thompson J, Fox M, Bremby R. Building multisectoral partnerships for population health and health equity. *Prev Chronic Dis.* 2010;7(6).

Fields D, Leshen E, Patel K. Analysis and commentary. Driving quality gains and cost savings through adoption of medical homes. *Health Aff (Millwood).* 2010;29(5):819-826.

Fisher ES, McClellan MB, Bertko J, et al. Fostering accountable health care: moving forward in Medicare. *Health Aff* (Millwood) 2009;28(2): w219-w231.

Fisher ES, Shortell SM. Accountable care organizations: accountable for what, to whom, and how. *JAMA.* 2010;304(15):1715-1716.

Fisher ES, Staiger DO, Bynum JP, Gottlieb DJ. Accountable care organizations: the extended medical staff. *Health Aff* (Millwood). 2007;26 (1): w44–w57.

Ford EW, Menachemi N, Peterson LT, Huerta TR. Resistance is futile: but it is slowing the pace of EHR adoption nonetheless. *J Am Med Inform Assoc.* 2009;16(3): 274-281.

Fraschetti R, Sugarman M. Successful Hospital-Physician Integration. *Trustee.* 2009;62(7): 11-2, 17-8.

Gittell J, Seidner R, Wimbush J. A Relational Model of How High-Performance Work Systems Work. *Organization Science*. 2010;21(2): 490-506.

Goldsmith J. Analyzing Shifts In Economic Risks To Providers In Proposed Payment And Delivery System Reforms. *Health Affairs (Millwood)*. 2010;29(7): 1299-1304.

Gosfield AG. The stark truth about the Stark law. Part I. *Fam Pract Manag*. 2003;10(10):27-33.

Greaney T. Thirty years of solicitude: antitrust law and physician cartels. *Houston Journal of Health Law and Policy*. 2007;72:189-226.

Griner P. Payment Reform and the Mission of Academic Medical Centers. *N Engl J Med*. 2010;363(19): 1784-1786.

Guterman S, Davis K, Stremikis K, and Drake H. (June 2010). Innovation In Medicare And Medicaid Will Be Central To Health Reform's Success. *Health Affairs*. 29(6): 1188-1193.

Health Care Cost Drivers: Chronic Disease, Comorbidity, and Health Risk Factors in the U.S. and Michigan. August 2010. *Center for Healthcare Research & Transformation Issue Brief*.

Heit M. and Piper K. Global Payments to Improve Quality and Efficiency in Medicaid: Concepts and Considerations. *Massachusetts Medicaid Policy Institute*. 2009.

Hellinger FJ. Antitrust enforcement in the healthcare industry: the expanding scope of state activity. *Health Serv Res*. 1998;33 (5 Pt 2): 1477-1494.

Hester J Jr. Designing Vermont's pay-for-population health system. *Prev Chronic Dis*. 2010;7(6):1-6.

Holahan J. The 2007–09 Recession And Health Insurance Coverage. *Health Aff (Millwood) 2010;*30(1):1-8.

Improving Health Care: A Dose of Competition. July 2004 Report from DOJ and FTC.

Institute of Medicine, Committee on Redesigning Health Insurance Performance Measures, Payments, and Performance Improvement Programs. *Rewarding Provider Performance: Aligning Incentives in Medicare*. Washington, DC: National Academies Press; 2006.

Institute of Medicine, Committee on Quality of Health Care in America. *Crossing the Quality Chasm: A New Health System for the 21st Century*. Washington, DC: National Academies Press; 2001.

Institute of Medicine, Roundtable on Evidence Based Medicine. *Workshop on The Learning Healthcare System*. Washington, DC: National Academies Press; 2007.

Institute of Medicine. *The Future of the Public's Health in the 21st Century*. Washington, DC. National Academies Press; 2002.

Jacobs P, Rapoport J. Regulation and antitrust policy in health care. In: *The Economics of Health and Medical Care*. 5th ed. Sudbury, MA: Jones and Bartlett Publishers; 2004: Chapter 16.

Jha AK, DesRoches CM, Campbell EG, et al. Use of electronic health records in U.S. hospitals. *N Engl J Med*. 2009;360(16):1628-1638.

Katayama AC, Coyne SE, Moskol KL. Another round of Stark law changes coming your way as early as October 1, 2008. *WMJ.* 2008;107(6):305-306.

Kerr EA, Krein SL, Vijan S, Hofer TP, Hayward RA. Avoiding pitfalls in chronic disease quality measurement: a case for the next generation of technical quality measures. *Am J Manag Care.* 2001;7(11):1033-1043.

Kocher R, Ezekiel EJ, DeParle NA. The Affordable Care Act and the future of clinical medicine: the opportunities and challenges. *Ann Intern Med.* 2010;153(8): 536-539.

Kocher R, Sahni NR. Physicians versus hospitals as leaders of accountable care organizations. *N Engl J Med.* 2010;363(27):2579-2582.

Konschak C, Jarrell L. *Consumer-centric Healthcare: Opportunities and Challenges for Providers.* Chicago, IL: Health Administration Press; 2010.

Kotter J, Rathgeber H. *Our Iceberg Is Melting.* New York, NY: St. Martin's Press; 2005.

Kotter J, Schlesinger L. Choosing strategies for change. *Harvard Business Review.* 1979;57(2):106-114.

Kilicoglu H, Demner-Fushman D, Rindflesch TC, Wilczynski NL, Haynes RB. Towards Automatic Recognition of Scientifically Rigorous Clinical Research Evidence. *JAMA.* 2009;16(1): 25-31.

Landrigan CP, Parry GJ, Bones CB, Hackbarth AD, Goldmann DA, Sharek PJ. Temporal Trends in Rates of Patient Harm Resulting from Medical Care. *N Engl J Med.* 2010;363(22): 2124-2134.

LeTourneau B. Communicate for change. *J Healthc Manag.* 2004;49(6):354-357.

Luft HS. Becoming accountable—opportunities and obstacles for ACOs. *N Engl J Med.* 2010;363(15):1389-1391.

McClellan M, McKethan AN, Lewis JL, Roski J, Fisher ES. A national strategy to put accountable care into practice. *Health Aff (Millwood).* 2010;29(5):982-990.

McDonald KM, Sundaram V, Bravat DM, et al. *Closing the Quality Gap: A Critical Analysis of Quality Improvement Strategies.* Rockville, MD: Agency for Healthcare Research and Quality; 2007. AHRQ Technical Review 9.

McIntyre D, Rogers L, Heier E. Overview, history, and objectives of performance measurement. *Healthcare Finance Review.* 2001;22(3):7-21.

MedPAC June 2009 Report to Congress: Improving Incentives in the Medicare Program. Chapter 2: Accountable Care Organizations.

Miller H. Pathways for Physician Success Under Healthcare Payment and Delivery Reforms. Report for the American Medical Association. 2010.

Mirabito AM, Berry LL. Lessons that patient-centered medical homes can learn from the mistakes of HMOs. *Ann Intern Med.* 2010;152(3): 182-185.

Moore, James F. (1996). *The Death of Competition: Leadership & Strategy in the Age of Business Ecosystems.* New York: Harper Business.

Morrisey MA, Alexander J, Burns LR, Johnson V. Managed care and physician/hospital integration. *Health Aff* (*Millwood*). 1996;15: 62-73.

Paulus RA, Davis K, Steele GD. Continuous innovation in health care: implications of the Geisinger experience. *Health Aff* (*Millwood*). 2008;27(5):1235-1245.

Pisapia J, Reyes-Guerra D, Coukos-Semmel E.. Developing the leader's strategic mindset: establishing the measures. *Leadership Review.* 2005;5:41-68.

President's Council of Advisors on Science and Technology. Report to the President realizing the full potential of health IT to improve healthcare for Americans: the path forward. December 8, 2010.

Prometheus Payment: On the Frontlines of Health Care Payment Reform. (July 2010). Project of the Health Care Incentives Improvement Institute® (HCI3) supported by the Robert Wood Johnson Foundation.

Raskovich A, Miller NH. Cumulative innovation and competition policy. Department of Justice Economic Analysis Group Discussion paper, September 2010.

Raths D. Is ICD-10 a Quality Initiative? Innovators will use ICD-10 to further their business models and clinical capabilities. *Healthc Inform.* 2010;27(9):24-28.

Rittenhouse DR, Shortell SM, Fisher ES. Primary care and accountable care—two essential elements of delivery-system reform. *N Engl J Med.* 2009;361(24):2301-2303.

Roadmap for Implementing Value Driven Healthcare in the Traditional Medicare Fee-for-Service Program. CMS Report. January 2009.

Robinow A. The Potential of Global Payment: Insights From the Field. *Commonwealth Fund Report.* 2010.

Robinson JC. Applying value-based insurance design to high-cost health services. *Health Aff* (*Millwood*). 2010;29 (11): 2009-16.

Schroeder R. Just-in-time systems and lean thinking. In: *Operations Management: Contemporary Concepts and Cases.* 3rd ed. New York, NY: McGraw-Hill Irwin; 2007; 408-411.

Schwartz RW, Tumblin TF. The power of servant leadership to transform health care organizations for the 21st-century economy. *Arch Surg.* 2002;137(12):1419-1427.

Senge P. *The Fifth Discipline: The Art and Practice of the Learning Organization.* New York, NY: Currency Doubleday; 1994.

Serio CD, Epperly T. Physician leadership: a new model for a new generation. *Fam Pract Manag.* 2006;13(2):51-54.

Shortell S. Challenges and Opportunities for Population Health Partnerships. *Preventing Chronic Disease.* 2010;7(6): 1-2.

Shortell SM, Casalino LP, Fisher ES. How the center for medicare and medicaid innovation should test accountable care organizations. *Health Aff* (*Millwood*). 2010;29(7):1293-1298.

Sisko AM, Truffer CJ, Keehan SP, Poisal JA, Clemens MK, Madison AJ. National health spending projections: the estimated impact of reform through 2019. *Health Aff* (*Millwood*). 2010;29(10): 1933-1941.

Sinaiko AD, Rosenthal MB. Patients' role in accountable care organizations. *N Engl J Med.* 2010;363:2583-2585.

Smithson K, Baker S. Medical Staff Organizations: A Persistent Anomaly. *Health Aff (Millwood).* 2006;26(1): w76-w79.

Steele GD, Haynes JA, Davis DE, et al. How Geisinger's advanced medical home model argues the case for rapid-cycle innovation. *Health Aff* (*Millwood*). 2010;29(11):2047-2053.

Steindel SJ. International classification of diseases, 10th edition, clinical modification and procedure coding system: descriptive overview of the next generation HIPAA code sets. *J Am Med Inform Assoc.* 2010;17(3):274-282.

Stoller JK. Developing physician-leaders: a call to action. *J Gen Intern Med.* 2009;24(7):876–878.

Suc J, Prokosch HU, Ganslandt T. Applicability of Lewin's change management model in a hospital setting. *Methods Inf Med.* 2009;48(5):419-428.

Taylor M. The ABCs of ACOs. Accountable care organizations unite hospitals and other providers in caring for the community. *Trustee.* 2010;63(6):12-14.

The President's Council of Advisors on Science and Technology, "Report to the President Realizing the Full Potential of HIT to Improve Healthcare for Americans: The Path Forward" (December 2010), 25.

Thorpe K, Ogden L. The Foundation That Health Reform Lays For Improved Payment, Care Coordination, And Prevention. *Health Aff (Millwood).* 2010;29(6): 1183-1187

Vermont Report of the Health Care Reform Readiness Taskforce, October 13, 2010.

Vest J, Gamm L. A critical review of the research literature on Six Sigma, Lean and StuderGroup's Hardwiring Excellence in the United States: the need to demonstrate and communicate the effectiveness of transformation strategies in healthcare. *Implementation Science.* 2009;4(35):1-9.

Weiner B. A theory of organizational readiness for change. *Implementation Science.* 2009;4(67).

Weiner JP, Kfuri T, Chan K, Fowles JB. e-Iatrogenesis: the most critical unintended consequence of CPOE and other HIT. *.J Am Med Inform Assoc.* 2007;14(3): 387-388.

Xirasagar S, Samuels ME, Curtin TF. (February 2006). Management training of physician executives, their leadership style, and care management performance: an empirical study. *Am J Manag Care.* 2006;12(2):101-108.

Zuvekas SH, Cohen JW. Paying physicians by capitation: is the past now prologue? *Health Aff* (*Millwood*). 2010; 29(9):1661-1666.

Glossary and Acronyms

Accountable care organization- Collaborations between physicians, hospitals, and other providers of clinical services that will be clinically and financially accountable for healthcare delivery for designated patient populations in a defined geographic market. The ACO is physician led with a focus on population-based care management and providing services to patients under both public and private payer programs.

Anticompetitive effects- business practices and actions that attempt to or have the potential for reducing competition in a geographic market leading to illegal restraint of trade and antitrust law violations.

Bundled payment- making a single payment for both the services provided by the hospital and the services provided by physicians during an inpatient stay for a particular diagnosis or treatment.[248]

Disruptive innovation- "A process by which a product or service takes root initially in simple applications at the bottom of a market and then relentlessly moves 'up market', eventually displacing established competitors."[249]

Ecosystem- "An economic community supported by a foundation of interacting organizations and individuals—the organisms of the business world. The economic community produces goods and services of value to customers, who are themselves members of the ecosystem. The member organisms also include suppliers, lead producers, competitors, and other stakeholders. Over time, they co-evolve their capabilities and roles, and tend to align themselves with the directions set by one or more central companies. Those companies holding leadership roles may change over time, but the function of ecosystem leader is valued by the community because it enables members to move toward shared visions to align their investments, and to find mutually supportive roles."[250]

Electronic medical record- A health information technology system that includes a clinical data repository, clinical decision support (CDS), controlled medical vocabulary, computerized provider order entry, pharmacy order entry, and clinical documentation

---

[248] Harold Miller. June 2010. Pathways for Physician Success Under Healthcare Payment and Delivery Reforms. Report for the American Medical Association (AMA). Part C. Comprehensive Care Payment. Page 26.

[249] Accessed online at http://claytonchristensen.com/disruptive_innovation.html.

[250] Moore, J. (1996). *The Death of Competition: Leadership & Strategy in the Age of Business Ecosystems*. New York: HarperBusiness. Pg. 26.

applications. These systems warehouse patient's personal health data for both inpatient and outpatient environments in use by physicians and clinicians to document, monitor, and manage health care delivery.

Electronic health record- This is a record in electronic format capable of being shared across multiple care settings. They may include data in on each patient's demographics, medical history, medications and allergies, laboratory test results, radiology results, vital signs, and billing information. Electronic health records are intended to feed into health information exchanges and the eventual National Health Information Network (NHIN).

Emotional intelligence- How leaders handle themselves and their relationships.

Fee-for-service payment- Payments for unbundled individual services (e.g. office visit, procedure, test, etc) payable to physicians or provider organizations from public or private payer organizations.

Global payment- Form of payment that provides a physician or provider organization a single payment to cover all the costs of care for a patient's treatment requirements during a "specific period of time" regardless of the number of inpatient episodes they experience.[251]

Health system- "Set of institutions and actors that affect people's health, such as organizations that care, health plans, educational systems, and city and county governments."[252]

Monopoly extension- Action of a firm that captures greater surplus from the market and promotes innovation and welfare growth rates.

Monopoly extraction- Actions of the firm that lengthens incumbent tenure, inhibits innovation and welfare growth rates when net intertemporal cost of innovation is negative.

Quality benchmarks- Clinical quality process or health outcome goals established by CMS or private payers for ACOs to achieve within a specified time period and for a specified beneficiary population in order to qualify for shared savings payments.

---

[251] Harold Miller. June 2010. Pathways for Physician Success Under Healthcare Payment and Delivery Reforms. Report for the American Medical Association (AMA). Part C. Comprehensive Care Payment. Page 26.

[252] Kottke T., Isham G. (July 2010). Measuring Health Care Access and Quality to Improve Health in Populations. *Preventing Chronic Disease*. 7(4): 1-8. Accessed online at http://www.cdc.gov/pcd/issues/2010/jul/09_0243.htm.

Systems thinking- Attaining an understanding of the interrelationships of complex entities and how the individual components can affect the functionality of the whole and serves as part of the foundation for the Learning Organization theory[253].

Value-based purchasing- Types of payments made as incentive payments for hospitals that meet performance standards based on specified quality measures tracked against specific conditions and measures in a given fiscal year.

Vision setting- The ability to describe the future for the organization and convey it in a meaningful way.

---

[253] Senge P. (1990). The fifth discipline: the art and practice of the learning organization. Copyright Doubleday/Currency, New York.

Acronyms

Acronym	Meaning
ACO	Accountable Care Organization
CIN	Clinical Integrated Network
CIP	Clinical Integration Program
CMS	Center for Medicare and Medicaid Services
CMMI	Center for Medicare and Medicaid Innovation
CMPL	Civil Monetary Penalties Law
EHR	Electronic Health Record
FFS	Fee-for-Service Payment System
GDP	Gross Domestic Product
HEDIS	Healthcare Effectiveness Data and Information Set
HIPAA	Health Insurance Portability and Accountability Act of 1996
HIT	Health Information Technology
IDN	Integrated Delivery Network
IFR	Interim Final Rule
IOM	Institute of Medicine
IPA	Independent Practice Association
MedPAC	Medicare Payment Advisory Council
MSPG	Multi-specialty Physician Group
MLR	Medical Loss Ratio
NHE	National Health Expenditure
P4P	Pay-for-Performance Payment System
PCMH	Patient-Centered Medical Home
PCORI	Patient-Centered Outcomes Research Institute
PHI	Protected Health Information
PHO	Physician-Hospital Organization
PQRI	Physician Quality Reporting Initiative
PPACA	Patient Protection and Affordable Care Act
VBP	Value-based Purchasing

Appendix A: CMS Board of Trustees Report (Excerpt)

2010 Annual Report of the Boards of Trustees of the Federal Hospital Insurance and Federal Supplementary Medical Insurance Trust Funds. August 5, 2010
Excerpt from Section II. Overview. Short Range Results

"The financial status of the HI trust fund is substantially improved by the lower expenditures and additional tax revenues instituted by the Affordable Care Act. These changes are estimated to postpone the exhaustion of HI trust fund assets from 2017 under the prior law to 2029 under current law and to 2028 under the alternative scenario. **Despite this significant improvement, however, the fund is still not adequately financed over the next 10 years. HI expenditures have exceeded income annually since 2008 and are projected to continue doing so under current law through 2013.**

The SMI trust fund is adequately financed over the next 10 years and beyond because premium and general revenue income for Parts B and D are reset each year to match expected costs. However, further Congressional overrides of scheduled physician fee reductions, together with an existing "hold-harmless" provision restricting premium increases for most beneficiaries, could jeopardize Part B solvency and require unusual measures to avoid asset depletion. In particular, without legislation, **Part B premiums payable in 2011 and 2012 by new enrollees, high-income enrollees, and State Medicaid programs (on behalf of low-income enrollees) will probably have to be raised significantly above normal requirements to offset the loss of revenues caused by the hold-harmless provision, raising serious equity issues.**

Part B costs have been increasing rapidly, having averaged 8.3 percent annual growth over the last 5 years, and are likely to continue doing so. Under current law, an average annual growth rate of 4.8 percent is projected for the next 5years. This rate is unrealistically constrained due to multiple years of physician fee reductions that would occur under current law, including a scheduled reduction of 23 percent for December of 2010. If Congress continues to override these reductions, as they have for 2003 through November of 2010, the Part B growth rate would instead average roughly 8 percent. For Part D, the average annual increase in expenditures is estimated to be 9.4 percent through 2019. **The U.S. economy is projected to grow at an average annual rate of 5.1 percent during this period, significantly more slowly than Part D and the probable growth rate for Part B.**"

Note: HI = Hospital Insurance; SMI = Supplemental Insurance

Appendix B: PPACA Section 3502

2010 Patient Protection and Affordable Care Act. Section 3502: Establishing Community Health Teams to Support the Patient-Centered Medical Home. Subsection (c). Requirements for the Health Teams.

"(c) REQUIREMENTS FOR HEALTH TEAMS.—A health team established pursuant to a grant or contract under subsection (a) shall—

(1) establish contractual agreements with primary care providers to provide support services;

(2) support patient-centered medical homes, defined as a mode of care that includes—

(A) personal physicians;

(B) whole person orientation;

(C) coordinated and integrated care;

(D) safe and high-quality care through evidence informed medicine, appropriate use of health information technology, and continuous quality improvements;

(E) expanded access to care; and

(F) payment that recognizes added value from additional components of patient-centered care;

(3) collaborate with local primary care providers and existing State and community based resources to coordinate disease prevention, chronic disease management, transitioning between health care providers and settings and case management for patients, including children, with priority given to those amenable to prevention and with chronic diseases or conditions identified by the Secretary;

(4) in collaboration with local health care providers, develop and implement interdisciplinary, inter-professional care plans that integrate clinical and community preventive and health promotion services for patients, including children, with a priority given to those amenable to prevention and with chronic diseases or conditions identified by the Secretary;

(5) incorporate health care providers, patients, caregivers, and authorized representatives in program design and oversight;

(6) provide support necessary for local primary care providers to—

(A) coordinate and provide access to high-quality health care services;

(B) coordinate and provide access to preventive and health promotion services;

(C) provide access to appropriate specialty care and inpatient services;

(D) provide quality-driven, cost-effective, culturally appropriate, and patient- and family-centered health care;

(E) provide access to pharmacist-delivered medication management services, including medication reconciliation;

(F) provide coordination of the appropriate use of complementary and alternative (CAM) services to those who request such services;

(G) promote effective strategies for treatment planning, monitoring health outcomes and resource use, sharing information, treatment decision support, and organizing care to avoid duplication of service and other medical management approaches intended to improve quality and value of health care services;

(H) provide local access to the continuum of health care services in the most appropriate setting, including access to individuals that implement the care plans of patients and coordinate care, such as integrative health care practitioners;

(I) collect and report data that permits evaluation of the success of the collaborative effort on patient outcomes, including collection of data on patient experience of care, and identification of areas for improvement; and

(J) establish a coordinated system of early identification and referral for children at risk for developmental or behavioral problems such as through the use of infolines, health information technology, or other means as determined by the Secretary;

(7) provide 24-hour care management and support during transitions in care settings including—

(A) a transitional care program that provides onsite visits from the care coordinator, assists with the development of discharge plans and medication reconciliation upon admission to and discharge from the hospitals, nursing home, or other institution setting;

(B) discharge planning and counseling support to providers, patients, caregivers, and authorized representatives;

(C) assuring that post-discharge care plans include medication management, as appropriate;

(D) referrals for mental and behavioral health services, which may include the use of infolines; and

(E) transitional health care needs from adolescence to adulthood;

(8) serve as a liaison to community prevention and treatment programs;

(9) demonstrate a capacity to implement and maintain health information technology that meets the requirements of certified EHR technology (as defined in section 3000 of the Public Health Service Act (42 U.S.C. 300jj)) to facilitate coordination among members of the applicable care team and affiliated primary care practices; and

(10) where applicable, report to the Secretary information on quality measures used under section 399JJ of the Public Health Service Act."

Appendix C: Case Studies

Case Studies: December 2010 Report on Medicare Physician Group Practice Demonstration (Report Excerpt)
Available at: http://www.cms.gov/DemoProjectsEvalRpts/downloads/PGP_Fact_Sheet.pdf

"Physician Group Practices

CMS selected ten physician groups on a competitive basis to participate in the demonstration. The groups were selected based on technical review panel findings, organizational structure, operational feasibility, geographic location, and demonstration implementation strategy. Multi- specialty physician groups with well-developed clinical and management information systems were encouraged to apply since they were likely to have the ability to put in place the infrastructure necessary to be successful under the demonstration.

The demonstration allows CMS to test new incentives in diverse clinical and organizational environments including freestanding multi-specialty physician group practices, faculty group practices, physician groups that are part of integrated health care systems, and physician network organizations. The demonstration has fostered a nation-wide learning collaborative among the groups who voluntarily participate in this demonstration as a result of their leadership in their communities and profession. CMS is working with the groups to identify successful health care redesign and care management models developed for the demonstration that can be replicated and spread across the health care system.

The ten physician groups represent 5,000 physicians and 220,000 Medicare fee-for-service beneficiaries. The physician groups participating in the demonstration are:
Billings Clinic, Billings, Montana Dartmouth-Hitchcock Clinic, Bedford, New Hampshire The Everett Clinic, Everett, Washington Forsyth Medical Group, Winston-Salem, North Carolina Geisinger Health System, Danville, Pennsylvania Marshfield Clinic, Marshfield, Wisconsin Middlesex Health System, Middletown, Connecticut Park Nicollet Health Services, St. Louis Park, Minnesota St. John's Health System, Springfield, Missouri University of Michigan Faculty Group Practice, Ann Arbor, Michigan

Performance Results
Performance Year 1 Results -- At the end of the first performance year, all 10 of the participating physician groups improved the clinical management of diabetes patients by achieving benchmark or target performance on at least 7 out of 10 diabetes clinical quality measures. Two of the physician groups -- Forsyth Medical Group and St. John's Health System -- achieved benchmark quality performance on all 10-quality measures.
In performance year one, two physician groups shared in savings for improving the overall efficiency of care they furnish their patients. The two physician groups, Marshfield Clinic

and the University of Michigan Faculty Group Practice, earned $7.3 million in performance payments for improving the quality and cost efficiency of care as their share of a total of $9.5 million in Medicare savings.

Performance Year 2 Results -- At the end of the second performance year, all 10 of the participating physician groups continued to improve the quality of care for chronically ill patients by achieving benchmark or target performance on at least 25 out of 27 quality markers for patients with diabetes, coronary artery disease and congestive heart failure. Five of the physician groups -- Forsyth Medical Group, Geisinger Clinic, Marshfield Clinic, St. John's Health System, and the University of Michigan Faculty Group Practice -- achieved benchmark quality performance on all 27 quality measures.

In performance year two, four physician groups shared in savings for improving the overall efficiency of care they furnish their patients. The four physician groups, Dartmouth-Hitchcock Clinic, The Everett Clinic, Marshfield Clinic, and the University of Michigan Faculty Group Practice, earned $13.8 million in performance payments for improving the quality and cost efficiency of care as their share of a total of $17.4 million in Medicare savings.

Performance Year 3 Results -- At the end of the third performance year, all 10 of the participating physician groups continued to improve the quality of care for patients with chronic illness or who require preventive care by achieving benchmark or target performance on at least 28 out of 32 quality markers for patients with diabetes, coronary artery disease, congestive heart failure, hypertension, and cancer screening. Two of the physician groups -- Geisinger Clinic and Park Nicollet Health Services -- achieved benchmark quality performance on all 32-quality measures.

Over the first three years of the demonstration, physician groups increased their quality scores an average of 10 percentage points on the diabetes, 11 percentage points on the congestive heart failure measures, 6 percentage points on the coronary artery disease measures, 10 percentage points on the cancer screening measures, and 1 percentage point on the hypertension measures.

In addition to achieving benchmark performance for quality, five physician groups shared in savings under the demonstration's performance payment methodology. The five physician groups, Dartmouth-Hitchcock Clinic, Geisinger Clinic, Marshfield Clinic, St. John's Health System, and the University of Michigan Faculty Group Practice, earned $25.3 million in performance payments for improving the quality and cost efficiency of care as their share of a total of $32.3 million in Medicare savings.

Performance Year 4 Results – At the end of the fourth year of performance evaluation, all ten of the physician groups achieved benchmark performance on at least 29 of the 32 measures. Three groups – Geisinger Clinic, Marshfield Clinic, and Park Nicollet Health Services achieved benchmark performance on all 32 performance measures and all ten of the groups achieved benchmark performance on the ten heart failure and seven coronary artery disease measures.

The PGPs have increased their quality scores from baseline to performance year 4 an average of 10 percentage points on the diabetes measures, 13 percentage points on the heart failure measures, 6 percentage points on the coronary artery disease measures, 9 percentage points on the cancer screening measures, and 3 percentage points on the hypertension measures.

In addition to the quality performance, five physician groups -- Dartmouth-Hitchcock Clinic, Geisinger Clinic, Marshfield Clinic, St. John's Health System, University of Michigan -- earned incentive payments based on the estimated savings in Medicare expenditures for the patient population they serve. The groups received performance payments totaling $31.7 million as their share of the $38.7 million of savings generated for the Medicare Trust Funds in performance year 4.

Care Management Strategies

One of the unique features of this demonstration is that physician groups have the flexibility to redesign care processes, invest in care management initiatives, and target patient populations that can benefit from more effective and efficient delivery of care. This helps Medicare beneficiaries maintain their health and avoid further illness and admissions to the hospital. The following provides an overview of the quality and efficiency innovations underway at each demonstration site.

Billings Clinic focuses on providing evidence-based care, including preventive services, at the time of each patient visit. This is accomplished by the creation of a summary that identifies gaps in care and redesigning workflow for nursing and support staff. An example is the improved management of patients with diabetes through the use of a diabetes patient registry, electronic medical record modules, a team of diabetes experts/educators offering a patient friendly report card, and a pharmacy driven insulin protocol for glycemic control in the inpatient setting. As a result of these efforts focused on diabetes care, a majority of the clinic's eligible physicians have been recognized through NCQA's Diabetes Physician Recognition Program for excellence in diabetes care. The Clinic also continues efforts to: (1) redesign heart failure care by leveraging an RN-directed telephonic computerized patient monitoring system; (2) decrease medication errors by using electronic prescribing and reconciling medications at every care opportunity; (3) expand the palliative care team; and (4) develop a community crisis center to benefit dual eligible patients with mental health related events. For more information, contact: F. Douglas Carr, M.D. at dcarr@billingsclinic.org.

Dartmouth-Hitchcock Clinic focuses on improving quality while reducing costs through implementation of evidence-based care initiatives. The clinic uses recognized experts to educate physicians and support staff in understanding evidence-based care guidelines. Electronic tools and reports including disease registries, dashboard reports to track progress on quality measures, and electronic medical record enhancements are used by the physicians and staff at the point of patient contact to proactively identify patients with gaps in chronic disease care and focus on preventive care. Evidence-based care implementation also requires changing workflow processes and roles for support staff. For example, in the primary care departments, the physician and nurse work together to provide a patient centered approach to care highlighted by patient and family involvement in developing and implementing the plan of care. Care is coordinated by nurses who target interventions to high-risk patients using motivational education on disease and personal health care through in-office visits and/or post hospital discharge phone calls. For more information, contact: Barbara Walters, D.O. at Barbara.A.Walters@Hitchcock.org.

The Everett Clinic is improving health care delivery to seniors by: (1) providing electronic patient reports to primary care physicians to use in addressing issues with diabetes, heart disease, hypertension, and mammogram and colonoscopy screening results; (2) coaching hospitalized patients and caretakers to guide them through complicated care processes during hospital stays and upon discharge; (3) having physicians follow-up with patients within ten days of hospital discharge to address any unsolved or new health problems; (4) partnering with local providers to deploy new palliative care programs in physicians' offices to improve end-of-life care for approximately 800 patients; (5) making delivery of primary care services more efficient and patient-friendly by removing non-value-added steps ("lean principles") ; and (6) implementing evidence based guidelines to improve appropriateness for ordering radiology imaging tests. For more information, contact: James Lee, M.D. at Jlee@everettclinic.com.

Forsyth Medical Group focuses on care coordination at transitions of care to promote safe, patient-centered services. Concentration on the frail elderly, high-risk diseases and poly-pharmacy issues identifies those patients at greatest risk for readmission and adverse events associated with multiple therapies. COMPASS Disease Management Navigators and Safe Med Pharmacists collaborate with inpatient services and systems to identify these at risk populations. Programs target inpatient discharges to assess the patient's understanding and adherence to discharge instructions and to navigate the patient back to the primary care provider for follow-up care. The Chronic Care Model transitions to a Patient Centered Medical Home with this emphasis on care coordination and self-management education for chronic conditions. Physician champions promote programs targeted to improve quality measures and patient outcomes. Educational materials continue to reach a broad range of patients with chronic disease and the scope of education was broadened to include end of life care, fall risk assessment and prevention and medication reconciliation and safety. The COMPASS Disease Management Program grew in both services offered to patients and contacts by nurse disease managers with an expanded emphasis on preventive care and intervening with patients with pre-disease for diabetes and peripheral arterial disease. For more information, contact: Nan Holland, R.N. at nlholland@novanthealth.org.

Geisinger Clinic focuses on: (1) A unique implementation of the Medical Home model of care including patient-centered, team based care across the continuum, practice-integrated case management, fully revamped payment incentives, and the proactive identification of high risk patients; (2) Transitions of care coordination and case management including medication reconciliation, enhanced access for early post discharge follow-up, self-management Action plans for chronic care exacerbation management, telephonic and/or device-based remote monitoring and associated order execution for beneficiaries with congestive heart failure; (3) Using its electronic health record to identify and systematically resolve care gaps to ensure comprehensive prevention and treatment of all medical conditions; (4) Automating identification, notification and scheduling of pneumococcal and influenza immunization services; and (5) Redesigned systems of care monitored by performance on "all or none" evidence-based bundles for diabetes, coronary artery disease, chronic kidney disease and adult prevention. For more information, contact: Ronald A. Paulus, M.D. at: rapaulus@geisinger.edu.

Marshfield Clinic is participating in the demonstration as a reflection of its mission to serve patients through accessible, high quality health care, research and education. The clinic expanded a number of on-going successful initiatives and accelerated the development and adoption of others including enhancements to its electronic health record to systematically expand a support structure to implement care management and coordination. Specifically, the clinic expanded its anticoagulation care management program across the entire system and developed a heart failure care management program with the goal of improving clinical care, improving quality of life and decreasing costs and hospitalizations. In addition, the clinic continues to promote use of its nurse advice line, develop clinical practice guidelines and monitor population-based clinical performance through clinical dashboards. For more information, contact: Theodore A. Praxel, M.D. at praxel.theodore@marshfieldclinic.org.

Middlesex Health System is participating in the project as a network of physicians affiliated with a community hospital. Interventions focus on processes to improve electronic linkages and communications among all providers for each patient and demonstrate quality and safety across the continuum of care. Building on a long history of close collaboration between the hospital, its medical staff and a commitment to the mission of community health improvement, the Hospital commissioned a community health assessment to identify service gaps and secure an understanding of the current and projected health needs of the service area. Services such as an inpatient COPD pathway and enhanced outpatient care for COPD patients were deployed to close existing service gaps. Care Management programs and support services designed to educate and promote patient self- management skills around chronic diseases such as heart failure, diabetes, asthma and Nurse Navigators for cancer patients are offered. Efforts to ensure appropriate immunizations, cancer screenings, support groups, smoking cessation program availability, medication safety, innovative palliative care, and use of tele-monitoring technology are also utilized. For more information, contact: Arthur McDowell, M.D. at Arthur_McDowell_MD@midhosp.org.

Park Nicollet Health Services started an inpatient palliative care program and continues to enhance their care of patients with diabetes and heart failure. An innovative telephone monitoring program was instituted for high-risk heart failure patients. Over 560 patients with heart failure have been enrolled into an automated telephonic program to improve their quality of life. Each patient makes a daily call to provide weight and symptom reports, allowing nurse case managers at the clinic to spot early signs of deterioration and intervene in their heart failure management. Electronic patient registries are the cornerstone of management for patients with chronic disease and have been combined with Park Nicollet's existing electronic medical record. As a result, patient information can be reviewed by the physician care team prior to upcoming appointments for unmet health care needs. Another improvement was initiating same-day lab testing prior to the visit for many of these chronic disease patients. Using these steps, along with pre-visit planning, significantly increased time for important face-to-face interaction with the provider when crucial decisions need to be made about treatment. For more information, contact: Mark Skubic at Mark.Skubic@ParkNicollet.com.

St. John's Health System developed a comprehensive patient registry to respond to the demonstration's quality improvement incentives. The registry is designed to track patient information, identify gaps in care, and ensure that appropriate and timely care is provided. A key element of the patient registry is the visit planner which is designed to complement physicians' established clinical work-flow process. It provides a "to do" list for physicians prior to each patient visit, with reminders for needed tests or interventions. The visit planner consists of a one-page summary for each patient showing key demographic and clinical data, including test dates and results. An exception list highlights tests or interventions for which the patient is due and provides physicians with reports on areas where patient care can be improved. The provider/clinic manger uses the decentralized reporting feature to generate un-blinded outcome reports from the registry at both the individual provider and clinic levels. In addition, a case manager was deployed in the emergency department to collaborate with the health system and community services to provide transition planning. A heart failure team has been designated to drive the coordination of heart failure care, provider education, and increase outcome success. Special groups are being convened to focus on diabetic retinal eye exams, mammography and colorectal cancer screenings. For more information, contact: James T. Rogers, M.D. at James.Rogers@Mercy.net or Donna Smith at Donna.Smith@Mercy.net.

University of Michigan Faculty Group Practice focus on improving transitional care and complex care coordination for Medicare patients. The group's transitional care call-back program contacts Medicare patients discharged from the emergency department and acute care hospital to address gaps in care during the transition between care settings. This program also provides short-term care coordination with linkages to visiting nurse and community services and coordination with primary care and specialty clinics. The group also developed a complex care coordination program with social workers and nurses who work with physicians to assist patients who have multiple risks, high costs and complex health status. In the hospital setting, the group developed a pharmacy facilitated discharge program for patients with high-risk medications and a palliative care consult service to work with patients and families to ease end of life transitions. In the second year of the project, these services were joined by a sub-acute service that brings geriatric faculty into local sub-acute facilities and an expanded geriatric inpatient consult service that provides expertise in geriatric medicine and transitional care. The group also has a heart failure nurse tele-management program that coordinates with its heart failure clinics. The group's quality program uses patient registries with relevant quality indicators and individual physician/provider feedback on the quality of care for their patients. For more information, contact: Caroline S. Blaum, M.D. at cblaum@umich.edu.

For More Information
The demonstration started April 1, 2005 and the fifth performance year ended March 31, 2010. As included in The Affordable Care Act, we are currently working on a transitional demonstration while the Medicare Shared Savings Program is being developed.
For additional information, visit the Physician Group Practice webpage at:
http://www.cms.hhs.gov/DemoProjectsEvalRpts/MD"

Appendix D: Joint Principles of PCMH

Joint Principles of the Patient-Centered Medical Home[254]	
Personal Physician	Each patient has an ongoing relationship with a personal physician trained to provide first contact, continuous and comprehensive care.
Physician directed medical practice	The personal physician leads a team of individuals at the prActice level who collectively take responsibility for the ongoing care of patients.
Whole person orientation	The personal physician is responsible for providing for all the patient's health care needs or taking responsibility for appropriately arranging care with other qualified professionals. This includes care for all stages of life; acute care, chronic care, preventive services, and end of life care.
Care is coordinated and/or integrated	—across all elements of the complex health care system (e.g., subspecialty care, hospitals, home health agencies, nursing homes) and the patient's community (e.g., family, public and private community-based services). Care is facilitated by registries, information technology, health information exchange, and other means to assure that patients get the indicated care when and where they need and want it in a culturally and linguistically appropriate manner.
Quality and Safety	• Practices advocate for their patients to support the attainment of optimal, patient-centered outcomes that are defined by a care planning process driven by a compassionate, robust partnership between physicians, patients, and the patient's family. • Evidence-based medicine and clinical decision-support tools guide decision making. • Physicians in the practice accept accountability for continuous quality improvement through voluntary engagement in performance measurement and improvement. • Patients Actively participate in decision-making and feedback is sought to ensure patients' expectations are being met. • Information technology is utilized appropriately to support optimal patient care, performance measurement, patient education, and enhanced communication. • Practices go through a voluntary recognition process by an

---

[254] Seven principles and descriptions come from the Patient-Centered Primary Care Collaborative. Available at http://www.pcpcc.net/joint-principles.

	Joint Principles of the Patient-Centered Medical Home[254]
	appropriate non-governmental entity to demonstrate that they have the capabilities to provide patient centered services consistent with the medical home model. ♦ Patients and families participate in quality improvement Activities at the practice level.
Enhanced Access	Care is available through systems such as open scheduling, expanded hours and new options for communication between patients, their personal physician, and practice staff.
Payment	It appropriately recognizes the added value provided to patients who have a patient-centered medical home. The payment structure should be based on the following framework: ♦ It should reflect the value of physician and non-physician staff patient-centered care management work that falls outside of the face-to-face visit. ♦ It should pay for services associated with coordination of care both within a given practice and between consultants, ancillary providers, and community resources. ♦ It should support adoption and use of health information technology for quality improvement. ♦ It should support provision of enhanced communication access such as secure e-mail and telephone consultation. ♦ It should recognize the value of physician work associated with remote monitoring of clinical data using technology. ♦ It should allow for separate fee-for-service payments for face-to-face visits. (Payments for care management services that fall outside of the face-to-face visit, as described above, should not result in a reduction in the payments for face-to-face visits). ♦ It should recognize case mix differences in the patient population being treated within the practice. ♦ It should allow physicians to share in savings from reduced hospitalizations associated with physician-guided care management in the office setting. ♦ It should allow for additional payments for achieving measurable and continuous quality improvements.

Appendix E: Commonwealth Fund Study
Excerpt from Commonwealth Fund Study on The Potential of Global Payment: Insights From the Field (February 2010)

"Global payment comes in many shapes and sizes, but has the common characteristic of holding providers financially accountable, to a greater or lesser degree, for the total cost of care provided to the patient population assigned to them. One critical element, according to the experts, is that financial incentives to manage patient resource use must exceed economic incentives to provide too much or too little care.

Global payment models vary based on the amount of risk assumed by the provider organization and the methods used to limit risks. Risks can be limited based on what services are included in the global payment and what, if any, adjustments are considered when evaluating provider performance. Risks can be limited based on what services are included in the global payment and what, if any, adjustments are considered when evaluating provider performance.

Sidebar: Capitation Problems Addressed in Next Generation Global Payment Models
- Incentive to skimp on care
- Incentive to skim risk
- No accountability for quality
- Limited ability to manage risk
- Limited data
- Patient and provider dissatisfaction with "gatekeeping"
- Lack of provider financial reserves
- Provider reluctance to assume risk

The potential cost exposure for professional services is minimal relative to the highly variable cost generated by the small percentage of patients who are hospitalized. Alternatively, provider organizations can be at risk for all covered services, but the risk amount may be limited to the approximate amount the provider would have received for those patients if they were paid on a fee-for-service basis.

Global payments are funded and administered in a wide variety of ways. Particularly with very large integrated provider organizations, an agreed-upon amount of money per member representing the total budget available to care for all needed services for patients under the provider's care is prospectively deposited by the payer in a provider-owned account. Any costs incurred outside the contracted provider organization are then drawn from this account either by the payer or the provider organization.

Alternatively, when the provider is at risk only for a subset of covered services for their patient population, a slice of the expected total cost per member is prospectively allocated into a provider-owned account or into a dedicated account held by the payer. Claims for services that are performed by providers that are not part of the provider organization are typically drawn from this account and the balance is available to the provider to compensate for the services they have rendered within their system.

Each payer–provider global payment arrangement considers multiple methodological variations. Typically, no two arrangements are the same for providers contracting with multiple plans and for payers contracting with multiple providers. Plans and providers report variations in global payment arrangements including:

- which patients are included (e.g., Medicare, Medicaid, commercial)
- which products are included (e.g., fully insured, self-insured, HMO, PPO)
- how to determine which patients are under the provider's care (e.g., patients specify and lock in provider, patients are attributed to providers based on de facto provider use)
- which covered services are included (e.g., all covered services, all services except pharmacy, all services except mental health, professional services only, primary care services only, etc.)
- methodology and technology used for risk adjustment
- methodology used for adjustment for catastrophic claims
- how risk is limited based on performance levels around a target, (e.g., in some types of arrangements providers can be at risk for +/– 10% of what their fee-for-service payments would have been, with the payer retaining the balance of the risk)
- how providers outside the globally paid organization are contracted and paid
- level of fee-for-service payments or withholds made prior to reconciliation
- timing and data sharing for reconciliation payments.

A full range of provider structures are operating successfully under global payment.

Large, integrated delivery systems are able to work well under global payment. However, since the vast majority of physicians in the U.S. are not part of such structures, conventional wisdom suggests that global payment can at best be applied only to a small subset of providers or that all providers will ultimately need to become part of such a system. The provider leaders interviewed for this project represented a wide range of organizational sizes and types. Very large, hospital-dominated systems; large multispecialty clinics with and without hospital ownership; mid-sized primary care practices; and IPAs representing very small primary care practices all have found ways to be successful in global payment programs. Some successful IPAs have expanded or are in the process of expanding geographically into new, previously unorganized markets. They are finding that the information and clinical support infrastructures they have refined over the years can be leveraged across a broader physician base."[255]

---

[255] Robinow A. The Potential of Global Payment: Insights From the Field. *Commonwealth Fund Report.* 2010. Page 3-5: What is Global Payment? (Excerpt), Page 13-14: Provider structures using global payments. Available at: http://www.commonwealthfund.org/~/media/Files/Publications/Fund%20Report/2010/Feb/1373_Robinow_potential_global_payment.pdf.

Appendix F: Challenges, Risks, and Mitigation Strategies
Compilation of Challenges, Risks and Mitigation Strategies for All Chapters

Chapter 2

Challenges	Risks
2a) Implementing an integrated performance reporting system.	2g) Revenue lost in transition to new reimbursement models.
2b) Achieving agreement across ACO participant PCMHs on integrated clinical guidelines and equitable savings allocation.	2h) Negative impact on individualized patient care services during the shift to population-based disease condition management.
2c) Aligning advanced PCMH objectives with ACO qualification level criteria.	2i) Lack of investment capital and acceptance of financial risk.
2d) Assigning patients to ACOs[256].	2j) Inability to hold an ACO accountable for a patient's care received outside their region[257].
2e) Having sufficient resources to manage large-scale complexity, overcome tradition, and change activities required across a multiyear ACO implementation.	2k) Not managing organizational change across ACO participants.
2f) Managing the impact on the revenue cycle impact for hospitals when chronic disease management has been optimized but payment methods have not caught up.	2i) Negative economic impact on consumers related to potentially higher out-of-pocket expenses and increased cost of navigating the care system.

---

[256] Luft HS. Becoming accountable—opportunities and obstacles for ACOs. *N Engl J Med.* 2010;363(15):1389-1391.

[257] Luft HS. Becoming accountable—opportunities and obstacles for ACOs. *N Engl J Med.* 2010;363(15):1389-1391.

Chapter 2, ctd.

Potential Mitigation Strategies
√ **Impact on patient care**: Use of predictive modeling tools[258] for identification of chronic illness population segments for targeted prevention efforts
√ **Impact on patient care:** Implementing care management programs[44] to proactively support and manage the patient's needs following treatment or interventions
√ **Lack of investment 1:** Engaging resources to establish financial plans that identify options for securing needed investments to cover capital, training, and expenses of the transition period
√ **Lack of investment 2:** Encouraging physicians in need of capital infusion to consider partnering with health systems and large entities
√ **Mitigating financial impact**: Physicians and providers negotiate rapid-cycle implementation of new payment methods to account for new and improved levels of healthcare services across the continuum of care
√ **Organizational transformation**: Utilize change management disciplines and process improvement methodologies to minimize risk of failure

---

[258] Boland P, Polakoff P, Schwab T. Accountable care organizations hold promise, but will they achieve cost and quality targets? *Manag Care.* 2010;19(10):12-6, 19.

Challenges	Risks
3a) Engaging physicians to develop and participate in a network initiative.	3f) Hospital systems may develop networks in isolation and thus fail to accrue a sufficient number of providers to adequately manage the patient population.
3b) Who drives the bus (will the ACO be physician practice-led or hospital-led)?	3g) Changes in leadership during the transition period.
3c) Navigating antitrust issues related to clinical and financial integration.	3h) Hospitals that move from a focus on inpatient to outpatient services may lose revenue in the near term.[259]
3d) Securing seed funding for the ACO startup.	3i) Failure to reach agreement with ACO participants on a savings distribution plan.
3e) Securing competent leadership to ensure the success of the ACO and mitigate risk of failure.	3j) Relying on a leadership style that does not fit the local ecosystem, resulting in setbacks for the ACO.

Potential Mitigation Strategies

√ **Engaging Physicians**: Engaging physicians in conversation about the development and management of an ACO is critical to their participation in the network. Early engagement is crucial to success.

√ **Who Drives the Bus:** Regardless of whether the ACO is led by a physician practice or a hospital, ensure that its board of directors is elected by relevant stakeholders from participant organizations and that it maintains its autonomy from the hospital's board. It is also important to ensure that the chair of the board is a licensed physician.[50]

√ **IDNs and CINs**: Engage payers early in planning an ACO startup to ensure alignment with payment model reform and incentives to mitigate loss of revenue during the transition period.

√ **Funding:** Proactively seek grant opportunities for startup funds through the Center for Medicare and Medicaid Innovation and other entities sponsoring ACO demonstration projects.

---

[259] Kocher R, Sahni NR. Physicians versus hospitals as leaders of accountable care organizations. *N Engl J Med*. 2010;363(27):2579-2582.

Chapter 4

Challenges	Risks
4a) Demonstrating greater value to the consumer with the ability to aggregate, analyze and manage data in significant ways.	4d) If indicia are not met, the FTC or DOJ can rule against the ACO and unwind the makings of the network.
4b) Moving quickly enough to remain competitive in a market while safe harbor requirements remain unclear or are in development.	4e) Moving too quickly or assuming changes that do not come to fruition.
4c) Maintaining the resources to monitor the changing landscape of regulations for the Shared Savings Program, HITECH Act, HIPAA, and antitrust laws.	4f) Losing competitive balance in geographic markets and creating anticompetitive practices that lead to market inefficiencies harming patients, consumers and employers.

Potential Mitigation Strategies

√ Consult legal counsel with expertise in antitrust and anti-kickback statutes.

√ Monitor changes in law as they are released.

√ Develop a strategy for horizontal and vertical relationships needed to form your ACO.

√ Develop an antitrust action plan to ensure compliance across the framework of federal antitrust laws along with state antitrust related laws and regulations.

Challenges	Risks
5a) Data aggregation across disparate systems at different levels of maturity.	5d) Not ensuring fully functioning IT interfaces across ACO participants (potential for patient data corruption, inaccuracies, or delays in transmission).
5b) Enabling a common or interoperable ACO technology framework across all participants and ensuring accessibility for providers outside the ACO.	5e) Allowing terminology conversions to create delays that impact continuity of care.
5c) Meeting stage 2 and 3 criteria for CMS meaningful use of EMR requirements for effective HIE as they will be defined in the future.	5f) Not achieving continuity of care and care coordination goals due to inadequate interface development.

Potential Mitigation Strategies
√ Ensure effective project implementation on semantic terminology and conversions.
√ Establish cross-functional committees to manage HIE implementation and track progress.
√ Engage clinicians and physicians jointly with IT professionals and vendors to ensure that all health data elements and disparate systems are accounted for in HIE required interfaces.

Chapter 6

Challenges	Risks
6a) Factoring in regional variation in patient conditions and service utilization.	6e) Cost and time to develop and test new measures may impede efforts to evaluate ACOs efficiency and performance improvement.
6b) Maintaining flexibility in quality benchmarks.	6f) Setting quality benchmarks may be unattainable for the some ACOs if volume of physician participation fluctuates (i.e. exclusive vs. nonexclusive contracting effect) or if beneficiary attribution changes due to voluntary participation.
6c) Identifying new innovations in care delivery processes to help ACOs reach quality benchmarks and spending targets.	6g) Not synthesizing Meaningful Use, HEDIS, PQRI measures could create duplicated work for overburdened and stressed physician practice groups if they are not merged with larger ACO support staff.
6d) Evaluating patient and care giver experience in an effective and timely manner that also clearly delineates responses and who the positive or negative feedback is applicable to for any given episode of care.	6h) Not factoring in ICD-10 transition to quality measure trends post 2013 may result in inaccuracies for evaluating ACO performance on health outcomes.

Potential Mitigation Strategies

√ Support requests for input to federal rule making processes with meaningful and well-constructed ideas to assist legislators in crafting best approaches for the industry.

√ Support industry stakeholder group nominations (i.e. PPACA Section 3014) with viable candidates that can aid efforts in performance evaluation, rule making, and gap identification.

√ Engage physicians with performance improvement teams early to identify new opportunities to improve processes, reduce waste, and achieve cost savings to effect transformation around the structure of care, process of care, and health outcomes at the population level.

Challenges	Risks
7a) Developing a transition plan to begin to assume risk while working in a largely indemnity market.	7e) Moving too early without new funding sources to underwrite the loss of inpatient revenues.
7b) Developing total cost of care accounting metrics.	7f) Inadequate tracking systems to manage clinical/financial risk meaningfully.
7c) Securing funding needed for infrastructure expenditures.	7g) Inadequate changes to physician training curricula to keep future physicians apprised of forthcoming changes that will impact their compensation arrangements in the future.
7d) Tracking, capturing, and distributing incentives and value-based payments to appropriate stakeholders.	7h) Unintended consequences that may arise from initiating shared savings program in relationship to impact on quality of patient care and services provided to a specific patient population.

Potential Mitigation Strategies
√   Begin to pilot shared risk initiatives to develop cores competencies.
√   Begin to explore total cost of care accounting vehicles.
√   Engage financial modeling expertise to forecast financial impact to all stakeholders based on changes to be made with clinical integration programs.
√   Plan for early launch of payer relationship strategy discussions to move toward multi-payer ACO model at an accelerated pace.

Index

Stark II, 80
Statements of Antitrust Enforcement Policy in
    Healthcare, 69, 89
Substantial financial risk, 101
Sutter Health, 55
Systematized Nomemclature of Medicine, 131
Systems thinking, 49, 210

T

Tax Relief and Health Care Act, 152
The Everett Clinic, 23
The Innovators Prescription, 106
To Err is Human, 1, 164
Trinity Health, 120
Triple Aim Project, 40
TriState, 93
TriState Health Partners
    See also TriState, 93
Tucson Medical Center, 26

U

U.S. v. LaHue, 261 F.3d993 (10th Cir.(Kan.)
    Aug. 17, 2001), 81
Unintended adverse consequences, 114
United Healthcare, 26
United States v. Greber, 760 F.2d 68 (3d Cir. Pa.
    1985), 81
University of Michigan Faculty Group Practice,
    23

V

Value-based insurance design, 7
Value-based purchasing, 210
Vermont Blueprint for Health Project, 39
Vertical analysis, 103
Veterans Health Administration, 105, 175
Volume driven system, 106

W

Waiver authority, 76, 80

8525392R0

Made in the USA
Lexington, KY
11 February 2011